DUQUETTE

MW01006254

SELLING YOURSELF TO OTHERS

SELLING
Yourself
to Others

The New Psychology
of SALES

By Kevin Hogan
and William Horton

Foreword by Jeffrey Gitomer

PELICAN PUBLISHING COMPANY
Gretna 2002

*The word "Pelican" and the depiction of a pelican are trademarks
of Pelican Publishing Company, Inc., and are registered
in the U.S. Patent and Trademark Office.*

Library of Congress Cataloging-in-Publication Data

Hogan, Kevin
    Selling yourself to others : the new psychology of sales / Kevin Hogan
and William Horton : foreword by Jeffery Gitomer.
        p. cm.
    Includes bibliographical references.
    ISBN 1-58980-007-9
    1. Selling—Psychological aspects. I. Horton, William. II. Title.

HF5438.8.P75 H64 2002
658.85—dc21

                                                        2002016926

Printed in the United States of America

Published by Pelican Publishing Company, Inc.
1000 Burmaster Street, Gretna, Louisiana 70053

For Christina, Katie, Jessica, and Mark

Contents

Foreword

A Giant Leap for Sales-kind

As I looked over Kevin Hogan's shoulder at a Las Vegas pai gow poker table, I reminded myself that salesmen are the easiest sold. And that they are as easily distracted as a moth flutters to the brightest light bulb. And that the lure of the dollar will bring people to the table, especially sales-people. And that the positive attitude of the invincible salesman is the mantra "losing is for others."

Vegas is a salesman's rudest awakening.

But Kevin, ever the winner in his own mind, ever the "outcome optimist," is certain he can beat them. That's what makes good salespeople great.

As a salesman myself, and a self-proclaimed expert at winning, when I visit Vegas I sit at a blackjack table for fifteen minutes with a few hundred dollars. As soon as I am ahead a hundred or two, I quit. And that's all I play for that trip. Makes me feel like a king to walk away with their money. And feeling like a king is what sales success is all about.

When I make reservations at a restaurant or give my name to the hostess, it's always "king." Nothing feels better than hearing "King, your table is ready" bellowing all over the restaurant.

I don't read current books on selling. Ruins my independent thought and creativity. I read the sales classic literature written fifty years ago or more. These books can only be found in used bookstores, and even though they are much less expensive than the shiny new ones, they contain the history and the philosophy of selling at its purest, and sales "answers" at their finest. They tell the way sales should be made. And, in fact, the easiest way to sell. The rare title *How to Sell Your Way Through Life,* written by

Napoleon Hill in the late twenties and early thirties, remains the best book ever written on the subject.

But when I read *Selling Yourself to Others* I was taken aback. This book is both a throwback and a leap forward. It embraces the concepts of yesterday (that rely more on the relationship and less on the hoodwinking), and it's a leap forward with the progressive thoughts and insights necessary for 21st-century sales dominance—both individual and corporate.

My personal philosophy (and trademarked phrase), "People don't like to be sold, but they love to buy," has never been portrayed in a more understandable and implement-able way than in this book. I found myself turning pages and nodding approval. Imagine a book on selling that brings a smile to your face as you absorb and agree with the content and concepts—and at the same time you can picture yourself using the techniques and strategies on your next sales call. This book makes you think and allows you to understand. This book gives you that feeling of certainty to scream, "YES! I can do this!"

As a reader of this book you are among the fortunate. You will learn by example and be able to assimilate by "aha!" This book is full of aha!

And that's just the beginning . . .

- This book is rich with winning examples, even if there is a temporary loss to help you understand the concept.
- This book is rich with stories that relate to everyday success.
- This book is a MindMap in every sense of the word. Learning the MAP concept was an incredible sales awakening for me that I will utilize forever—and so will you.
- This book takes you inside the psychology all the way to the biology of selling. If there is a DNA of selling, this book unlocks the genetic code.
- This book has a universal model of sales and selling that anyone can adapt for one's own and implement in his or her career—and you can do it without affecting the "sales model" your company shoved down your throat during "training."
- This book covers the gamut of sales, from shaking hands to shaking in your boots. From hypnotic language to secret words. With laws you can obey and strategies you can't wait to employ.
- This book presents the winning side of the selling process and enhances the model of professional salespeople, in spite of the fact that there is

(as in all professions) an occasional loser in the profession. More than that, it explains what has caused salespeople to lose in the past, and how to re-understand and retool for the win on the next appointment.

- This book enables and empowers the reader to understand "why" people buy and what can be done to influence that decision.
- This book identifies human desires in a way that anyone can relate to and grasp.
- This book has a voice. It speaks the language of sales as a winning process, and it tells readers how to win in any environment.

And this book puts sex back in selling. More than seventy years ago Napoleon Hill wrote about sex as the strongest drive in the world. This book reinforces that validity and adds new insight about the real thoughts of buyers and sellers. It turns sex appeal into sales appeal.

Here are a few IMPORTANT "don'ts" about this book:

Don't read this book without a hi-liter and laptop. Capture the gems and convert them to your selling process the minute you read them.

Don't try to read this book too fast. The slower you go, the more you will learn. The more sales-power you will assimilate.

Don't read this book once. Read it at least twice.

Don't leave home without the book if you're going on a sales call. Just don't.

And in the words of the great Harvey Mackay, "Don't read this book, study it."

In the author's own words they say, "Reading this book will help you sell. Utilizing the tools in this book will ensure you success." And they are correct.

The Death of a Salesman may be fifty years old, but the rebirth of the selling process is alive and in your hands.

I guess the only real problem I have with this book is that I wish I had written it.

JEFFREY GITOMER
Author of
The Sales Bible
Customer Satisfaction Is Worthless,
*   Customer Loyalty Is Priceless*
Knock Your Socks Off Selling
YES! A Wonderful Alternative to No

Acknowledgments

No book is the product of one person or, in this case, two co-authors. Many people have influenced our thinking and provided support for us when we most needed it.

Both of us would like to thank the wonderful people at Pelican Publishing Company for putting this book into the hands of the people who really want this information—Dr. Milburn Calhoun, Nina Kooij, Joseph Billingsley, and everyone at Pelican who worked at making this book better than what we gave you to work with. Thank you.

Thanks to Jeffrey Gitomer, author of *The Sales Bible,* for his support. Thanks for writing a rock and roll foreword. Jeffrey remains the superstar in the field of selling. Nobody does it better.

We also want to thank Richard Brodie for his contributions in the chapters about the sixteen desires. Richard's thinking in memetics and his understanding of genetics has helped us appreciably in making this book "scientifically accurate." (All mistakes remain the authors', and not of those who helped us in the writing or idea creation of the book.)

I (Will) would like to thank all the people who have helped me in this quest to write an easy to read and useful sales book. First, my co-author and friend Kevin Hogan for his getting me to dig down and do better than my best; my wife, Christina, who not only helped but is my guiding light (and she remembers the rules of grammar); my father, who taught me do just do the next right thing; my daughter Erika for making me proud; and the rest of my extended family, who make it all worthwhile.

I have to acknowledge all my mentors: Elsom Eldridge, John Grinder, George Bein, Richard Bandler, and Scott McFall. A special thanks to James Heil, Robert Labrie, and Rich Alexander for their help, and to my martial teachers Bill and Bret Holhman for their insights and sharing the secrets of the martial way.

Finally, I want to thank every student I have ever taught, from courses in psychology to the martial arts. I always learn from every teaching. And I want to thank YOU for having the insight to buy this book NOW.

I (Kevin) personally want to thank many people who provided me with love, attention, support, ideas, and appreciation throughout the long days and nights of writing this volume: Katie Hogan, Jessica Hogan, Mark Hogan, Elsom Eldridge, Richard Brodie, Jeffrey Gitomer, Dianne Olson, Devin Hastings, Katherin Scott, Ron Stubbs, Jeannie Taylor, Terence Watts, Andrzej Batko, Jacek Santorski, and all of my wonderful friends, colleagues, and family.

I (Kevin) also want to point the readers toward the great writers and motivators that influenced me and my career but never knew it: Napoleon Hill, W. Clement Stone, Dale Carnegie, J. Douglas Edwards, Tom Hopkins, Zig Ziglar, and all of the greats in the field of success philosophy and selling power. All the rest of the pioneers are listed in our extensive bibliography.

Introduction

Getting to Yes

There are two kinds of people in any business.

1) People who generate revenue.

2) People who spend those revenues.

This book is written for those who generate revenue. This book is written for the person who sells. This book is written for you.

Without you, the economy dies. Without you, the federal government goes broke. Without you, the stock market collapses. Without you, every corporation in the world is bankrupt. This book is going to show you how to capitalize on the science and art of human influence. Whatever your current income is, you deserve more. You are paying everyone's bills. It's that simple.

People who sell for a living are the best-paid people in the world, but they deserve so much more because it is the person who sells that makes the world go around. This book is our tribute and our gift to you. It is a literal instruction book that reveals how to sell more and achieve great success.

The first thing you will notice about this book is that it's different. Most sales books show you lots of ways to "close the sale." We'll show you a few, but books that focus on closing the sale miss the point of selling. We want your customer to beg you to hire you, your company, buy your products and services. Our objective is to focus on what really drives the selling process.

Closing sales is a result of asking someone for an agreement. As you will see, closing sales will take on an entirely new meaning after reading this book. It becomes easy. Instead of using the ancient warrior mentality of selling, where you have to beat your customer over the head 6.7 times before she says "yes," you now have the science and psychology of selling at your fingertips to make the process a pleasure instead of a contest.

You will see the phrase "Mind Access" sprinkled throughout the text. Therefore you really should know what mind access is and what a Mind Access Point is. I coined the phrase "Mind Access" in 1996. It is a phrase that encompasses unconscious communication and the instinctual drives that move us in one direction instead of another.

A Mind Access Point (MAP) is any stimulus-response "mechanism" that has been conditioned in a person's mind either genetically or through life experience. This book shows you how to avoid setting off negative stimulus-response "mechanisms" while carefully and ethically pulling the strings that encourage your customer to say "yes."

Mind Access is much more than a number of powerful techniques for making money and gaining compliance through the selling process. Mind Access is also a philosophy of success that encompasses your whole life. People who read this book will easily improve their sales. If you apply what you learn here, your life will literally change. You will double, triple, or quadruple your income. You will be happier. You will be more excited about life. Therefore, before you help other people get what they want, you want to make a commitment to yourself. You want to commit to yourself and those you love that you will take good care of yourself and those around you. Turn these pages and commit now!

After decades of studying psychology you learn that commitment is NOT just a mental process. We know that people who commit to something, to anything, in writing are far more likely to fulfill their commitment than those who verbally say they will do something. Because this is true, we want you to participate in the simple act of signing your name below as a commitment to your success.

Commitment

Whether you are influencing yourself or others, the power of commitment is critical. Promise yourself now that you will be great and live your dreams. You probably have heard or read about a decades-long Harvard study that revealed that **3 percent of students who wrote down their life goals in college out-earned the remaining 97 percent of all Harvard**

students. The power of written goals and signing your name to your promise of your future is absolutely essential in your success plan. What follows are the keys to long-term success.

1) Becoming a black belt in selling (My co-author is a black belt in several forms of karate, so I'm adopting this phrase as a rapport-building mechanism!) requires committing yourself to mastery and the cessation of dabbling. Only people who are experts in communication truly become successful in sales and life. Today, you commit to becoming an expert in communication. Conscious and unconscious, verbal and nonverbal. Interpersonal and textual skills are all necessities to long term success.

2) Commit to find a coach, a mentor and a model. Who are people who can assist you in your quest for excellence in persuasion? Who are people who can assist you in your quest for excellence in life? If you don't know of anyone, you can call the International Institute of Coaching at 1-800-398-4642. Salespeople all too often try to be go-it-aloners. I want you to have someone to keep you going to the next level . . . and the next one after that!

3) In a notebook, write down everything you will tell your coach about what motivates you. What are you moving toward in life? What are you moving away from in life? What things do you want to experience more of? What are you tired of? What don't you want in life anymore? Write down everything, and we mean EVERYTHING. Write down everything that relates to your family, friends, values, beliefs, attitudes, your lifestyle, everything.

4) Develop a mastermind group. The word "mastermind" was popularized by the success philosopher Napoleon Hill. A mastermind is a group of people focused on creating and directing the success of themselves and others in the group. Once you decide upon who will be in your mastermind (your coach, your mentor, your motivators), give your coach your e-mail, fax number, and phone number.

5) Ask your coach or mentor to call you twice each month to keep you inspired and keep you on course for sales excellence and happiness in life. Get your mentor to fire you up and give your mentor permission to help you when you miss your mark.

6) Your coach or mentor should sign the Commitment to Achievement below, which you can copy on a separate sheet of paper. If you don't have a coach yet, sign anyway and begin the process now! Remember: The 3 percent earned more money than the 97 percent. Do you think commitment matters? Here's your chance.

Commitment to Achievement

1. I am 100 percent committed to taking action on the information I learn in this book in my everyday life. I know that my success or failure in using the skills I learn in this book are based solely on my effort and practice.

2. I am 100 percent committed to be completely responsible to and for myself. No one but me can take responsibility for what I learn from this program and its applications in my life. If I don't apply the material I learn from this program, I know I am destined for mediocrity. I know that my emotions drive my behavior and I will begin taking charge of my emotions today.

3. I am 100 percent committed to becoming a flexible communicator and flexible in my behavior. I know and understand that I am the key to my own success by being the most flexible person in every communication I enter into. I have the widest variety of possible behavioral choices of any person I meet. I know exactly what result I want at the beginning of each encounter. I always take appropriate action. I constantly monitor feedback and change my approach when necessary.

I am 100 percent commited to becoming part of the top 3 percent.

Signature_____

Coach_____

Here is the first key question of this book:

Question: What is the difference between the top 20 percent of salespeople who earn 80 percent of the money and the 80 percent of salespeople who earn 20 percent of the money?

Answers:

The top 20 percent of salespeople are expert communicators. They know how to ask questions and discover the needs and desires of others.

Those who dwell in mediocrity do so until they have powerful reasons to move in a different direction . . . or any direction.

Salespeople who don't live up to their potential have not set and planned for powerful goals.

Outstanding salespeople are experts in two things. One is the field in which they are selling. The other is in communicating at the unconscious level.

Most people who are currently involved in the sales professions are influence-impotent because they do not have compelling reasons and goals to take advantage of their potential knowledge. They do not understand how other people think, and they do not know how to motivate themselves so they can catch fire to act on knowledge.

Why are you going to be different? What benefits and reasons do you have to become an expert?

WHY?

. . . is the most important question in the journey of success.

1) Find the BIG WHY your customer needs your products and services and you will be influential, you will be successful, and you will become wealthy.

2) Find the BIG WHY you must be successful and you will be.

When you know what motivates a person you can influence them. When you know what motivates yourself you can change your own behavior.

Mind Access Points (MAP): Become an Expert

Recent research reveals that a waitress who touches a customer as she gives him the bill is more likely to get a larger tip on average than a waitress who doesn't touch her customer. That is a MAP. The waitress purposefully and ethically "pulls the string" (or pushes the customer's button, if you will) and because she does so, she gets a larger tip.

She knows either consciously or unconsciously that her tips are larger if she makes contact with her customer. There are thousands of MAPs installed in the minds of your customers. Knowing which strings to pull and when to pull them will determine how many sales per contact you have, and the volume of sale per contact will go up as well if it applies in your business.

With all of the knowledge you are about to discover, how will you actually utilize this information? What is the process to go from being in awe of what you are going to learn to mastering it?

Mastery

There are five basic steps to becoming a master salesperson. You must do these five things if you are going to be in the top 20 percent who earn 80 percent of the money.

1. Find an excellent model. A model is someone who has done what you want to do. You must discover how they do what they do. This book in many ways includes an ideal model of sales success. The authors are revealing not only their secrets of success but the secrets that have been scientifically tested and proven by the best salespeople in the world.

2. Repeat and duplicate the work of your model. As you learn the skills, attitudes, thought processes, and actions of your model, you duplicate what they do.

3. Regularly utilize the skills that you are practicing. This book contains hundreds of MAPs that you will want to practice. Practice is the mother of skill.

4. Integrate the skills you are learning into your behavior. Always choose as models people who have the highest values and beliefs that you

are comfortable with. As you begin to experience success, you want to be happy with your new patterns of behavior.

5. Reinforce the skills you are learning. Each day notice where you are on Maslow's learning curve, which you will find below.

The Sales Learning Curve

Abraham Maslow, one of the leading psychologists of the 20th century, discovered that we all go through a four-step process in self mastery. (He used slightly different terminology, as you may remember from your psychology classes in school!)

1. Unconscious Incompetence. Stage one in learning is where you don't even know that you are ignorant of what is effective in selling.

2. Conscious Incompetence. Stage two in learning how to sell is where you become aware that you do not know how or why people buy in each specific situation.

3. Conscious Competence. Stage three in learning how to sell occurs when you become an effective salesperson at the conscious level. In other words, you are able to pay attention to the communication styles, MAPs, buying profiles, etc. of your client, *and* discuss your products and services at the same time.

4. Unconscious Competence. Mastery is the fourth and final stage in learning how to sell. Once you have reached the level of unconscious competence, you are no longer consciously aware of what you are effectively doing in the sales process. At this point you have become a master and you sell as naturally as you drive or walk. At this stage you sell your products and services to the vast majority of people you interact with.

Thought Exercise: How these four elements occur in all learning and not simply learning how to sell using MAPs. Are there any exceptions?

> *Mind Access Point (MAP). Knowing when and where to touch someone can dramatically increase your income.*

Dozens of the world's largest corporations have *some* of the research you are about to learn. No one has all of what you are about to learn because much of this research in selling at the unconscious level is unique. Some of it is so cutting edge that it has been released only in the eighteen months prior to the writing of this book!

Obviously not all MAPs can be taught in a book. Hundreds of strategies and techniques relate to vocal intonation, vocal pacing, tone of voice, tiny facial expressions, and specific body postures and motion that are simply impossible to capture in the printed word. Don't worry. You can learn them, too, either through our audio and videocassette programs or at live seminars. We promise you that we will hold nothing back. You will learn the complete lexicon of unconscious persuasive communication.

Becoming a black belt in selling gives you the ability to pull mental strings to get the predictable responses that have been programmed into your customer, often in childhood or before. MAPs all occur below the level of conscious awareness. In other words, few if any people are aware of why they are making a decision if a MAP is being pulled. This puts immense power and responsibility into the hands of the expert with the techniques you are about to learn.

When you bought this book you really hired us to teach you the MAPs that are the most applicable to you as a person who sells products or services. You have hired us to show you specifically what to do to increase your sales-per-call ratio. You have hired us to show you how to simplify the sales process for you. You have hired us to show you how to communicate with another person's unconscious mind in a simple, easy-to-understand manner.

If you carefully utilize the strategies and tools in this book, we promise that you will make more "sales per call" from this moment on, for the rest of your life. We guarantee it.

Most books you have read about selling have focused on selling your product or service to someone or some group at the conscious level of thinking. On a random chance basis that is nothing more than a numbers game. Ten cold calls might get you an appointment in the old system of thinking. Ten appointments might earn you a sale using the old-school methodologies. If you want to be able to decide who you are going to allow to buy from you, and who you are going to pass by, then you can begin incorporating the concepts and techniques in this book immediately.

Why would anyone release this powerful technology to the public? Wouldn't it be better to just keep this information closely guarded and use it only for one person's or corporation's benefit?

No.

We have an ulterior motive. As I write this confession, I need you to know that we have made some predictions. First of all, you are learning new information, new strategies and techniques. Some of this information has never appeared in text before. We know by the unconscious law of reciprocity (see Chapter 10 for the ten Unconscious Laws of Persuasion and Selling) that once we give you this information you will almost certainly be appreciative and want to do something nice for us. Question: If I show you how to earn $10,000 more next year than you did last year, would you tell ten friends about this book? Of course you would! That's what reciprocity is all about!

Salespeople make the world go around. The more sales that are made, the better the economy. The better the economy the more expendable income there is. The more expendable income there is, the more people can afford to own a copy of this book or utilize our programs. This is the ultimate win/win technology. Selling awesome and life-changing products and services is how great people and great companies get to use that adjective.

For years only the largest corporations in the world had many of these strategies and techniques available to them. In recent years, we have discovered many nuances in successful selling. Many more have been discovered by social psychologists and have NEVER been talked about until now! Even more techniques have been leaked from the major corporate advertising firms.

The problem that faces the salesperson is finding out what works and what doesn't. This book solves the problem for you. Everything in this book is tested, tried, and true. Everything in this book works.

Everything you read in this book has been thoroughly studied and researched. The tools, techniques, skills, and patterns you are about to read about work in real life regardless of what you sell. There can be no doubt that much of what you are about to learn about the science of selling is new to you and unknown by everyone else in your office. You will not be bored with the scientific jargon that has helped us discover this information, but you will be given an extensive bibliography that will help you do further research into selling and specifically selling to the unconscious mind. Why all the attention on the unconscious mind?

The unconscious mind is where the sale is really made. The unconscious mind is the storehouse of memory and emotion. It makes up 99.999 percent of all of your experience. Your conscious mind is the part of you that is aware of what you are reading at this moment. It is engaged in some "critical thinking" and learning processes, and that is about it. Most people sell to the conscious mind, and that is why most people fail in selling.

Selling is much more fun when *you* decide whether the other person is going to buy from you instead of the other way around. The difference between selling to the conscious mind and the unconscious mind is the difference between random success in selling and selling almost everyone you want to.

In *The Psychology of Persuasion: How to Persuade Others to Your Way of Thinking* (Kevin Hogan, 1996, Pelican Publishing), I showed you how to be more influential, make more money, and improve your personal relationships by utilizing the powerful techniques of persuasion.

From the many letters and e-mails I received (and continue to receive), it became clear you wanted more . . . much more. I know you are already making more money, and that is exciting news. The cry was heard, and here is the beginning of the answer to the voices that yelled, "more, more, MORE!"

The difference between this book and *The Psychology of Persuasion* is very simple. This book goes beyond altering someone's behavior. As you learn the material in this book you will discover that many MAPs were "programmed" into you and your customers before birth. That means many of your behaviors are shaped in your genes, in your DNA. Better? We make it simple to understand, easy to apply, *and we promise that you will learn how to change people's minds by simply appealing to them at an instinctual level!* Nothing is more compelling. Nothing.

What I'm saying is that this book takes you straight to the double helix, the DNA, and you don't even have to know how DNA works or even what it is to use the techniques in this book. We did the research, applied the techniques in real selling experiences, and have simplified them into easy-to-master themes and concepts. All you have to do is push the right buttons.

The Microsoft Approach

We want you to be the dominant force in selling what you sell. Your name will become equated with your product or service. What was Microsoft's goal? To make good software? Nope. To sell lots of software? Nope. Microsoft's goal was to dominate the market by becoming the operating system in every computer on earth. Did they succeed? No. They are in only 97 percent of the computers on earth.

I guess they will have to suffer the embarrassment of knowing that all of their competitors combined only have 3 percent of the market. Microsoft really did it right, didn't they? They produced the friendliest software on earth and decided they wanted everyone to use it. This is what we want you to do. We want you to be the salesperson this side of Tokyo, and we want you to decide who will be buying your products and services.

There is one important point we should discuss. *If you sell something to someone who cannot benefit from your product or service, you will not develop the long-term relationships that are necessary for success in business.* A black belt in the martial arts doesn't prove his skills by harming the helpless. He proves his skills by defeating the competition. This book shows you how to eliminate the competition. Never sell to anyone who doesn't benefit far more from purchasing your product than the price they pay you! With this one cautionary note, you can know that the edge you have over your competition is literally in your hands . . . and it is enormous.

This extraordinary technology picks up where *The Psychology of Persuasion* leaves off and comes very close to what would be the ultimate in unconscious communication: psi abilities. We haven't broken that barrier yet, but you don't need to be any closer. You're knocking on the door!

Using the tools you learn in this book, you will eventually be able to almost "read" people's minds. You will be able to know what program is running at each given moment and easily "see" what strings are "in play" and ready to be pulled. *You will be in control of each communication you participate in.* Your confidence will soar. People will literally beg you to sell them your products.

Hi! This is William Horton writing for you now. Kevin gets so excited about selling I can't get a word in edgewise! I'll see you in Chapter 5 ("Rapport!"). I wanted to wait until then but I decided to cut in now. I want to share something with you before letting Kevin come back! If you have ever seen Kevin Hogan speak to an audience in person, you can see his enthusiasm and passion or selling and communication. You should know that he never "sells" any products in front of an audience, yet people shout from the audience about how they can buy his audio and video programs.

It is truly a startling phenomenon. In part, his success in selling is based upon his reputation of giving his all. In part it is because people know that they are always getting the cutting, no, the bleeding edge, from Kevin. This book will show you how to do what Kevin does. (Now, we'll let Kevin come back. I'll see you in a bit!

Mastering MAPs means that you will be able to move people to the point where they seemingly cannot control themselves. They will demand to buy from you. You will never "sell" anything again.

I want to share with people a tremendous value in return for their buying the book. What I do is provide huge value to the reader, and in return you always remember where you got the information and tools that changed your life. Zig Ziglar once said, "They don't care about how much you know until they know how much you care." That is a Mind Access Point, and that is our philosophy in teaching you.

> *If you truly care about your customers, they will demand your services and they will be loyal to you for a lifetime.*

Napoleon Hill, the great success philosopher, said to "go the extra mile" for people.

Are You READY?

Say "Yes," or **"YES!"**

What will you learn as you turn the pages in this book?

- How to predict human behavior with accuracy.
- Specifically what to do to create demand for your products or services.
- Exactly what the motivating forces are within each individual and among groups as wholes.
- How to alter your products or services so people insist that you allow them to buy from you, NOW.
- How genes influence your customers' behavior, so you can pull their genetic strings.
- All the keys to writing powerful copy that backs up verbal claims and makes for great personal presentations.
- The limitless potential of unconscious communication.

Unconscious Communication: Reaching the Only Decision Maker You Will Ever Need

What is unconscious communication? Before we define it, let's see if we can give you two vivid examples to prime your mind to understand the concept before putting it into words.

1) Have you ever met someone with whom you had instant chemistry?

2) Have you ever met someone whom you knew you didn't like, before they ever uttered a word?

In both cases, unconscious communication was occurring long before anyone spoke.

Unconscious communication includes the sending and receiving of verbal and nonverbal communication as it is perceived by the unconscious mind. The unconscious mind is that part of our thinking that we are not aware of at any one moment. It's always there and it's always paying attention. In fact, it's always communicating.

What are some other examples of unconscious communication?

- The way a person smells may or may not register at the conscious level of thought but it "speaks volumes" at the unconscious level. The scent you wear, or whether you wear none at all, alters the entire perception of any selling situation you enter into.
- The exact body posture and gestures you have can trigger positive or negative emotions in anyone you meet. People aren't aware of these triggers at the conscious level but the unconscious mind immediately detects them.

For example: If your buyer (your client) was physically struck by a parent as a child, just viewing a hand raised above the head can create fear. At the conscious level the buyer doesn't know that he rejected you on the basis of something that happened to him as a child, but the unconscious mind knew instantly that it didn't like the salesperson.

- Where you sit at a table will increase or decrease your chances of making the sale, as will how you sit in that chair.
- When making a presentation, whether you use a podium, and/or how you use it can make or break a sale before you utter a word.
- Wearing contact lenses will make some sales presentations more likely to sell and others less likely to sell. This book will teach you how to know whether to wear glasses or contacts.
- Jewelry sends messages at both the conscious and unconscious level. You'll learn all of the correct types of jewelry to wear and when to wear

jewelry. Each prospect you meet will be different, and you will need to make adjustments.

• Your physical appearance will make and break sales. This book will show you when casual is a must, when an expensive coat and tie are demanded, what skirt lengths a female salesperson should wear, and how the unconscious mind perceives differences in dress.

• The unconscious mind processes the tonality of words and phrases while the conscious mind processes the language. The tonality will normally overcome the actual words and phrases. Do you know when to change your tonality?

• There are words that the unconscious mind almost always says "yes" to. The conscious mind finds them irrelevant but the unconscious mind makes the decisions. Read on and you will learn what they are.

• How close you stand to a prospect will determine whether or not he is instantly turned off to you and your products and services.

This book brings to your fingertips (which, by the way, also send unconscious signals to everyone you meet) the secrets of MAPs. We all have coded into our brains thousands of stimulus-response experiences. Any person can knowingly or unknowingly pull your strings and you react immediately without conscious thought. Each of these is a Mind Access Point. If you master only twenty of the hundreds of techniques to gently touch other people's MAPs, you will increase your sales volume without ever needing to increase the number of contacts and prospects you see.

Every presentation you make from this day forward is going to be much easier. As you find yourself becoming more skilled at unconscious communication, you will find that you rarely ask for a sale. "Closing the sale" will quickly become a thing of the past or, at worst, a mere formality. Your customers will literally *demand* that you sell them your products and then they will develop loyalty to you in a such a way that makes future selling a mere formality. *That isn't a promise, it is a guarantee.* Utilizing unconscious communication is a skill that takes some time to master.

As you practice one technique each day, you will find yourself in control of every sales situation you enter. You're on your way to being in charge from this day on.

Turn the pages and learn how these MAPs developed in each of us. Then learn how to pull the right strings and push the right buttons with each of your customers. Enjoy!

CHAPTER 1

Why You Are a Salesperson

Before we begin discussing the science of selling, we should remember that we all are attracted to this profession because of our desires and values. No one chooses to sell because they want a simple 9 to 5 job. Here is a fact I want you to always remember:

> *Salespeople are the income providers of every other person on earth.*

Every single person on earth who is not in the business of selling is completely in debt to those who do. There is no customer-service department without the salesperson. There is no government without salespeople. There is no military funding without salespeople. Every single monetary exchange begins and ends with a salesperson.

> *There are two kinds of people in the world: those who generate money and those who consume it.*

Every person on earth owes an eternal debt of gratitude to sales-people because without salespeople there would be no jobs for anyone.

Salespeople are more than special; they make the world go 'round. The profession of selling is literally the most important profession on earth. Without you there is no government. Without you and other salespeople there is no economy, no retirement, no Medicare, no military . . . there is nothing. You're making the world go 'round. Thank you!

The Birth of a Salesman\Autumn 1972
Selling: My Only Hope

I (KH) started selling when I was ten years old. I had to. I was the oldest of five children and we had no money. My stepfather was going to die in less than eighteen months and Mom's time was divided between her job and taking care of Dad, who was confined to a hospital bed in our home. It was a heck of a way to live. We lived in a "lower-middle class" suburb of Chicago. If I wanted to have money for anything (and I did), I would have to sell something.

I sold my services in the wintertime as the kid on the street who would shovel your driveway. $1 per hour. The Chicago winds would blow out of the north and off the lake with a bitter coldness that I'll never forget. Sometimes I'd take the $3 I would earn and give it to Mom. Sometimes I'd keep the money and buy Pepsi and Reese's. In the summer, I would sell my services cutting people's lawns or pulling weeds. (I hated pulling weeds.)

Realizing that there was no hope for me in the lawn and garden services, I knew at age ten I would have to do something where I could utilize my time in a far more efficient manner. I saw an ad in a Sunday newspaper for Cheerful House Greeting Cards. I read that I could earn from fifty cents to two dollars for each box of cards sold. I immediately sent the company my $10 for a sample kit. ($10 was a lot of money in those days.)

In return, Cheerful House sent me five boxes of Christmas cards. Some quick math calculations revealed that if I just sold the five boxes I'd make one dollar per box sold! The sales literature said that there would only be four "selling seasons" per year, so whatever money was going to be earned would have to last a LONG time.

I got home from school the next day, and as soon as my paper route was done I was ready to go make some real money! I knocked on my neighbor's door. It was Mrs. Gossard. I showed her my cards and she bought a box. My first dollar was earned! Then I went to Mrs. Singer. (She couldn't buy a box.) Mrs. Hendricks bought two boxes, Mrs. Serdar bought a box. Mrs. Makela bought a box. Lots of other people didn't.

I was gone until 8 P.M. and had knocked on thirty doors and sold about eighteen boxes of cards. I looked at my watch as the sun was setting. I knew I had to go home and help put the kids to bed. I had checks totaling about $60, of which my math whiz brain figured $20 was mine.

Mom was so excited when she saw the order sheet. I told her that I'd give her all the money I earned. She replied, "No. You earned it; you are going to keep it."

Wow! The next day I left the neighborhood to start selling in a neighborhood I never went to. I was out from the time my paper route was done until sunset. I sold only four boxes of cards. Some of the people's houses were scary looking and, being a skinny little kid, I decided that I wouldn't go back there again! Nevertheless, I made about $4. I showed Mom when I got home and she told me that it was mine to keep.

The problem was that I knocked on about fifty doors to earn that $4. I couldn't believe that more people didn't buy my Christmas cards. They obviously weren't as smart as the people in my neighborhood. The next day was Saturday and I remember getting up, delivering the Saturday morning *Waukegan News-Sun* (it had to be delivered by 7 A.M.!), cutting the lawn, and then at noon off I went on my bicycle. I went into neighborhoods I had never been to and knocked on over 100 doors that day. I didn't stop to eat lunch . . . or dinner. I sold six boxes of cards.

I got home to find that there was no Hamburger Helper left. (I was eternally grateful.) I told Mom that I didn't have a very good day. I had made $6, but I was driving across highways and I was kind of scared of the neighborhoods I was going into. She suggested I stick with the neighborhoods where people knew me and that way I wouldn't be crossing the highways anymore. (She would later tell me she was scared to death that her son was going into some of the neighborhoods!)

We totaled the order sheet. I had sold twenty-eight boxes of cards. My total earnings would be about $30. I would get paid after I delivered all of the cards to my customers. I couldn't wait!

I learned a lot that week.

I learned that people were more likely to buy from me if they knew me. I realized that if people had the money, I could talk them into buying an extra box for someone else as a gift.

I learned that selling cards was a lot better than cutting the lawn, pulling weeds, shoveling the snow, or delivering the newspaper.

I learned I could only work four weeks per year selling cards. Selling cards was going to make me $100 next year but I'd need to think of something else to sell if I was going to make more money.

More importantly, after delivering the cards to the people a few weeks earlier, I realized how much fun it was to see people smile and say, "Thanks, Kevin." "They're beautiful." "You got those to me faster than I expected."

Most importantly, I made $30 for about twenty hours of work that was not physically killing my scrawny ten-year-old body!

I sold greeting cards for the next four years as a source of income. I sold flower seeds and vegetable seeds. (I also continued to sell my body shoveling snow, pulling weeds, cutting lawns, and doing anything I could.) The most fun was selling cards, though. The women were (for the most part) fun to talk with, the work was all sitting down in their living rooms, and some of them even gave me cookies and milk those few days a year when I was selling. I was actually having fun working at something.

The ad from Cheerful House Greeting Cards changed my life. Not because it made me rich. It didn't. It gave me hope that I could escape living in poverty. The Boy Scouts wouldn't need to bring me clothes and turkey dinners on Thanksgiving any more. (The Boy Scouts delivered clothing and food to our home on Thanksgiving on a couple of occasions. I remember appreciating the clothes and food . . . and hating being needy.) I knew that whatever I was going to do when I was older, it would be selling.

I was right.

I discovered as a ten-year-old that the ability to think quickly and talk with people could give me a chance to escape being poor and maybe . . . just maybe . . . be rich. Selling was hard work in some ways, but it was fun. It certainly beat "physical work!"

Selling would give me security, freedom, independence, and the ability to be productive, to be valuable to other people. It was something I could do well.

Fast forward to 1998.

Autumn 1998

I've been earning a six-figure income for a few years. I've owned my own business, consulted or sold for other people since 1987. The idea of receiving an hourly wage and punching a time clock is almost a phobia. Business is good. I have several books in print, including one, *The Psychology of Persuasion,* that is doing pretty darned well in the bookstores. But . . .

I've stalled. I've stagnated. I've been earning $1,000 to $2,000 per speech I give. Nothing wrong with that, but I've been there and done that.

What is going on? No one is offering me more than that. I am baffled. People compare my speaking style to Anthony Robbins and my physical and offstage presence to Kelsey Grammar, David Letterman, and Drew Carey. Now, what more could a guy want? That's enough talent to feed off for FOUR lifetimes.

Enter Dottie Walters, the author of *Speak and Grow Rich.* (Dottie owns the world's most prestigious speakers bureau and publishes *Sharing Ideas* magazine for national speakers.)

I see her Speak and Grow Rich course listed next to mine in the Open U catalog. I have no time to take a full day off and learn what I already know, regardless of whom it is with. But for years I have been wanting to meet Dottie. She would now be about seventy, or maybe older . . . and it was her book *Speak and Grow Rich* that helped me focus my world on teaching and speaking in public for a significant portion of my current living.

I decided to take the Saturday off and go see Dottie. If nothing else, I should thank her for being inspirational in my life!

I experienced her class with about twenty other students. I enjoyed watching the woman speak for five hours. She was able to keep the group enthralled with stories she had no doubt told for decades. Her approach was simple and somewhat "grandmotherly." She was kind and direct. I was in love. (Not to mention that watching her do back-of-the-room sales was inspiring!)

I didn't get what I came for, though. I hadn't really learned anything "new." But I was in love. I approached her after everyone had left the class and her grandson had finished packing the few books and videotapes that hadn't been snatched up by the audience.

"Dottie, I'm Kevin Hogan. I want you to know you have been an inspiration in my career."

"Thank you, Kevin."

She looked up into my eyes. She was tired. I've been here before. The last person wants to keep you forever. You (I) have been on stage for six hours and you want to find the bed in the hotel and fall flat on your face and have them wake you in fifteen hours for breakfast.

"Dottie, I want you to have this." (I hand her my book *The Psychology of Persuasion.)*

"Thank you, Dear."

O.K., Kevin, her brain is fading. Either ask or get the hell out of here. She has a date with a hotel pillow and you are being as charming as a bottle of mental Drano.

"Dottie, I have one question for you. I have been doing about $1,500 per speech for the last couple of years. It doesn't change. They don't offer more than $2,000. What do you suggest? You tell me, I'll do it. Anything. What is going to take me to the next ($5,000+) level?"

"Have you asked, Kevin?"

"Pardon me?"

"Have you asked for $5,000?"

"Well, not really. I mean . . . no . . . you know, I haven't."

She put her hand on my arm and patted me like I was a little child.

"Well, Honey, just ask." She looked at my book and smiled. "Just ask."

"Thanks, Dottie, I will."

As I walked out of the door on that brisk Minneapolis afternoon, I wondered just how stupid I must have looked. Successful author towers over sweet woman asking the dumbest question on the face of the earth. Thank God no one would ever know about this moment.

Fast forward one month.

Early Winter 1998

I have a sore throat and a terrible cold. My nose is stuffier than it ever has been. I feel terrible. CNBC is on in the background. The market is not doing well and I'm not making money today.

(Ring)

"Who could that be?" I talk to CNBC when no one else is around.

"Kevin Hogan, can I help you?" (It didn't sound like that . . . but maybe they bought it on the other end."

"Is this Dr. Hogan?"

"Yes it is." (Dr. Hogan has actually left the building for dead. This is his associate who has not yet succumbed to the flu.)

"Oh, you sound terrible. This is Richard Marks (not his real name) with the Sales Association (not their real name either)."

"How can I help you?"

"Well, we were at your web site and are looking for a speaker for our winter meeting in Minneapolis. What are you charging nowadays."

Here it is, Kevin. You spent the last month finishing Talk Your Way to the Top. It's over. The book is at Pelican Publishing Company. What are you going to tell this guy? Your voice sounds like hell. You've just yelled at CNBC. You . . . just ask, Honey. Just ask.

"Five thousand dollars is my fee, but I'd sure like to know more about your group and what you are looking for."

Richard tells me about his group, tells me they want me to talk about "body language," and asks if I will settle for $4,000, which is what his budget is approved for.

What's the difference between 4K and 5K anyway? You're working for ONE HOUR, Kevin? You moron. It's an hour drive and you are working for an hour. Just ask, Honey . . . just ask.

"No, My fee is $5,000, and I think I can give you exactly what you are looking for. An hour of massive entertainment combined with an hour of data, all happening simultaneously."

"I'll have to check for approval on $5,000. I'll call you back. Thanks, Kevin, we'll talk soon."

I thought to myself, *"You stupid moron."* (CNBC *was running a commercial with Ringo Starr in it . . . I could use a little help from my friends . . . Ringo . . .)* "What the heck are you thinking? Guaranteed $4,000. Been paid that once for a full day, never for an hour, and you say $5,000. Idiot. Idiot. Idiot."

Sue Herrera talks with Ron Insana about how the market is taking a hit today and I'm feeling like a bigger idiot by the micro-second. The phone doesn't ring for the rest of the day.

Fast forward to next day.

(Ring)
"Kevin Hogan."
"That really you?"
"Who's this?"
"Richard Marks."
"Hi, Richard, good to hear your voice." *(I'll take the $4,000. Just offer it again now and I'm yours.)*

"Kevin, we got the $5,000 approved and would like you to . . . blah blah blah blah . . . *(Get out of here. DOTTIE, I LOVE YOU . . . just ask, Honey . . . I never doubted you, Dottie, I swear to . . . just ask . . . and I wrote* The Psychology of Persuasion. *I mean, how long does it take to realize that you are unable to follow your own advice? Just ask, Honey. DOTTIE, YOU ARE THE GREATEST!)*

"How does that sound, Kevin?"

"Yes, absolutely. Let's run through the details again. My head is foggy from this flu."

Deal closed. Check received in six business days. That was the last time I doubted that still, small sweet voice in my head. Dottie is with me always.

Have you ever suffered from low self-esteem? We all do. I tell you this story because every time I think of it I remember that I'm worth an enormous amount to people, to society, to myself. I also think of my childhood because it reminds me that no matter how tough things get, they aren't going to be that bad ever again.

When you sell, **you** *determine your outcomes.*

Whether you are ten years old or seventy years old, you are going to determine your own fate in selling. You are a free agent and can choose to sell almost any product or service you want. Once you have the product or service picked out that you want to sell remember this fact:

People don't buy your product; they buy you.

You must represent a great product or service. What you sell is critical to your self-image and your self-esteem. It needs to be the best, and if it isn't, dump it and go get on the team that is the best. Every product has problems. Every service has its weaknesses. My question is, did you pick the best of the group? If not, go sign up with the best. Because once you do, the rest of the story is about YOU!

Selling is an inside job. It all takes place inside people's minds. Selling is a simple science that encompasses beliefs, values, attitudes, lifestyles, emotions, feelings, and psychological shifts. Selling is the most wonderful profession on earth because it gives you what you want:

✓ Freedom
✓ Security
✓ Productivity
✓ Independence
✓ Sense of Accomplishment

No longer are you a slave to anyone. You are your own boss and you are the master of your life. You'll never work forty hours again. You'll work fifty or sixty because they are for YOU and the people you love. Selling is the solution to the destructive "dollars per hour" mentality that exists everywhere. You'll never get paid an hourly wage again. You'll be "unemployed" every day for the rest of your life and you will never feel more in charge of your own life!

Dr. Horton (WH) and I (KH) will take you on a journey through your mind and the mind of the people you are selling to in this book. You will be given all of the tools you need to earn a six- or seven-figure income. If you're really ready to run your own life and learn the new science of selling, please continue reading!

CHAPTER 2

21st-Century Selling: The Ultimate Selling Model

Win/Win Relationships Create Near-Term Wealth and Long-Term Happiness

There is a special energy about selling. Occasionally, the sales transaction is experienced as a chess game where there are two opponents who must buy and sell from each other, and only one will ultimately win and one will ultimately lose. Far more often **the sales setting is one where both the customer and salesperson MUST win.**

In some selling situations, you will never see the buyer again. Selling a house, a timeshare, or a car is typically a one-time interaction between the salesperson and the customer. The pressure experienced by both salesperson and customer is far greater in each of these settings because it is a "one-shot deal." A win/win scenario is still critical to the long-term success of the customer's finances and the salesperson's reputation. The "feel" of these kinds of transactions is very different from long-term relationship selling, though.

Insurance salespeople have a slightly different kind of pressure on them. People who sell to a customer every week or month (pharmaceuticals, for example) have an even different type of pressure. One thing is certain: Engaging in Win/Win deals will make you sleep at night and be proud of the work you are in.

My (KH) personal insurance agent is Denis Dunker of Cannon Falls, Minnesota. In all but two years of my adult life he has served as my casualty insurance agent. He has always utilized MAPs effectively and ethically in working with me. On many occasions in the past I have "demanded" that my coverage be improved. That is one of the telltale signs of someone who is a master at walking on someone else's mind map! When the customer demands the salesperson sell them more and more, the salesperson has become a master.

Every couple of years Denis makes it a point to drive the forty-five minutes to get to my home in the Twin Cities. He drives past several other State Farm insurance agencies on the way up here for a visit or a luncheon date. In theory, I should have had my business with one of those agents he drives past, but Denis has built a long-term relationship, a friendship, and has always shown great respect and interest in my work.

Those are all important to me, and they are all related to many of the sixteen basic desires you will learn about in the next two chapters.

> *All people need respect and friendship.*

Denis probably didn't know that being a friend and respecting someone's work is part of my instinctual drive. He simply likes people and works hard to do what is in his customer's best interests. Today Denis is a wealthy man and has a substantial client base that will take care of him and his family for the rest of his life. He never has asked me buy an insurance product I didn't want. In fact, he has never "closed" a sale with me. He has always allowed me to "close myself."

He utilized my personality, which includes analyzing data, being in charge, being a decision maker, and has acted as my advisor instead of what other less astute individuals may have done . . . and lost my business. Here is Denis's key to success:

> *Build rapport and ask questions!*

Denis has taken care of me for over twenty years and hopefully will do the same for the next twenty years. He is an unconscious master of selling, and I don't think he is fully aware of it. On his next island vacation trip, I'm sure he'll not be too concerned as he sits on the beach with his wife sipping from the tall glasses. That's what happens when you care about people. They demand you sell to them . . . because they know you care . . . just like Zig Ziglar said.

When I think of Win/Win on a different level, I think of the great expense and the great fun involved in a trip to Disneyland.

When was the last time you went to Disneyworld or Disneyland?

Remember how much fun everyone had? The rides were great. The shows were great. Meeting the cartoon and fantasy characters was a thrill for the children. The day or weekend at Disney may have been the focal point of the vacation. You look at your pictures from Disney and think of how thrilled the kids were to get there.

In between the parking lot and the park was a ticket booth where you paid over $100 for your day of fun. You may have been shocked at how much the price had gone up since the last time you had been there. Looking back, was it worth it? You bet. You paid a lot of money to allow your family to have a great deal of fun. It was definitely worth it.

It was a Win/Win deal. Disney's tradition is to continually generate enormous revenues from the masses of the world populace in exchange for an experience of great fun and enjoyment.

Win/Win thinking is not a platitude with a wink attached to it.

Win/Win is at the core of every long-term, successful business venture and sales meeting in the free world. Win/Win thinking is the foundation for every technique utilized in this book.

Two Levels of Awareness

Sales are made and lost on two levels of awareness and communication. One level is called the conscious level of awareness. The other is the unconscious level of awareness. After you read this book, there will no longer be anything mysterious about the unconscious level of awareness. The unconscious level of awareness is that which you are not consciously aware of but are still responding to in your mind and body. Communication is ongoing at both levels of awareness all of the time during the sales setting and no one is ever *fully* aware of what is happening at both levels of awareness.

Here is what is even more fascinating. **Before two people see each other in the sales setting, many sales are made and broken.** Even before a customer and a prospect ever meet (or even know they will meet), sales are made and broken. You will shortly learn how to prepare for what used to be largely unknown in the sales process: the beliefs and attitudes of yourself and those of your customer.

The Four Features on the Sales Map

The 21st-century Selling Model begins with an understanding of the beliefs, values, attitudes, and lifestyles of both the salesperson and the customer.

What do these four words mean and why are they important to your success?

Beliefs are what people know to be true, with or without enough evidence to have made a rational determination that the belief itself is actually true. Beliefs are what someone else knows to be true. This doesn't mean that the customer is right or wrong. It's their belief. It's foolish to argue about beliefs. It's foolish to debate beliefs. People's lives are supported by their beliefs and people are normally slow to change them.

Values are what people hold in esteem or significance in their life. Some people consider love, happiness, peace of mind, money, security, freedom, justice, and companionship among the highest values in life. There are hundreds of values. Values arise from the core desires and drives that unconsciously motivate us. Values are normally more difficult to change than beliefs. Therefore, don't try. Better: Utilize the values of another person. Acknowledge them and appreciate them.

Attitudes are people's states of mind or feeling as they pertain to specific issues. Unlike values, which are overriding themes in a person's life, attitudes are specific. They relate to specific things in life.

Lifestyles are how people live, considering the means, values, beliefs, and attitudes they currently have. Lifestyles are all about how we behaviorally respond to our beliefs, attitudes, and lifestyles.

Beliefs, values, and attitudes are unconscious "filters" of our experience. We see everything in life through the glasses of our beliefs, values, and attitudes. Once we open our eyes to our own beliefs, attitudes, and values, it is easier to understand other people's values, attitudes, and beliefs. In the course of an average day, we don't discuss our attitudes, values, and beliefs, but we do perceive and experience life based upon these filters.

Once you know a person's beliefs, values, attitudes, and lifestyles, you can ask him for anything in an appropriate fashion and he will in all but the rarest instances say "Yes!"

Understanding your own beliefs, values, attitudes, and lifestyle comes first in the selling process. Long before your customer meets you, you spend time with your belief systems, values, your attitudes about life and your work, and live within a certain lifestyle that often make or break sales before you meet the woman who will say "Yes!" to you today. Take a few moments to learn about yourself first, and understanding others will be easy.

Values:
Opening the Doors of the Mind

Take twenty minutes and write down the answer to each of these questions:

A) What are the ten most important things to you in life?

humor

passion

independence

friends

money

time

health

beauty

truth

fairness

B) Rank the above ten values in order by placing the numbers one through ten by the value.

C) Write the ten values in the spaces provided below. Below each write specifically how you know when you have that value. (If you wrote love, for example, then write next to the word exactly how you know when you have love.) Take your time. This isn't as easy as you might think!

My Top Ten Values and Evidence of Them

1) _____

_____

_____

2) _____

_____

_____

3) _____

_____

_____

4) _____

_____

_____

5) _____

_____

_____

6) _____

_____

_____

_____

7) _____

_____

_____

_____

8) _____

_____

_____

_____

9) _____

_____

_____

_____

10) _____

_____

_____

Understanding your values is the beginning of sales mastery. Your values are what you move toward. These are the states of mind and "things" that you want most in life. One element that separates great salespeople from those who are mediocre is the ability to discover what is important to others in business, relationships, and life. As you learn what is important to others, you work hard to meet their values and needs and find that what you hold in highest esteem, while wonderful for you, is not what you are selling. You must sell your products and services to meet the values, beliefs, attitudes, and lifestyles of others around you.

Magical Questions
that Open the Doors to the Mind

There are three magical questions that allow you to uncover another person's values instantly. They are very simple to learn and once you can utilize them in any context, your personal power as a salesperson is enhanced dramatically.

The reason you want to know another person's values is that once you know what is most important to another person in the sales setting, you are virtually guaranteed to "make the sale."

Generally speaking, you want three pieces of information.

1) What is most important to you in X?

(X is in "buying" or "considering the purchase of your products or services.")

"What's most important to you in deciding how much life insurance to buy?"

"What is most important to you in deciding what computer system to use?"

"What is most important to you in buying a new home?"

"What is most important to you in deciding what to invest in for your retirement?"

Your prospect or customer will respond with whatever is important to him or her. He may respond with one word like "quality" or "service," or he may respond with a twenty-minute monologue that you will recap into one or two sentences. Regardless of how your prospect responds, his response and your summary of his response now become "Y."

2) How do you know when you have Y?

(P) Prospect: I want a car that is a good value.

(M.S.) Master salesperson: "How do you know when you have a good value in an automobile?"

(P): I want enough life insurance to protect my family when I die.

(M.S.): "How do you know when you have enough life insurance to protect your family?"

(P:) I want a house that is big enough for my whole family to live comfortably in.

(M.S.): "How do you know when a home is big enough so your family is comfortable?"

[Once the customers respond to your inquiry, they do so by stating something that is often ambiguous. For example, they may say, "We like quality." Therefore, the master salesperson wants to know, "How do you know when you have a quality X (house, automobile, mutual fund, insurance company)?" This is called "evidence" in this book.]

3) If I could give you Y, would you Z?

If you can meet their highest value, quality, using the example above, will they work with you, or hire you, or buy your product? It is very difficult to say "no" at this point because of the framing of questions 1 and 2. Consider the following examples:

"If you can be certain that this is an A+ rated insurance company, will you feel comfortable?"

"If you can be certain that this is the best value in automobiles, will you feel comfortable owning it?"

"If you feel sure that this is a quality home, will you feel comfortable living here?"

The Fourth Magical Question

On occasion the customer will say no to a "stage-three question." If that ever occurs, you have one more magical incantation that will turn the key.

4) What else is most important to you in buying/owning an X?

At this point you merely cycle back through the value-elicitation process noted above. There are times when the customer does not know what is most important to him in the purchase of your product. Question four eliminates the concern and continues the magic cycle to a positive solution!

You now know the magic formula for eliciting values. This is one of the single most important factors on the journey of success that you will learn in this book.

Two charts appear below. The first chart is an assessment of what men and women value the most in life as far as their "ends values" are concerned. Ends values are states of mind such as happiness, freedom, and love. This chart was compiled from a study in which a number of values were shown to participants. The participants then created a hierarchy of those values. This first chart will help you have a basic understanding of what you will discover in the marketplace when you begin eliciting values from your clients.

The value you can gain from this important ranking is twofold. First, you see the values that shape America. Second, you can observe the difference between men and women and their hierarchies.

The second chart reveals the personality traits that Americans value most. If you can mirror the American values, you will appeal to the greatest number of people:

Ends Values and Composite Rank Orders
for American Men and Women
(adapted from *The Nature of Human Values* by Rokeach)

Terminal Values	Men (665)	Women (744)
Comfortable Life	4	13
Exciting Life	18	18
Sense of Accomplishment	7	10
World at Peace	1	1
World of Beauty	15	15
Equality	9	8
Family Security	2	2
Freedom	3	3
Happiness	5	5
Inner Harmony	13	12
Mature Love	14	14
National Security	14	14

Pleasure	17	16
Salvation	12	4
Self Respect	6	6
Social Recognition	16	17
True Friendship	11	9
Wisdom	8	7

Instrumental Values and Composite Rank Orders for American Men and Women

Instrumental Value	Men	Women
Ambitious	2	4
Broadminded	4	5
Capable	8	12
Cheerful	12	10
Clean	9	8
Courageous	5	6
Forgiving	6	2
Helpful	7	7
Honest	1	1
Imaginative	18	18
Independent	11	14
Intellectual	15	16
Logical	16	17
Loving	14	9
Obedient	17	15
Polite	13	13
Responsible	3	3
Self-controlled	10	11

Changing Values in America

American values are not remaining static, however. Each year we re-shape our society and the individuals within the society re-shape themselves. It is a slow process but definite changes are clearly apparent. Notice how many values and attitudes have been re-shaped in just the last two decades.

Changing Values in America

(adapted from: *The Futurist*)

Old	New
Self-denial ethic	Self-fulfillment ethic
Higher standard of living	Better quality of life
Traditional sex roles	Blurring of sex roles
Accepted definition of success	Individualized definition of success
Faith in industry/institutions	Self Reliance
Traditional family life	Alternative families
Live to work	Work to live
Hero Worship	Love of ideas
Expansionism	Pluralism
Patriotism	Less patriotism
Unparalleled growth	Growing sense of limits
Industrial growth	Technology/Info Age
Receptivity to technology	Technology Orientation

The United States and Canada are changing countries. Values and beliefs are shifting with time and growth. You become an expert in Mind Access by having the foundational knowledge necessary for sales success as detailed in this book. You become a sales success by applying the strategies and techniques you learn in this book in your everyday life.

The 21st-century Selling Model

There are hundreds of ways to present information to clients, customers, prospects, and buyers. The 21st-century Model of Selling is really just one of our top ten favorite models of selling.

When we are making our presentations and proposals to others in the sales process, we should note the following key elements are occurring whether it is a one on one lunch date or a public speaker before a group of 1,000. This model has been proven effective and we recommend you utilize it in your business.

Specific strategies for each of the elements below are detailed elsewhere in the book. For now, we want you to have a useful framework for selling.

Some of this will be very familiar to you. A few of the points may be new distinctions that you had forgotten about, or perhaps they are brand new to you!

1) Establish and Maintain Rapport

Rapport can be defined as being "in synch" with another person. Generally, people are more likely to be in rapport with someone else if they like that person. How do you know if you are in rapport with someone? Answer this question:

Does the person respond to you in a positive manner?

If so, you are in some degree of rapport. Remember what Zig Ziglar said: "They don't care what you know until they know that you really care." Therefore, you will want to begin to develop a sense of empathy and genuine interest in t others. Rapport occurs on different levels of communication. You can be technically skilled at acting and appear to be in rapport, but if you don't sincerely care about your customer and the people you are working with, what is the point? There are several methods of developing rapport.

2) Use Content to Build Rapport

Discover what their interests are and if you are already not in tune with the interest, learn about it. *People love to talk about what they love and what they know about!* When I (KH) lead sales training seminars, one of my favorite stories about building rapport is the "learning about fishing" story.

Living in Minnesota, many of my clients are avid fisherman. How would I connect with my clients knowing absolutely nothing about fishing? I grew up a Chicago Cubs fan, a child prodigy in mathematics, and even though I lived very close to Lake Michigan, unlike most kids, I never enjoyed fishing. In Minnesota, a big deal is made every year when it is time for the "opener." To my mind, "opener" means opening day at Wrigley Field. To the mind of many of my customers, the only Wrigley they know about is the chewing gum. It seems I am doomed at meeting many of my clients at more than a superficial level until one day . . .

I decided to learn about fishing by asking all of my clients that love fishing to tell me their favorite fishing stories. I began asking questions that to them must have seemed absolutely ridiculous. Over the last few years, I have built an array of knowledge and stories about fishing. I can direct you to all of the best lakes for fishing and I can tell you what to fish for at these lakes . . . and I've never been fishing in the state, not once.

You can build a great deal of rapport and long-term friendships by showing and experiencing sincere interest in what is important to other people. Sharing the experiences of your client's hobbies, lifestyle, and interests is called "using content to build rapport."

3) Use Processes to Build Rapport

There is more to building rapport than swapping fishing stories. Becoming in synch with another person or a group can take a great deal of skill, in addition to the sincere interest that is necessary in building relationships. Many customers will not feel comfortable discussing their families, hobbies, and lifestyles with you, a perfectly nice, perfect stranger. How does the ice get broken when stories are very uncomfortable for the customer? Many of your customers were taught as children to not talk to strangers. Many of your customers were taught to keep private matters private. How do you help these customers become comfortable with you?

4) Pacing

When in doubt, an effective way to begin building rapport with anyone is by pacing. Pacing is essentially synonymous with the term "matching" or "mirroring." In other words, be like your customer, because he likes people who are like him. There are a number of techniques that can be used to effectively pace your client, to begin building rapport. An entire chapter will go into much greater detail about building and enhancing rapport. Rapport is one of the pillars to success in sales and in life.

5) Use Your Voice

Imagine that your customer is in an upset mood. He has a sharp edge to his voice and you get to make your presentation. Many salespeople attempt to get him out of his mood with enthusiasm or a cheery story. In fact, the rule of thumb is *"when in doubt, pace your client."* If your client has an edge in his voice, let your voice have an edge. If he sounds angry, let yourself be angry, however briefly, with something that occurred today as well. This vocal pacing will help put you in synch with your client. Eventually you will lead your client out of the negative frame of mind, if you choose to. (There are many times when a negative frame of mind is necessary to making a sale.)

There is more that you can do with your voice than match the tone of your client. We all speak with a measurable average number of words per minute. Many people drawn to the sales profession happen to speak quickly. Part of this experience is due to the nature of the business where we are obligated to be quick and to the point. Unfortunately, if your client speaks slowly and you are speaking quickly to meet a time constraint, you probably will lose the sale.

People tend to speak at a rate that is consistent with how they process their thoughts and internal representations. If people tend to think in pictures (movies), they tend to speak very quickly. People who tend to speak very slowly process information through their feelings and emotions. In between are what we call the radio announcers. These people are those who speak with a more rich and resonant voice. They normally think in words.

> *Building rapport as a salesperson is critical. One specific strategy is to speak at the same rate and pitch of voice as your client.*

6) Why Pace Breathing?

Admittedly, one of the more difficult pacing techniques is that of pacing your customer's breathing. Breathing is one of the most unconscious of all body functions, and pacing of breathing is one of the great rhythm generators of all time. Two people in the heat of sexual passion often are breathing at the exact same pace. Two people sitting side by side in deep meditation often experience the same exhale and inhale points. When leading a group in hypnosis, hypnotherapists find that having the group breathe together actually creates a wonderful bonding rapport in the room. It is this Mind Access Point that you will now enter.

As you watch your client breathe, begin to breathe in when she does. When she exhales, begin to exhale when she does. It is best to practice this pacing technique when you are not in verbal communication with people. For example, if you are waiting in line somewhere, and someone is talking to someone else, begin to pace his breathing. You can practice this at home by pacing someone who is unaware that you are doing it. Our research shows that by pacing another person's breathing, the liking between the two people rises!

7) Physiology and Posture

Unlike pacing someone's breathing, pacing someone's posture and physiology is much easier. If you sit erect and stiff and your client is seated in a comfortable, slightly bent over manner, you are not likely to develop the rapport you hope for.

Pacing physiology too closely can be a mistake. If every move your client makes is mirrored immediately back at him, he will begin to feel uncomfortable. The most effective manner of pacing physiology is to match the posture and general body position of the other person. When we discuss "leading," below, you will learn how to appropriately test your pacing skills with your client and be certain you have established rapport.

8) Leading

Developing a sincere interest in relationships and friendships with others is the first step in the sales process. Pacing your customer is the second step. Leading comes third. A lead is successful when the person follows you. If you are sitting across from your client and you both have similar physiology and you are both enjoying each other's company, you have an opportunity to now begin leading, which is the beginning of the active process in selling.

Will the client now follow you into the sales presentation? You have been following him for minutes and minutes. You've matched his vocal pacing and his physiology. You have shared mutual interests. Now it is time to take a nonverbal break from pacing and start leading. If your client follows your lead you have successfully built rapport at the unconscious level and you can begin your sales presentation momentarily. There are a few key methods of determining if you are in rapport with your client. We will move on to them now.

9) Lead with the Tone, Rate, or Pitch of Your Voice

If you have been successfully matching your client, you have an opportunity to lead by altering one of your vocal qualities. You may, for example, increase your speaking rate a little bit and induce a more enthusiastic attitude in the tone of your voice to help you bridge the conversation to your product. The context of your discussion will help determine when and if this is appropriate.

When you notice that the client follows your lead with a more enthusiastic voice, an increased rate of speech, a higher or lower tone of voice, you can feel assured you have successfully developed rapport.

10) Leading with Physiology, Posture, Movement

The simplest movements you make will often be mirrored identically by a customer that is in rapport with you. Imagine that both you and your customers have been sitting with a hand to chin for several minutes. Now, imagine that you believe you are ready to "test" to be certain you are in rapport. If you are sitting at a restaurant, you can take your hand to pick up a glass of water and watch to see what your client does. If he follows you by also picking up his glass of water, or even picking up a pen or a napkin, you have successfully led your client to the next stage of the selling process.

> *If your customer does not follow your lead, you need to begin the process of building rapport again.*

11) Induce Reciprocity

Building rapport begins within you. The entire process of building rapport is built upon the foundation of concern, caring, compassion, interest, and a desire for the well-being of your customer. Pacing and leading is a process that creates comfort for you and the client to know that you are moving along at a pace that is appropriate for the client. The entire process of building rapport, pacing, and leading could be as little as one minute and as much as an hour or more. After rapport has been established you can enter into the body of your presentation.

There are many ways to begin the sales presentation, but my favorite is to give my client something. I regularly give a book that I (KH) wrote called *The Gift: A Discovery of Love, Happiness and Fulfillment* to my clients. You may not have a book to give, so here are some ideas to consider when deciding how you will induce reciprocity.

What you will give to your customer to induce reciprocity will be in part based on the average profit per sale and the significance of your gift.

> *People don't really buy products or services. They buy YOU!*

You should know that gifts tend to be reciprocated with sales in direct correlation to the dollar value of the gift that is given. Specialty items such as pens, date books and calendars are perceived as advertising items and do not induce reciprocity. You must think of something appropriate that you can give to your customer that will be appreciated.

Inducing reciprocity is not just a sales technique. It is a way of life. There is almost a metaphysical energy that seems to emanate from the giving of gifts. Expect nothing in return when you induce reciprocity. The simple act of giving helps you develop a caring and compassionate personality. *That* is what people are buying when they buy from you . . . YOU!

12) Share Part of You with Them

Show your confidence in your customers by helping them with one of their potential clients (or problems). In other words, offer to help them in any way you can. Can you make a phone call for them as a referral? Can you help them bring more business to their store by taking fifty of their business cards? What can you do to freely help them with their business that is above and beyond the scope of your sales call. OFFER TO HELP.

I've done this for years in selling and marketing and you can't believe how many times my kindness has been returned a thousand times over, over the years. Would you be willing to write them a testimonial on your letterhead for your customer to show HIS customers? That is the kind of treatment you would like from your customers, so why not offer it first!

13) The Common Enemy

Nothing binds two people, groups, or nations like a common enemy. Find their enemy and align yourself with their viewpoint. Do they hate the IRS? Do the same people try to hurt your mutual businesses? Jibe with them. Once someone shares with you who his enemies are, you have built a relationship for life. Drugs? Gangs? Taxes? Unemployment compensation insurance? Lawsuits? Government? Criminals? What are the common threats to business and society that you both dislike and you both know hurts your business?

You won't find a common enemy in every sales interview, but if you are thinking of the theme, the opportunity to put both of you on the same side of the table will occur during 50 percent of your interviews. Once you have a common enemy you have a sale and a lifetime relationship.

14) Tell a Short Story about Someone Like Them

If you can build a reservoir of stories *(short stories)* about people who have become your customers, you can utilize this selling tool. Tell today's customer about another customer who recently bought from you. This customer should be someone they remind you of. You can build an entrancing sales presentation around such stories, and they make great lead-ins to the core of your presentation.

15) Respect

Sincerely show respect for the person via a compliment. Always be looking for things to like about other people. Compliment them. A little respect goes a long way, and you cannot under estimate the value of a sincere compliment of respect in the selling environment.

16) Knock Their Socks Off

The shortest amount of time we spend with any client is normally that of the actual sales presentation. When you do actually begin the process, the very first thing you do is this: *Blow them away with an astonishing claim, an amazing fact, something that few would know. Show them something amazing that no one else has shown them.* Make the biggest claim that you can substantiate. The client will always remember and consider this introduction. Start strong, finish strong. Your claim for your product or your service should be colossal, and it must be true. Knock their socks off.

17) Always Give More than You Promised

Napoleon Hill always made sure his audiences knew the principle of going the extra mile. Follow the example of those who sell who become millionaires. If you promise something, make sure that your customer gets exactly what you promise and then some. Remember that phrase: . . . *and then some!*

18) The Power of Understatement

After making your big fat claim, you can quickly work your way into your sales presentation. This is the time to make sure you don't over-inflate your product or service. You made your big fat claim, now support it with the power of understatement. In other words, if your mutual fund portfolio has a track record of 12 percent return per year over the last ten years, then understate that by saying, "Now, if you average 10 percent per year . . ." For ten years you have earned a 12 percent return, but you are being conservative for your client and he knows it *and appreciates it.*

19) Be Precise: Then Beat Your Precision

If you know that this automobile is going to get your customer nineteen miles per gallon, tell him that. Then tell him a secret: " . . . but if you use Mobil One oil, you can literally add an extra three miles per gallon of gas and that translates to an extra $100 of gasoline savings per year." Be precise, then be better than being precise.

20) Get It Done Faster, Easier, Better

You live in an age where your customer wants everything to be better, cheaper, faster, quicker, smarter, easier, more luxurious. So promise what you can, and then deliver . . . and then some. If they tell you that your competitor will get them X, then if you can really do it, you tell your customer that you are going to get them X+2. Never be beaten because of the lack of going the extra mile. What can you do for your customer that no other agent will do for them? What can you do for them that no one else in the business does? Answer these questions, then do it.

21) Be on the Edge of Your Seat

Pay attention with baited breath to every word your customer has to say. It should be clear that what your customer has to say is the most important thing in either of your worlds at that moment . . . and it is. If these were the last words you would hear while you were alive, you would want to know what your customer has to say. Live your sales presentation as if the significance of each word will change your very life. Relationships are cemented when you do this. With the attitude of respect, going the extra mile, and intense excitement about your customer and his life, you won't need to use a multiplicity of closing tactics "on your customer." He will demand that you sell him your product *now.*

22) Closing the Sale

As you begin to experience this kind of a relationship in selling situations, the idea of closing is literally just that of consummating the relationship. Your customers know you care, they know you have their best interests at heart. You know their values and what is important to them in life and in the process of this sale. They know that you are going to help them solve their problems, and they know that you will be there for them when you need them. It's the same as a friendship. Specifically how you want to do your paperwork is up to you. Simply ask a question or make a statement.

Your customer is your friend. You are now involved in a relationship that will be long in duration and loyal in nature. Aside from leading the customer to take action now, you don't have to "close" in the traditional sense of the word.

"Okay, John, we can wrap this up and do lunch again next week on me. I'm thinking a half-million life insurance, level-term twenty years. By then you are likely to be self-insured. Agreed?"

"Janet, can I make a suggestion? You have $80,000 ready for retirement. You still have thirty years until you are going to need the money. I know you are averse to risk and I know that bonds and money market funds aren't going to do it for your retirement. Are you ready to divide the money evenly between small cap growth and large cap growth funds?"

"Bill, in my mind you need to be careful not to overextend yourself on your payments. I think you should finance for four years. If you go six years, most of the extra money is interest and that's a waste of money. In addition to that, it will be forever before you own equity in the car. On the other hand, if you find yourself in a bind you can always refinance later on. Most banks will look at this as a new or virtually new car for the first year. Take it home now and pay it off faster and then you own it. Okay?"

"Christina, as I look at this your company will be able to save thousands of dollars with our new system F90. You could spend a lot more on other systems I sell but this is the one that will optimize your return on investment. But, it's up to you. What do you want to do?"

Now, I know what you are thinking.

"They can say no!"

"These aren't alternative choice closes!"

Nonsense.

People don't buy because they don't need a product, they don't trust you, you haven't shown benefit to having the product, they don't like you, they don't have the money, and perhaps a few other stray reasons.

The 21st-century Model of Selling is one that is based upon the foundation of trust and liking. It demands Win/Win or No Deal scenarios. If the customer can't benefit from your product, you wouldn't ask them to buy it. And if they don't have the money, they can finance it or simply not buy it. If financing is a reasonable and ethical option, and it normally is, then you can make the product affordable for the customer in payments. Your customer is your friend. No longer are they enemies that salespeople have to outwit.

The customer is your friend. They are someone to be cared about and nurtured. When they see that in you, you won't need to worry about hundreds of closing lines and techniques. It turns out in real life that closing is actually the easiest part of selling.

Building rapport, identifying the driving needs (those that they see and do not see) and wants of your client, and understanding how and why your customer buys is really where the time in the selling process needs to be spent. That's what the next several chapters will cover in detail.

CHAPTER 3

Meet Your Customer: Part One

A boss, seeking desperately to motivate his low-morale employees, decided to give everyone in his company a generous raise. He expected the extra money to make his employees happy and increase their productivity. Instead, employees were resentful.

"He's just throwing money at us" was a common response. "He doesn't care about what's really important to us." It wasn't that he didn't care, but rather that he had no clue what motivated his employees—what drove them.

According to the latest academic research, there are sixteen core desires found in human nature. These are the desires that motivate us to move in one direction or another. The desires all take place at the unconscious level, though on occasion we may actually become aware of our desires, our instinctual drives.

Salespeople, on average, have a very high desire for competition. That's one of the sixteen basic desires and without that desire you probably couldn't be successful in selling. Lots of people have a very low desire for competition. These are people who should not be in sales! The basic desires include the desire to have power, the desire for tranquility, the desire for having a family, and the desire to belong. There are numerous others that round out the sixteen. In the next two chapters we will catalog them all and have you learn how to enter into the MAPs that trigger the desires.

Each of these desires can be objectively measured, which is nice for you and me because then we know that someone didn't just dream these sixteen up one night and write a book. The sixteen core desires have been thoroughly researched at Ohio State and I'm convinced that:

> *Understanding the sixteen desires that humans experience makes motivating others and getting them to want to buy from us not only easy but virtually instantaneous.*

Where did these sixteen desires come from? They came from our evolutionary drive to reproduce, locate and eat food, and the fight-or-flight response. All sixteen desires stem from these basic drives. The remaining desires all come into play because they assist the core desires or attempt to "control" or squelch them in some fashion. The interplay between genetic predisposition and environmental factors is obvious in the sixteen desires, and it is something you will not only become proficient at identifying but also something you will learn to utilize.

Your customer is nothing more or less than a human being. (We know you have often wondered it this were really true, but rest assured . . .) Your customer is alive and here today (in part) because she is a carrier for her genes and more specifically for her DNA. DNA is something that replicates over millennia, and you and your customer are both alive today because your genes "found a way to replicate."

Before we go any further, I know you probably believe in God and that God made you in his image. You are probably right. If you are right and he did, then the DNA that has replicated is probably going to have some staying power! Let's do a mini-lesson in evolution to see just who and what you are so you can see what MAPs will trigger strong responses in your customer.

You don't have to believe that your ancestors are apes to utilize this information! In fact, understanding the theory of evolution allows you to understand just how unique you are and how many things had to go right for you to be here.

Nothing you are about to read will ask you to set aside your belief in God or your religion. What you are about to read is what happens after God puts your great-great-great-great-great-grandparents on earth and they begin to have children and reproduce. Enjoy!!

In every cell of your customer's body there is DNA. On this DNA there are genes for which we now finally have a complete roll call. We don't know what they all "do," but we "know" them all. (The census has been taken; their "jobs" will be discovered later.)

Because the material in this chapter is so vital to the science of selling,

I want you to get a free mini-lesson about evolution and genetics from the inventor (author) of Microsoft Word and author of *Virus of the Mind,* my friend Richard Brodie. Richard has one of the brightest minds on earth. I've had the privilege of his friendship and have been his travel companion on many occasions when we discussed the significance of what he will now share with you. Richard's ability to explain the complexities of evolution and genetics in an easy-to-understand fashion is something that always leaves me awestruck.

Brodie wrote:

> The theory of evolution by natural selection explained the facts well enough that it held on for a long time. But Darwin had never heard of DNA.
>
> The selfish-gene theory shifted the evolutionary spotlight from the fittest individuals onto the fittest DNA. After all, it is the DNA that carries the information passed from one generation to the next. The individuals of a species don't, strictly speaking, replicate copies of themselves. Parents don't clone themselves to produce children who are exact copies. Instead they cause copies of pieces of DNA to be reproduced in a new individual. The pieces of DNA that are best at causing themselves to get replicated become most numerous, and it is they that participate in the survival of the fittest, not whole individuals.
>
> Those pieces of DNA that play this game, causing themselves to be replicated by whatever means, are called genes. The fact that evolution seems to revolve around their well being rather than ours makes them selfish genes.
>
> Paradoxically, one way that scientists confirm the selfish-gene theory is by noticing unselfish behavior in animals. Female worker bees have evolved to labor all their lives to support their mother, the queen, and have no children themselves, because by a genetic quirk their mother's offspring share more DNA with them than their own offspring would. It serves their selfish genes better to behave that way than to go off on their own.
>
> (From *Virus of the Mind: The New Science of the Meme,* by Richard Brodie, 1996)

Four "drives" are critical to the survival of genes (yours, your customers', your children's, your friends', all of your "relatives" who live in every nation on earth). All of these drives or programs are running all the time but they are running at the unconscious level in your mind. You probably don't ever think about these drives in the course of the day.

They are simply part of you and every living creature on earth. Understanding and appealing to these drives is what will double your sales . . . or triple them . . . or more.

1) **The first is food**. We all need to have food to keep the body alive that allows the genes to live in your body. You are hosting your genes and your genes "want" your body to eat. They don't much "care" what you eat but they "want" you to eat until you reproduce and copy them into other little customers. (Genes don't think, by the way. They simply have instructions for influencing your physical appearance and behavior.)

2) **The second thing necessary to the survival of genes is the ability to flee in the face of danger.** If it makes more sense to the survival of your genes to run from danger than fight, you will instinctively do so. Now, remember that YOUR genes are not only in your body. Many of them are also in the bodies of YOUR children!

3) **The third thing necessary to the survival of genes is the ability to fight in the face of danger.** If it makes more sense to the survival of your genes to fight than flee, you will instinctively do so. Now, once again, remember that your genes are not only in your body. They are also in the bodies of YOUR children! In addition, also remember that some of the same genes are in the bodies of other humans as well. As Richard points out in *Virus of the Mind,* if your family is together and you all come into danger at the same time, it may be in your genes' best interest for you to intervene between the threat of danger and your children. Sacrificing your life for your children is selfish on the part of your genes. It's all part of how genes get replicated.

4) **The final thing necessary to the survival of genes is reproduction. You must reproduce or your genes will not be copied.** The desire to have sex is the key "moving toward" program that is running your life. Your genes are "telling you" to make as many babies as you possibly can. Your genes don't care if you just got laid off from work. Your genes aren't interested in your financial situation or changing diapers. They simply "want you" to reproduce. To your genes there is no distinction between reproduction and having sex. Therefore, anything that you can do that appeals to the desire to have sex is going

to appeal to the unconscious minds of the majority of people on earth. We will have a lot to say about this later!

Each human being is driven instinctively by these four needs. In fact, these four needs form the foundation of what are known as the sixteen basic desires. Before we arrive at the core desires of human experience, let's take a careful look at the four programs that are running our life:
1) The desire to eat. — *for your whole life*
2) The desire to flee from danger. — *risk*
3) The desire to fight when in danger. — *do sth*
4) The desire to have sex/reproduce.

Remember this key point:

> *You don't fulfill these desires to keep you alive. You fulfill these desires to allow your genes to survive.*

Question: If you only knew these four astonishing facts about your genes (and we might as well say your "self"), how would you sell your products and services?

Answer: You sell your products and services so that they appear to meet the needs and desires of each of these four key drives. In general, any sales message that meets your instinctual needs is likelier to be acted upon than messages directed at other desires.

This may seem obvious (or not!) but how do we apply this immediately into our careers as salespeople?

Look at some specific examples:

Life Insurance: If your customer buys life insurance his genes are protected. His children will survive until they are old enough to reproduce. His children will be able to eat and his children will be able to have the resources to ward off danger. Now, you don't say that when you are selling life insurance. You frame your presentation in such a manner that these points become clear.

Real Estate: If your customer buys a home from you, she has a place to cook her food. She has a place that is safe from the dangers of the world for her and her children (her genes). She also has a place where it is safe to reproduce and nest.

Clothing: If your customer buys clothing from you, she has (hopefully) improved her appearance so that she looks more attractive, thus increasing her chances for reproducing her genes. Buying new clothes will (hopefully) also help her stay more attractive so she is more likely to be viewed in a positive light by others for mating, continued mating, or so she can earn more money to protect her genes.

> *Almost every product or service has a connection with at least one of our instinctual drives, and by highlighting these drives we make our products and services far easier to sell and far more attractive to the buyer.*

If you sell clothes at Macy's you probably won't find your sales going up if you say, "Oh, and if you buy this skirt you will ultimately have lots of sex and marry a guy who has lots of money to take care of your biological need to reproduce."

Framing your communication so that it is artistically grounded in science is going to be the key. The woman you are selling clothes to already knows at the unconscious level that clothes that enhance her appearance will improve her "face value." Your job as the sales person is to reinforce the fact that "you look absolutely stunning in that dress."

Emerging from the core desires and needs to have sex, avoid or ward off danger, and eat come thirteen other desires. Dr. Steven Reiss of Ohio State is the first individual I know of to successfully catalog each of the sixteen basic desires. Others (William James, for example) have recorded most of the human desires, but Reiss, in my opinion, is the first to scientifically categorize and distill them all. The balance of this chapter will discuss the sixteen basic desires and how they relate to selling.

(For further reading about the sixteen basic desires, I recommend *Who Am I? The 16 Basic Desires that Motivate our Actions and Define our Personalities* by Stephen Reiss.)

THE SIXTEEN CORE DESIRES

Perhaps the responses we show under stress are those that are most telling about our motivations. We will do a great deal to avoid pain but what specifically will we do? As noted earlier, we are going to be protecting our genes' survival and those responses may indeed be "calculated." But what response protects the genes the best? Over time however, people may miscalculate and develop tendencies to respond to a majority of fearful situations in a flight-or-fight mode.

When you become afraid, do you tend to respond to fear by fighting or fleeing? Most people don't really know themselves very well so let me give you a few examples to consider:

1) You see a police officer on the highway while you are speeding. Do you challenge him to come and get you (fight) or slow down (flight)?

2) The IRS sends you a notice that you are going to be audited. Do you go in and fight like hell or do you start making up receipts and reconstructing records (flight)?

3) A tall stranger approaches you (you are alone) on the street late at night. Are you prepared to run or fight?

4) Your boss yells at you about something. Do you scream back at him? Do you quietly apologize?

As you can see, there are many situations that can represent danger to an individual. Now that you have thought of a few of them, you can look at the continuum of behaviors below and how people see themselves and others along the continuum. Which side of the spectrum do you tend to be on? Notice that timid people (people who consider themselves wise enough to flee from danger) see themselves as cautious, prudent, and careful. They see other people who may consider themselves to be brave as foolhardy and reckless. Where do you see yourself?

With this thumbnail sketch of evolution we now turn to the first three (four) core instincts and desires.

Desire for Tranquility and the Flight-Fight Response

Many people move toward tranquility as a basic human desire. When this is thwarted, people respond with the flight-fight response. Show people danger and they go into preparation mode. They prepare to fight or flee. In order to do so they may need your product or service!

What is the danger if your customer doesn't buy your product or service from you now?

You sell new automobiles.

✓ What is the danger if your customer doesn't have a new car?
✓ What is the danger if they have one of the other types of cars?
✓ What is the danger if they own one of those SUVs that tip over?
✓ What is the danger of not having the best for your family?
✓ What is the danger of waiting for a different day to buy from you?

You sell skin-care products.

✓ What is the danger to your customer's skin if they don't buy your lotions?
✓ What is the danger to their appearance if they don't buy from you?
✓ What is the danger of using the competitors' products?
✓ What is the danger of waiting for another day to buy?
✓ What is the danger to your "face value" if you don't protect your skin?

You sell yourself as a personal coach.

✓ What is the danger to your customer if he doesn't hire you?
✓ What is the danger to your customer if he doesn't utilize you regularly?
✓ What is the danger to your customer if he uses a less-qualified coach?
✓ What is the danger to your customer if he waits to hire you?

I will answer one question for each of the above examples for you, then you respond to the rest.

1) If your customers don't buy a new car from you they put their family at risk. They are running the most important things (their loved ones) on earth in a ten- or twenty-year-old vehicle. The brakes could fail, the car could stall at an intersection, the tires might not give you the ten extra feet you need to prevent a serious accident. Question: Is it worth it? I didn't think so.

2) If your customers don't buy skin care products from you they put themselves at risk on many levels. First, the fact that they are considering skin care shows they care about themselves. Do you know how many people don't care about themselves? Do you know what this does to people's self-esteem? Do you know how this affects everyday life for the person? Their level of happiness or depression? On another level, the skin is the

largest organ in the human body. It needs to be cared for. Skin care products will keep it looking better for a lot longer, and that makes your customers not only feel better about themselves but lets other people see them in their best light. Other people will respond better to your customer who will look more attractive because of your products. That isn't fair, that's just the way life works.

3) You are a personal coach. If your customers don't hire you then you have possibly created harm for them. You charge $200 per hour, but let me ask you this. If your customer could have saved or earned $10,000 in exchange for that time, isn't it worth it? If you could have coached them to save their marriage, are you willing to put a dollar figure on that? If you could have shown them five ways to draw more interesting people into their lives, do you really believe that isn't worth $500? A person's daily life is all he has. Are you going to let your shyness about your personal income stand in the way of another human's rich experiences?

As you can see, a big part of your job as a salesperson is to highlight the risks inherent of not buying your services from you, now. That's the big picture of danger. Now let's fine tune utilizing your customers' instinctive responses to dangers so they become buyers.

You will notice that throughout the rest of this book you will find many continuums of behavioral experience. On one side will be one desire, say, "timid." On the other side will be the other end of the continuum, in this case it's "brave." Now at some times in your life you are brave and others you are timid. However, research clearly shows that you will respond typically from one point on the continuum.

I want you to find where you are on these continuums. Then look at how you perceive yourself to be by reading "Believe themselves to be." Next look on the other side and see how others think of themselves. Finally, go back to the next set of descriptions under your side. It says, "Others believe to be." This means that other people perceive you in this fashion! (What is THIS information worth to you?) On the other side, you will be shocked by how accurate the phrases are that describe how you feel about others.

That's how these charts work. (For more details about each of the desires, see Reiss's *Who Am I?*)

DESIRE FOR TRANQUILITY

Timid ———————————————— **Brave**

the brave see themselves as

Believe themselves to be:

Shy	*Fearless*
Cautious	*Courageous*
Wary	*Bold*
Prudent	*Daring*
Careful	*Confident*
Mindful	*Valiant*

Believe others to be:

others believe them to be

Imprudent	*Fainthearted*
Reckless	*Cowardly*
Foolhardy	*Neurotic*
Unaware	*Worrier*
Daredevil	*Overprotective*

others see the brave as

Imagine a tax accountant is attempting to sell his services to a fairly timid person when it comes to personal safety. When it comes to the rest of his genes (their children), he is quite the opposite from what might be predicted from our previous discussion. Perhaps part of the conversation might go like this:

> "Mr. Johnson, when you give me your tax information I want you to be as careful and prudent as you can. I don't want you to get into any trouble. But your kids deserve to live as well or better than they are and not have all of this extra money going to the government, which is going to blow it on pork projects. Let me shoulder the responsibility for going to war with the IRS. I'll be up there on the front lines fighting for every dollar you deserve."

Wow! Mr. Johnson gets to be prudent and the tax accountant is going to be courageous on Mr. Johnson's behalf. She's going to fight the war for Mr. Johnson. He can live with that! She will shoulder the responsibility and fight for Mr. Johnson. She has closed the sale!

This is just one example of being aware of people's response to dangerous situations and then utilizing that information into a communication for the purpose of making the sale.

The following exercise can help you double your income. But there is a danger. If you don't do it, you will probably stay in the same income bracket you are in for eons. Do the risks of skipping this exercise outweigh racing through this text, which you bought to change your life?

Exercise:

Write down all of the possible dangers your customer could face by not buying your services/products from you, now. Write down the possible dangers to your customer if she waits, even one day. Write down all of the dangers in light of the evolutionary needs we have discussed. Do this now. (If you don't you will fail to see the value of this information and are unlikely to utilize this material. That means no increased sales. Please do this exercise!)

THE DRIVE TO EAT

People have an instant response when presented with food. If they like the food that is presented (in thought, on television, on radio, or set on a plate in front of them), a MAP is about to be entered. If you show people food (that they like) and you associate it with your product or service, you are on the right track.

Do you sell groceries, fast food, own a gourmet restaurant, or have anything to do with the multi-billion-dollar food (or dieting for that matter) industry? If so, you have an obvious MAP you can enter into. The need for food consumption is one of the core desires. Utilize that fact!

Are you in that multi-billion-dollar, multi-level marketing business that sells herbs and vitamins? Nutritional supplements you call them, right? It's a terrifying thought to consider that *all* the food you are currently eating isn't giving you enough or the right nutrition isn't it? *It could threaten your very survival!*

It's funny, though. Every time someone approaches me to buy their supplements they tell me how much better I will feel, how healthy I will feel. Those are fine reasons to use such a product, but wouldn't it be more effective to simply tell me, "Kevin, you're forty years old. If you want to make it to ninety on your current diet, well, you are hallucinating. Supplement Q810ZX is going to keep you out of the nursing home and on the beach frolicking, if you know what I mean. . . ."

Now, I don't know about you, but there's something there that appeals to me. There is food, there is danger, there is frolicking. (What is frolicking anyway? I don't know, but my genes seem to be responding to the notion.)

You can tell people you sell herbs and vitamins or you can tell them that they will still be frolicking when they are ninety. Are we on the same page?

BUT! Maybe you don't sell Reese's or own a McDonald's. What can we do for you? How could your product or service possibly relate to food consumption? (Food consumption is an obvious survival need for both your customer and his genes, but so what?)

Question: If you sell Mary Kay cosmetics, what does that have to do with food?

Answer: Maybe nothing . . . maybe everything. If you sell Mary Kay and you know that cosmetics help a woman appear more attractive to men, then they bring certain benefits to the woman. She appears more attractive and therefore she attracts a wider range of men. She has more choices as to whom she can be with. Her genes have a better chance of being replicated, and her genes have a better chance of being passed on in further generations if she can locate men that will help her provide a safe environment in which to raise children.

It sounds so simplistic. It sounds very old fashioned. Here's the reality: It's (the DNA, the genes) millions of years old and it isn't interested in the feminist ideology or much of anything except getting the genes replicated. Finally, the fact that the genes are more likely to get copied—they will be cared for—means that food consumption will not be a problem.

Appealing to the evolutionary need of food consumption is absolutely critical in the selling process. (Have you ever wondered why successful salespeople close a lot of deals at lunch? Even they don't know . . . but now you do.)

✓ After all, we all have to eat.
✓ It puts the food on the table, you know.
✓ You don't work, you don't eat.
✓ An apple a day keeps the doctor away.

(By the way, do you see how "danger" is threaded into the last two common phrases? Welcome to the world of scientific selling.)

> *What subtle implication of easy access to food can you link to your product or service? What implication of limited access to food can you link to your product or service if your customer doesn't buy from you?*

You sell automobiles.

✓ Who will be the first person your customer takes to his favorite restaurant in his new car?
✓ How will having this new vehicle make access to his basic needs easier?
✓ How will having this new vehicle make your customer more aware of his own physical body?
✓ How will having a new vehicle help your customer feel like going shopping?

DESIRE TO EAT

Hearty Eaters ——————————— **Light Eaters**

Believe themselves to be:

Connoisseur	*Physically Fit*
Happy	*Slender*
Sensual	*Healthy*
Gourmand	*Sensible*

Believe other half to be:

Self denying	*Lack willpower*
Unhealthy	*Unhealthy*

The desire to eat, to be nourished, is something we always consider as important in the science of selling. I find it useful to close deals over lunch and dinner, and so do others. Research shows that people are more likely to say yes when dining than when doing business in an office setting. Certain foods have certain effects on brain chemistry of course, and this is part of the reason. We also have many traditions about sharing food and "breaking bread" as way of bonding and celebrating.

Many people in the United States do try to control the instinctual need to locate and eat food. It is extremely difficult for most people who are overweight, for example, to actually lose weight and keep it off. Whether food is abundant or not, people look and consume as much as they can. It's prepared into the nature of who you are. Ninety percent of all people who diet will gain their weight back in less than two years.

So how will we utilize the evolutionary urge to find and eat food in the sales process?

First, it's very important to place the implications of having no food or too much food in the customer's mind. Second, on a cautionary note, you should know that people who are extremely overweight or underweight have serious problems and this becomes an area that salespeople should avoid. Entering minds through MAPs is necessary to increase sales but we don't need to encourage anorexia, bulimia, or obesity!

The Icing on the Cake

It's obvious from the previous chart that people who are light eaters perceive themselves to be sensible, slender, and healthy. So when they go out to eat with us, doesn't it make sense to have something that will be healthy for us both? Wouldn't it also make sense to eat something along the same lines that our customer does to show our wisdom as far as being healthy goes?

It's also obvious from the distinctions in the chart that people who are heavy eaters consider themselves to be happy and sensual in nature. I'm sure that we will be able to model this behavior for one lunch ourselves and not raise a fuss about the amount of food they consume. Hearty eaters love to talk about food. I'm certain that you will find ways to weave their favorite restaurants and meals into the conversation.

Sex, Romance, and Sensuality

Here is the key to your sales success. Here is the key to most people's buying pattern. The drive to reproduce (the behavior for which is romance, flirting, and the act of sex) is virtually unparalleled in humans. We could write a book about how this single drive is what life is all about.

Because this drive has been suppressed for over 3,000 years by many world cultures and religions, there are many tricky nuances about specifically how to utilize this drive in the process of selling. The genetic urge for reproduction runs squarely up against many of society's moral values that make it wrong to want to reproduce. Therefore when using the Sex MAP you have to be very careful indeed.

Men and women both want to be perceived as attractive. Men are hard-wired to spread their seed everywhere and do so as often as they can. Women are hardwired to find a secure location for their offspring and fill it with as many babies as possible with one mate who will provide for that brood. That's at the unconscious level of course.

These very specific instinctual needs then meet society. For the most part in the 21st century the evolutionary urges are regulated by laws. You're generally permitted one wife if you are a man and there is a limit to the number of children that is considered "reasonable." To be sure there are some religions that encourage the birth of many children. These organizations even make rules that make it almost impossible to not have kids. However, almost all of these organizations see the folly of having multiple wives and set ground rules so it can't happen.

All of this is very interesting and it makes you want to talk about it all day, but what does sex have to do with selling?

Just about everything.

There are several reasons people enter into the selling profession and most of them relate to three of the four core instinctual drives . . . and one of the other thirteen basic desires plays a very strong wild card in the mix.

Salespeople as a group tend to be fighters. They are aggressive and face challenges daily that they overcome, get around, move beyond, and they love to win. Every day for a salesperson has an element of danger in it. Salespeople wake up unemployed every morning. If they sell they live another day, if they don't they must return to working for someone else. You may work for a big company as a salesperson and think that you work for the big company. You don't. It works for you. You are paying the salaries of the rest of the employees with all of the net profits from your salary after you are paid.

Only when you become a liability do you actually work for the company. This happens when your net profits do not pay for your salary and commissions. There is something incredibly attractive about people of the opposite sex who are in control of their own destinies. Women in particular are attracted to providers—and what are salespeople? They provide for everyone.

Salespeople work to eat first. This doesn't mean they are overweight or even hearty eaters. Not in the least. But salespeople work to eat. People who have jobs that pay the same amount every week don't work to eat. They work for their total sustenance. They have no control over their lives in any meaningful sense of the word. No one eats until the salesperson eats. No one. If no sales are made, no other employee gets his paycheck. Once again the salesperson is the provider. They work to eat first, and nothing is more attractive (to women in particular) than someone who can provide food for the group. Most salespeople don't know this but now you do!

Salespeople have intense sex drives. (At least, the best salespeople do.) Selling is one of the few professions or jobs that requires proactive action on the part of the individual. Consider these professions and avocations: Attorney, medical doctor, chiropractor, psychologist, social worker, teacher, priest, etc. Almost every profession or job that is not a sales position requires people to come to them. In selling it's the opposite. You have to go to other people. Salespeople therefore must have an enormous set of strengths to overcome everything from rejection to the fears of interpersonal communication with every type of human being.

Salespeople are, generally speaking, fearless in the communication setting. They are the ultimate adaptors. They have the ability to communicate with every type of person and therefore they are the most interesting people to communicate with. They have adventures to tell that are unparalleled by other professions. Salespeople are ultimately attractive to others. The drive to reproduce keeps the salesperson successful. The salesperson is someone who channels his intense evolutionary desires into profits.

The sex drive coupled with the desire to eat and the flight/fight response come together to create a lean, mean fighting machine known as a salesperson.

Now that you know that you are driven by your instincts in such a fashion, let's look at our customers.

Your customer has the urge to reproduce, too. You aren't the only person who "feels this way."

> *Your customers will buy your products and services if at the unconscious level they know this will improve their ability to reproduce.*

Please remember that genes don't think. They just replicate, and they have their orders to replicate. Those orders are causing drives in your customer.

Question: How does your product appeal to your customer's instinctual drive to reproduce?

Answer: Almost all products and services will help this desire or can be linked to this desire if you think about it in the right fashion.

You sell mutual funds and stocks.

✓ Who is buying your product? (Men.) Who is attracted to men with resources?
✓ How might your customer benefit sexually from having more money?
✓ How might your customers be perceived more attractive if they are successful?
✓ How does owning stocks and mutual funds NOW make your customer more attractive in contrast to waiting?

You sell real estate.

✓ How might your customer benefit sexually from buying property or homes?
✓ How might your customers be perceived as more attractive if they own a beautiful and elegantly decorated home?
✓ How does owning real estate NOW make your customer more attractive in contrast to waiting to buy later?

You sell automobiles.

✓ How might your customers be perceived as more attractive if they own a new car?
✓ How does buying a new car now make your customer more attractive in contrast to waiting?

"So you know, Charlie, if you buy a home, own Cisco and IBM, and get a new Lexus, you're going to have some amazing sex this week."

While that might be true, we aren't going to quite frame things this way in the sales process.

"Can you imagine how you will look flying down the highway in that new Lexus? Man, I'm telling you, you will be unbelievable." (His unconscious mind fills in all the blanks.)

"Isn't owning your own place what it's all about?" (For a man, the unconscious mind fills in the blanks.)

"When you two own this home, you will be able to finally settle down."

(For women, "settle down" equals "make babies" at the unconscious level.)

"Won't your wife feel more secure if you go ahead and invest in stocks that will ensure your long-term security?" (The woman is nodding her head. It's biologically wired in!)

Appealing to the needs of reproduction, sex, and desire for sensual experience is a powerful motivator. Every man's magazine (such as *Maxim, FHM, Details, Arena, Loaded, Playboy, Penthouse*) is sold with a cover that features a beautiful woman. Every woman's magazine *(Cosmopolitan, Mademoiselle, Ladies Home Journal, People, Entertainment Weekly)* is sold with a cover that features a beautiful woman. Attraction and desire sell. Period.

Appealing to the nesting instinct sells too. *Better Homes and Gardens, Country Living, American Home*—all are sold to women who want to nest and "settle down." They want to stay put and make their surroundings safe, secure, and attractive. These desires are hardwired in to the woman's genes and they are exhibited in her behavior. What are you doing to sell to these unconscious urges and needs?

Have you ever gone into the Romance section at Barnes & Noble? There are thousands of books there with the same cover, same theme, and same story. Women devour this material like men devour pornography. Women want to be romanced and they can't get enough of it. How are you linking your product or service to these needs?

Here is the continuum of the urge to reproduce in human beings. Find where you are on the continuum, then see if how you perceive others matches the chart. It should. Then see how people on the other side of the spectrum perceive you. This will help you sell more efficiently both to people who are like you and people who are very different.

SEXUAL DESIRE

Pleasure-Seeker	Ascetics
Believe they are:	
Flirtatious	Conservative
Romantic	Virtuous
Sensitive	Saintly
Carnal	Spiritual
Lustful	Cerebral
High Sex Drive	Self Controlled

Believe other half to be:

Puritanical	Wild
Prudish	Hedonistic
Hung up	Lacking in Control
Impotent	Superficial

There are also large numbers of people who have successfully suppressed their sex drive. These people are sold by tapping into the MAPs of self-control and virtuosity. As you listen to what people say when they talk to you, discovering their most powerful drives will be simple. As with all skills, it just takes practice!

In the next chapter we will look at the balance of the drives that all emerge from the three core drives that we have discussed. By now, I think you are starting to see how your instincts drive your behavior, and you are now probably starting to see an emerging picture of others around you that may have been foggy until now.

CHAPTER 4

Your Customer:
An Open Book

Each drive in this chapter emerges from the core drives in Chapter 5. However, they are definitely distinctly different and are important in developing a complete picture of yourself and, more importantly, your customer. After you have read this chapter, your customer will essentially be an open book.

Salespeople tend to be very competitive. They have to be to survive. They certainly have a strong tendency to cooperate with their clients but they are definitely competitive with others in their profession. However, let there be no question that some people are energized by competing as part of a team. Still others love to compete one on one. Which are you? (Remember you may fall in the middle of the continuum!) You may find that you are on one end of the spectrum at home and on another at work.

DESIRE TO COMPETE OR SEEK VENGEANCE

Competitive ——————————— **Cooperative**

Believe themselves to be:

Competitive	Cooperative
Go-Getter	Conflict-avoidant
Winner	Kind
Competitive	Forgiving
Aggressive	Turn other cheek
Will get even if necessary	

Believe others to be:

Competitive	Cooperative
Failure	Bent out of shape
Loser	Aggressive

Non-assertive	Competitive
Passive	Angry
Always wants to win	Always need to win

Vengeful behavior probably began as a way to punish aggressors who stole possessions from the individual or the group. Those who would take revenge upon others may have been the protectors of the community. Perhaps 10,000 years ago they were higher on the totem pole in the society and had to protect the group from outsiders. These vengeful people became leaders because of their drive for "justice" and need to be "the best."

Vengeance, of course, has its downside in behavior. Men still kill out of jealousy in our civilized society. The need to get even can be very intense, especially in men.

Individuals who have a difficult time controlling their anger, those who compete, and those who seek revenge fall on the competitive side of the spectrum. People who tend to avoid competitive situations definitely fall on the other side. These critical distinctions help us sell our customer. Imagine that your customer falls on the competitive side of the spectrum. Here is how we want to enter his MAPs:

You sell securities (stocks and mutual funds).

✓ "What matters most is what you end up with at the end."
✓ "Don't you deserve more because you've worked harder?"
✓ "Aren't you as good as the rest of them?"
✓ "Don't you deserve as much as anyone else?"

You sell real estate.

✓ "Would you like to own the nicest house in the neighborhood?"
✓ "Is it important that you get the best price possible?"
✓ "I know you. You just want the best."
✓ "What it all comes down to is are you getting the best deal."

You sell advertising.

✓ "Whose image do you want to pop into people's heads first?"
✓ "Don't YOU want to be known as the go-to guy?"
✓ "Do you want a bigger ad than (your competitor)?"
✓ "What do you think the best long-term strategy is to knock them out?"

Drive to Nest

Research continues to show that better-educated and higher-IQ people are having fewer and fewer babies. (How's that for an evolving mess?) What is going on here? I'm not certain, but understanding a person's drive to have a family is very important indeed. Obviously this drive emerges from the instinct to reproduce but it is not the same thing. Wanting to have lots of sex is not to be confused with wanting to have lots of children. Your genes don't know the difference, but your 21st-century brain sure does.

I often look around the office of my customers to see if they have several pictures of the wife and kids or if they have the one obligatory picture of the family . . . probably several years old. That helps me understand this most important desire.

Stephen Reiss notes that if raising children is essential to your happiness, then you fall on one side of the spectrum. If having kids is mostly difficult, you fall on the other side of the spectrum. There seems to be no difference between men and women on average with the desire to raise children, so be careful of stereotyping!

When I listen to people talk about their children I want to know how much affection for those kids is resonating in the person. (I am not interested in how people view other people's children in most cases.) If they say, "My kids are great," I haven't heard anything to MAP into. They may say, "My kids are my reason for living. They make me thank God every day." That I can MAP into, and here's how I do that:

You sell cars.

✓ "Won't your kids love having this new car?"
✓ "Doesn't it make you a proud dad to be able to bring this home?"
✓ "What have your kids been asking you to get?"
✓ "How important are your kids in your decision to buy a safe car like this?"

You sell securities (stocks and other financial investments).

✓ "Do you factor in your kid's future when you make your investments?"
✓ "What's it feel like to be a responsible parent in an age where no one cares?"
✓ "What weight do you assign to your kids when making these decisions?"
✓ "Are you looking for enough to put the kids through college?"

As you consider the continuum below, where do you fall on it? Are you responsible and domestic? Do you just relish every moment with your children? Are they the center of your universe? You're on one side of the spectrum. Do you sense kids are more work than they are worth? Do you feel that children conflict with your desire for freedom? Are kids going to just tie you down for twenty years? You are on the other side of center.

THE NESTING INSTINCT

Family	Non-Family
Believe themselves to be:	
Cocooner	Out and about
Domestic	Independent
Responsible	Free
Believe other half to be:	
Selfish	Burdened
Irresponsible	Tied Down
Immature	Imprisoned
Unaccountable	Obligated

Exercise: The desire to nest and raise children is common and dominates the decision-making process of most parents. How does your product or service MAP into both groups? Answer now before going on!

The Desire to Connect with Others

It is an interesting fact that people who have many friends and rich relationships tend to be healthier, live longer, and heal faster when they are sick. There is an inborn drive to connect with other people that serves an important purpose in ensuring the replication of those little genes. In ancient times it was very important to gather together in groups so you could survive everything from attacks by enemies to animals.

The same instinct can be seen in the modern world. People tend to live in cities. The cities are expanding to where there was once just farm land. People may not like everything about being in close proximity to others but for the most part it is how we feel comfortable.

To be sure, there is a significant percentage of the population that feels the need to live in rural areas or lead very private lives, tucked away from others. This is not the norm, however, and it is not the drive that has per-petuated the safety that is found within a group.

Social connections for the individual can be very important. Each week many people take time out of their everyday lives to congregate at their local church. They renew friendships and make new ones with like-minded individuals. The same experience is true of people who go to Rotary, Lions, Kiwanis, and other fraternal organizations. Similarly, most people tend to find more security in working for a BIG company in con-trast to a small company.

The drive to connect with others is powerful, and there is a price that may have to be paid for those who don't connect with others. Everything from the safety the large group provides to the healthier life one experi-ences with lots of connections makes it clear this instinct pays dividends.

Not everyone prefers the group, though. They've fought the desire to be one of "the group." They've "gotten over" the need for acceptance. They might just want to be left alone to appreciate the solitude of peace and quiet. The stress and hustle and bustle just aren't worth the effort for these people.

Wouldn't it be useful to MAP into the specific thinking that is driving your customer?

Where do you fall on the continuum of connectivity? Do you feel hap-piest when you are in a group? Do you feel like there are groups to which you "belong?" Do you like to have fun with others? Do you consider yourself a very friendly person? If so, you are on the side of the instinc-tual drive to connect with others.

On the other hand, do you tend to be serious and studious? Do you find time alone preferable to time with others? Do you find the group repul-sive? Do you find yourself lonely or alone (in either a positive or negative sense)? If so, you are on the other side of the fence.

Now, as you think about your customers, think about where some of them fall on the spectrum.

DESIRE TO CONNECT WITH OTHERS

Sociable ———————————— **Private**

Believe themselves to be:

Sociable	Private
Warm	Intimate
Approachable	Secret

Friendly	Serious
Fun	Unhappy
Lively	Lonely

Believe other half to be:

Cold	Out There
Reclusive	Loud
Aloof	Lack Depth
Private	Superficial
Serious	Shallow
Shy	Boisterous

You sell cars.

✓ "Won't it be fun to go out in your new car?"
✓ "Traveling becomes fun again with this car, doesn't it?"
✓ "Won't it be nice to drive up to the office in this one?"

You sell real estate.

✓ "Won't it be nice to throw a party in your beautiful new home?"
✓ "Isn't it going to be fun entertaining here?"
✓ "Isn't it nice to have a neighborhood with so many nice people?"

You are a travel agent.

✓ "Won't it be fun to take spring break in Orlando with all the people?"
✓ "Won't it be great to take a cruise and meet people just like you?"
✓ "Can you imagine Las Vegas at Halloween and all the people you will see?"

Exercise: Write key questions and sentences that will help you enter your customer's Mind Access Points. Include sentences and questions for people on both ends of the spectrum, not just the side of the instinctual drive!

Seeking Power

Power is the ability to influence the behavior of others.

Poland's leading magazine is called *wProst*. It's as influential in Poland as *Time* is in the United States. *wProst* did an extensive interview with me in 2000. They printed the interview and a nice photo to boot. The caption read something like, "Kevin Hogan, The Guru of Business Psychology." *wProst* lent power to my work for the people of Poland, who didn't know me from your brother-in-law.

On my next trip to Poland, I received the royal treatment. Everyone from the people in the hotel to the people who came to the sales conference I spoke at in 2001 wanted autographs and pictures. Why? Because *wProst* said I was the Guru of Business Psychology.

Particularly interesting about this specific experience is the fact that the millions of people who read this magazine believe what they read. The magazine, like magazines in all countries, shapes opinions about who or what is important. It creates perceptions in people's minds that may or not be accurate. In my case, the stamp of approval was important for my message to be well received. I used that instant rapport in many ways that were useful for the audiences to whom I spoke.

Power is a two-way street. People have to be willing to give someone power, and someone has to desire the power for the power to be utilized on a long-term basis. Power is a fascinating subject, but let's see how to tap the drive for power with your customer.

The word alone creates images in your mind. The drive to reach the top of some pecking order (to become a big fish in a small pond) is common among men. They seek power in different ways. Some strive to political power. Do you know how many multi-millionaires there are in the U.S. House of Representatives? Why would a man who is a multi-millionaire spend millions of dollars of his own money to get a job that pays $133,600 per year?

Power.

Other men seek power in different ways and on different levels. The evangelist who is enlightened seeks the followers to listen to his message. The author wants people to read his book, and the judge wants to be the representative of justice. The police officer wants the power to control behavior and the mayor wants the reins of the city. Some people want to have the biggest burger joint, the biggest airline, the prettiest wife, the most fans, the most clients, the most money, and on and on. They all want power and to some degree they get some power.

Unfortunately, the drive for power can get ugly. The striving and acquisition of power can cause wars and literally cost millions of people their lives. Power is a potent drive that can help individuals to do great good or ill. This deep desire of human nature is chiefly a drive of male behavior in contrast to female behavior. (Understand that both men and women want power. The point is to what degree the genders want power. There is no question that great power is sought and acquired by far more men than women.)

Whether your customer is male or female isn't that important. Everyone (almost everyone) wants to influence human behavior. We all want our children to obey. We want the neighbors to change some of their behavior. We want the idiot at the stoplight in front of us to turn left so we can get going. We all want to influence the behaviors of other people. This is the striving for power.

> *How does your product or service help your customer acquire power?*

If your customesr can see how you can help them become more influential—and power IS influence—then you can virtually guarantee a sale.

Look at the following continuum and see where you fall from the standpoint of the desire to have power. If you find yourself to be ambitious, influential, working sixty hours per week, and have a dominant personality, you fall on one side of the spectrum. If you aren't particularly ambitious, tend to be people-oriented and are a good support person, you probably fall on the other end of the spectrum. Find yourself on the continuum first, then consider where your customers tend to fall on the spectrum.

SEEKING POWER

Leader ——————————————— **Follower**

Believe themselves to be:

Enterprising	Simple
Aspiring	Humble
Motivated	Undemanding
Ambitious	Not ambitious
Influential	People oriented
Hard-working	Submissive
Dominant	

See the other half as:

Allergic to work	Lofty
Unmotivated	Demanding
Lazy	Domineering
Weak	Not caring
Unsuccessful	Controlling
Workaholic	

How do you use the drive of power to sell?

You sell cars.

✓ "Doesn't driving a Mercedes give others the impression of you that you want them to have?"
✓ "Doesn't owning a new car make a statement about what you can have?"

You sell real estate.

✓ "Some people say it's a good investment to have the least expensive house in a neighborhood. Doesn't it say something to have the nicest house in the neighborhood?"
✓ "When people see this house, how will they respond to you?"

You sell securities.

✓ "Money is power and power is freedom. Isn't that what you want?"
✓ "Doesn't having money mean that you can do anything you want?"

Exercise: Write key questions and sentences that will help you enter your customer's Mind Access Points. Include sentences and questions for people on both ends of the spectrum, not just one side of the instinctual drive.

Seeking Status

Everyone wants to be important to someone else. Some people want to be important to larger groups. Status and power often dovetail, but not always. The desire to be perceived as important is a driving force in human nature. In the last five years news groups on the internet have created an interesting battleground for status. People who never have been well known publicly can obtain social status (good and bad) in various small groups by posting regularly to these various groups. Everyone looks the same in text so people with time on their hands can be seen as players in whatever field of interest they feel they have a right to make public comments about.

"Fifteen minutes" is a well-known phrase in America that refers to amount of time everyone supposedly will be famous during their lifetime. Many people want more than fifteen minutes. Some people are motivated by their drives and desires to be seen as having "more" or to become well known in certain ways. Some people will buy a mansion. Someone else might drive a ridiculously priced house or wear an enormous diamond. All of these are status symbols. The people that produce status products realize this and can command a premium for these types of products.

Some of your customers may only need to be important to their family. Some may feel the need to be important to a large group. Knowing where the MAPs are is vital. Do you find yourself buying the best or the most expensive things in certain areas? Do you buy things to impress other people? If so, then you fall on one side of the spectrum.

On the other hand, you may find yourself unimpressed by royalty, status, prestige, and the accoutrements thereof. If you don't care what others think, then you fall on the other side of the spectrum. First determine where you lie on the continuum, then think of your customers and decide if they are driven by status.

DESIRE FOR STATUS

Social Climber ——————— **Egalitarian**

See themselves as:

Social Climber	Egalitarian
Moving up	Equal to everyone else
Prestigious	Libertarian
Important	Fair minded
Worthy of recognition	Democratic
Prominent	Down to earth

See others as:

Social Climber	Egalitarian
Unknown	Stuffed shirt
Insignificant	Highbrow

Unimportant	Snob
Low class	Arrogant
Poor taste	Showoff

How do you use status to sell your product or service?

You sell securities.

✓ "Imagine how people will look at you when you are retired, compared to the rest of the people who don't care about their futures."
✓ "When you are wealthy from all of these investments, please remember the little people who helped you get there."

You sell cars.

✓ "Just imagine how you are going to look driving this new car!"
✓ "People will think you have really made it when they see you driving this!"

You sell real estate.

✓ "There is no doubt that this house is a statement. You have arrived."
✓ "This house says that "you have worked hard and you deserve the best.""

Exercise: Look at your product/service now and decide what phrases, sentences, and questions you could ask someone on either end of the elitist/egalitarian spectrum.

Seeking Independence

The group offers protection and social contact. Those are two elements absolutely necessary for the perpetuation of your genes! Once secure in those two factors, the individual comes to an age where it is time to set out on his own. In ancient days this was necessary to find food. The group had formed. Lots of people congregating together in one place is not going to be positively correlated to having animals stop by to sacrifice themselves for the community dinner.

The desire to strike out from the collective is very important indeed. Today we find that people often need to make a change after having relied on the group for so long. In ancient days there was much more work to be done than in our 21st-century society. Capturing food and preparing it was a hard day's work . . . if not a week or months. The need for self-reliance is not only an instinctual need but it is a key drive for success and achievement in life.

People who are "independent" feel they are self-reliant. They say things such as "If you want it done right, you have to do it yourself" or "I just want to be free." And indeed, like a bird put in a cage, the individual struggles to become free. The birdcage becomes a prison though, and over time the individual becomes reliant upon others. The need for self-reliance is conditioned from the individual and he learns a new set of behaviors. These we will call "interdependent." Interdependence serves many functions.

Interdependent people are easier to love because they are home more often! They appear to have more invested in the personal and social aspects of relationships, and they are more connected with others in their homes and their community. Interdependent people see themselves as loving people who are much more devoted to their spouses and families than independent people.

As you look at the continuum for independence/interdependence, where do you seem to belong? Are you more freedom-seeking and autonomous, or do you tend to act far more devoted to those around you than the average person?

DESIRE FOR INDEPENDENCE

Independent	Interdependent
Believe themselves to be:	
Self-sufficient	
Reliable	
Self-reliant	Loving
Autonomous	Trusting
Free	Devoted
Resistant to the herd spirit	
Believe the other half to be:	
Immature	Inflexible
Weak	Prideful
Dependent	Strong-willed
Needy	Bullheaded

How will we link into the MAP of your customer who has a strong drive for independence?

You sell securities (stocks, bonds).

✓ "Won't it be nice when you can rely solely on yourself when you are older?"
✓ "Have you ever known anyone who was wealthy who wasn't his own investor?"
✓ "Do you find that having money build up makes you more independent thinking?"
✓ "Would you say that investing for your future will give you financial freedom?"
✓ "Isn't it nice to not be a slave to anyone?"

You sell Mary Kay distributorships (or any face/face direct sales).

✓ "Isn't nice to be able to do something on your own?"
✓ "Doesn't it feel good to be your own boss?"
✓ "What's it like being on your own?"
✓ "How good does it feel to know that you aren't a slave to someone else?"

You sell real estate.

✓ "Isn't nice to not be a slave to rent any more?"
✓ "What's it like to have your own home finally?"
✓ "Isn't it nice to live well and build your independence at the same time?"
✓ "How is buying this home going to help you achieve financial independence?"

Exercise: Look at your product/service now and decide what phrases, sentences, and questions you could ask someone on either end of the independence/interdependence spectrum.

Desire of Curiosity

Sherlock Holmes. He searched and found the clues that pointed him to the truth. In his cases there was always a villain who left a trail of clues, albeit minute and often almost impossible to notice. Holmes was the great detective. He told fascinating stories of his travels, he was aware of every move someone would make, and he was brilliant. Holmes would have made a terrible detective had he not been curious.

Richard Brodie, whom you met in the last chapter, introduced me to a friend of his on a recent trip we all made to Las Vegas. Jeffrey Gitomer had just arrived in town. I was familiar with his book *The Sales Bible* and his masterpiece about customer service called *Customer Service Is Worthless, Customer Loyalty Is Priceless.* I had never heard Jeffrey speak but I knew from his writing style he was going to be a no-nonsense kind of guy.

We met at a little restaurant just off the Strip. Jeffrey and I were both exhausted from flying into town. We exchanged pleasantries and immediately he began.

"I see you wrote this book *The Psychology of Persuasion.*"

"I did. Have you read it yet?"

"No."

"I thought your *Worthless/Loyalty* book was great."

"Good job, Kid." (He called me Kid. For future reference: As of the publication of this book, I will be forty. Had I been much younger, the reference to Kid would have been particularly annoying. However, because of the fact that Jeffrey is at least ten years my senior, I forgave him . . . in less than a week.)

"How's *Loyalty* doing?"

"It's fine. Define selling for me in two words."

I drank my wine, or most of it, at that request. Selling in two words. Geez, Jeffrey, summarize *War and Peace* in two words. This is what I get for being last at the table. Richard has obviously prodded you into getting inside of my head and pushing buttons instantly. Okay, here we go.

"Build rapport."

"No. Guess again."

Guess again? Build rapport is a heckuva answer for this off-the-cuff "Who Wants to Be a Millionaire?" at Batista's restaurant. I look at Richard. He is restraining a smile. His girlfriend, Heather, has not restrained her smile. She is clearly thrilled that I am getting tutored.

"I can't guess heads or tails on a two-sided coin. You tell me, in two words, Jeffrey. Summarize selling."

"Ask questions."

Well, duh. You have to ask questions or you're just a videotape that is constantly replayed over and over . . . and . . . why didn't I say that? It's a better answer than "build rapport." This is the kind of guy I could really be annoyed with, if I wasn't ready to learn so much.

"Good answer."

"I know."

Ask questions. Why? Because we don't know their answers. We can only imagine we know their answers until we ask. Then we know their answers. That's what selling IS all about. (By the way, lest you think the distinction had been previously lost on me, there is an entire section in *The Psychology of Persuasion* highlighting the significance of asking questions!)

Aristotle was a philosopher some two millennia ago. He wrote about curiosity, and I think there is a lot to be learned from his writing. There are four things that humans are intensely curious about:

---

1) We want to know what things are made of.

2) We are curious about the forms and shapes that things take.

3) We are curious about the beginnings and causes of things and events.

4) We are curious about the purposes or goals of people, things, and events.

We were curious about these things thousands of years ago and we still are.

Begin to tap into people's curiosity!

Genuine curiosity about all that goes on around us is a survival and success mechanism. Curiosity helps individuals become capable of solving problems and that once again helps keep our genes flowing! People who are very curious consider themselves to be intelligent, thoughtful, and aware.

On the other side of the spectrum are people who are not interested in intellectual pursuits. They tend to live simpler and more practical lives. They consider themselves "street smart," having learned from experience. Interestingly, people on both ends of the spectrum consider people on the opposite ends to be boring and this brings up a critical point:

The only way to avoid being boring is to ask questions!

Your only hope to not bore someone to tears is to be certain you know where they are on the Curiosity continuum! Simply communicating our wealth of knowledge and interests to another person is one of the riskiest communication behaviors there is. If you have someone on the other end of the spectrum as your listener, they won't listen for long.

Look at the following continuum. Where do you find yourself? If you are often seeking intellectual pursuits, trying to find out why you are here, are in search of the truth, and generally want to know "more," then you fall on the intellectual side of the spectrum. On the other hand, if you find yourself to be more of the "street smart" and practical, down-to-earth type, you fall on the other side of the spectrum. Now that you have "found your self," think about some of your customers. Where do they fall on the continuum?

DESIRE FOR CURIOSITY

Intellectual ———————————— **Non- Intellectual**

Believe themselves to be:

Intellectual	Non-Intellectual
Engaging	Sensible
Fascinating	Sane
Smart	Practical
Interesting	Down-to-earth
Aware	Street Smart

Believe the other half to be:

Intellectual	Non-Intellectual
Boring	Boring
Ignorant	Nerd
Superficial	Arrogant
Dull	

How do we frame our questions and statements to MAP into another person's desire of curiosity?

You sell real estate.

✓ "Are you looking for a home that is close to a church?"
✓ "How many rooms will you need internet access in?"
✓ "Will you use one of the bedrooms as an office or library?"

You sell securities.

✓ "Would you like a complimentary, ninety-day subscription to *Investors Business Daily?*"
✓ "Would you like a list of the best investment web sites?"
✓ "Are you interested in technical analysis of these stocks?"

You sell cars.

✓ "Would you like to look at what *Consumers Reports* has to say about this car?"
✓ "Would you like to see what Edmunds.com shows the value of your trade in is?"
✓ "Are you interested in seeing how this car compares to our competitors?"

Exercise: Consider your product or service. How can you MAP into the thinking of your customers with the desire of curiosity? Write down several questions, statements, and themes.

Desire for Acceptance

"You better go back to driving a truck, son." That's what the manager of the Grand Ole Opry told Elvis Presley in 1955. The manager had determined that Elvis simply didn't have what it would take to be a star. A person who lacked in self-confidence never could have gone on to fight his way to the top. The non-assertive individual desiring acceptance of group norms would immediately have packed his guitar and decided to go back to driving that electrician's truck. Thankfully the need for acceptance by the group is over-ridden in cases like that of Presley.

I spent an enormous amount of time researching and writing a book. The first draft was written in 1991. I submitted the manuscript to a publisher that in less than two years would go bankrupt, and my manuscript was returned. That was 1993.

Beginning in late 1993 I began submitting the manuscript to publishers all over the United States. Week after week I would receive rejection letters. Many of them said that I had no chance of being published without an agent. But I was convinced that the book was an excellent piece of work that would help people sell and persuade others to their way of thinking.

I was **certain** that if people read the book they would love it and, more importantly, that the book would help change their lives. As of 1995 I had received over 240 rejection letters for *The Psychology of Persuasion.* Then I wrote one letter with a personal touch.

For years I had admired Zig Ziglar. He was always one of my favorite authors and speakers. I knew he was published by Pelican Publishing Company, a family-owned firm in Louisiana. I wrote Pelican and told them that I was going to be the next Zig Ziglar. I had already begun a somewhat successful speaking career, had self-published two books by this time, and was ready for a hardcover. Trust me, I told them. I'll make it happen.

After all those 240 rejections, Pelican said yes. Since that time I have been in a Win/Win relationship with Pelican, and we're still receiving great reviews and inquiries to speak about *The Psychology of Persuasion.* Had I followed my "common sense," I never would have sent out any manuscripts after the first 50—and certainly none after 100. I was absolutely certain though that I was going to be a popular author.

Today, of course, you see *The Psychology of Persuasion* in bookstores from Los Angeles to Warsaw and from London to New Delhi. It has been published in China and Brazil.

Defying the voice that said "give up" that had been programmed in by the group was something I never questioned. I was certain that *The Psychology of Persuasion* was a great book. I've never regretted not listening to all the other people who told me I was wasting my time . . . and getting a real job that "paid benefits." I'm a salesman. Paid benefits . . . geesh.

The desire for acceptance is what keeps people in large groups though and the desire for acceptance has its benefit. People who desire acceptance tend to "go with the flow" better than people who are defiant in the storm. People who "go with the flow" tend to experience less stress and make fewer waves.

There are a lot of benefits there. More calm, more relaxed. Virtually everyone would prefer that they be accepted and liked by the group. That said, not everyone **needs** to be accepted, and herein lies this desire. Those people who need to be liked tend to be very non-assertive by nature. They are literally needy.

As you look at the continuum below do you find yourself being more a "go with the flow" kind of person, or do you see yourself as being more assertive? Which side of the continuum are you on?

DESIRE FOR ACCEPTANCE

Go with the Group ——————— Assertive

Believe themselves to be:

Insecure	Assertive
Lacking in self-confidence	Confident
Not Assertive	Self-assured
Go with the flow	Persistent

Believe others to be:

Conceited	Needy
Too confident	Immature
Slick	Overly sensitive

How do you sell the person who needs acceptance?

You sell cars.

✓ "This is the most popular car out there."
✓ "This car will make you look and feel great."
✓ "Don't feel pressured to buy this car. Just drive it and see if it feels right."
✓ "This car is safe and reliable. You will feel comfortable owning it."

You sell securities.

✓ "I work for people who don't feel comfortable investing on their own."
✓ "I've been doing this for fifteen years. Why don't you let me take the pressure off you and show you what will make your future more secure?"
✓ "This is a simple growth mutual fund. Nothing aggressive. Just consistent and steady."
✓ "Most people who want a solid future will have a balanced portfolio. Does that sound like you?"

You sell real estate.

✓ "This is a pretty conservative home that you will feel safe in."
✓ "This is a pretty conservative neighborhood. I think you will be comfortable here."

✓ "Would you like to handle getting a loan on your own, or do you want me to take all the stress out of it and do it for you?

Exercise: Consider your product or service. Decide now how you will communicate with people on both sides of the acceptance spectrum. Write down sentences, questions, and themes that will appeal to people on both sides of the continuum.

Desire to Have Honor

We aren't really "just" animals anymore. Consciousness is something that is experienced by just about every living person. The need to be decent to people is something that is respectable. This need certainly has its root in the evolving race we are in.

If people didn't cooperate with others there would be no economic expansion, no long-term relationships, and eventually the groups that collect into urban areas would all turn on each other and self-destruct. That doesn't happen, though, because many people have honed the desire to be honorable into a key personal value.

Obviously, the counterpart has its place, too. There is a certain amount of checking and double-checking that takes place in honorable people. Sometimes there are so many reassurances that need to be made that things don't ever get done. Sometimes expedience is more useful than principle.

In ancient days disloyalty was severely punished. In times of war, loyalty can be severely punished. You can be certain that loyalty and honor are rooted deeply in our behavior. Always remember that many have grown to make the trade-offs that disloyalty offers. A sense of individuality and freedom come with expedience. Breaking away from the group to strike out on your own becomes important to many.

As you look at the continuum below. Where do you find yourself? Are you more focused on principles, loyalty, morals, and duty, or are you more of an opportunist, practical minded and expedient?

THE DESIRE OF PRINCIPLED LOYALTY

Principled ——————————— **Expedient**

Believe themselves to be:

Principled	Expedient
Devoted	Resourceful
Dedicated	Quick-thinking

Patriotic	Problem-solving
Moral	Practical
Have character	Opportune
Dutiful	Like everyone else
Loyal	Pragmatic

Believe others to be:

Disloyal	Self-righteous
Self-serving	Holier than thou
Lacking Character	Sanctimonious
Impractical	

How do you MAP into your customer's mind with the instinct of loyalty?

You sell securities.

✓ "If I can help you begin to meet your financial goals, will you work with me long term?"
✓ "If I help you succeed, will you refer me to the rest of the people in your family and at the office?"
✓ "I see you've done well with Fidelity over the years. Do you want to stick with Fidelity Select Funds or would you rather switch to another company?"

You sell advertising.

✓ "If I can help you make money, will you let me structure your marketing program as well?"
✓ "If I write you an ad that pulls, will you refer me to your non-competing buddies?"
✓ "If I write you an ad that makes money, will you give me a list of names I can call to help get the same results?"

Exercise: Consider your product or service and prepare questions, statements, and themes about how specifically to sell to people on both sides of the spectrum of loyalty.

Desire for Altruism

No doubt about it, we all have our altruistic moments. Some people live a life of altruism. Mother Theresa may have been the best-known altruist of our times. People who sacrifice something of themselves for others are often living up to a higher value or spiritual level. This doesn't mean that altruism isn't rewarded many times over, though.

Altruism is as old as the ancients. Altruism pays off for the individual when the individual believes that his behavior is being seen or felt on another level. At this level people feel as if they are attaining their highest good and that they are truly making a difference. Self-sacrifice brings self-satisfaction, and that is a very good thing indeed!

Of course many people have overridden the desire to be altruistic. We call these people realists. Realists tend to be more focused on the self as opposed to others. This is neither good nor bad, but once again the realist is either moving away from the group or attempting to move higher up in the group. The idealistic tend to stay centered in the group.

As you look at the spectrum of behaviors below, where do you find yourself? Do you find yourself mostly caring, compassionate, self-sacrificing, and altruistic? If so, you fall on the left side of the spectrum. If you find yourself more pragmatic, realistic, and self-focused, then you are on the other side of the continuum.

DESIRE FOR IDEALISM AND REALISM

Idealistic ————————————— **Realistic**

Believe themselves to be:

Idealistic	Realistic
Caring	Pragmatic
Selfless	Practical
Humanitarian	Real world
Giving	Sensible
Compassionate	Looking out for #1
Visionary	Realistic

Believe others to be:

Idealistic	Realistic
Self centered	Idealistic
Heartless	Dreamer
Insensitive	Meddlesome
Unfeeling	Unrealistic

How do you sell someone who has the desire for idealism?

You sell securities.

✓ "If you find you make a lot more money than you think, would you want me to set up a giving program for you?"
✓ "How do you see yourself using your money if you become wealthy beyond your plans?"

You sell direct sales products or services.

✓ "A portion of all sales go toward . . ."
✓ "Would you like us to donate a portion of the proceeds toward . . . "
✓ "Not only would you be purchasing your new X for yourself but you will have made a difference for me, and I appreciate that.

You sell business opportunities.

✓ "The real nice thing about owning your own business is you can turn around and help other people help themselves."
✓ "The great thing about being in business for yourself is that you ultimately decide how you will help people."

Exercise: Consider your product or service and prepare questions, statements, and themes about how specifically to sell to people on both sides of the spectrum of altruism.

Desire for Order

Once people collect things, or collect groups of people around themselves, they have a desire to be organized. People like to have "stuff" but they often want to be neat about it! Being organized is a signpost of control for a lot of people. Being organized means that the person is in charge and this is a key to motivating others. We want people's behavior to be neat and orderly as well. We tend to identify organization with intelligence, although there is no evidence to support such a belief.

Some people really enjoy the ability to live without a script. Some people look at a speaker who knows all of his lines as the most boring speaker in the world. Others appreciate the organized and well-prepared individual. People who are organized like processes and algorithms. These people like taking direction and feel all alone if they don't have the direction.

Having considered the two ends of the spectrum, do you find yourself neat, in control, socialized, orderly, organized, enjoying the process? On the other hand, do you enjoy spontaneity? Do you prefer being flexible instead of having to do things the same way all the time? If so, you are on the other side of the continuum.

DESIRE FOR ORDER

Organized ———————————— Flexible

Believe themselves to be:

Neat	Flexible
Tidy	Natural
In control	Spontaneous
Socialized	Unrehearsed

Believe others to be:

Sloppy	Too perfect
Dirty	Controlling of others
Out of control	Concerned with trivia
Messy	Neat freaks
Disorganized	Rigid

How do you sell the organized person?

You sell real estate.

✓ "Will this house provide you with the space you need for all of your stuff?"
✓ "Where do you see all of your stuff going in this house?"
✓ "Will having the den as an office help you keep the rest of the house neater?"

You sell clothing.

✓ "How will other people see you in this new coat and tie?"
✓ "Does this suit present the image you are looking to project?"
✓ "Does this outfit give you that 'take charge and in control' appearance?"

Exercise: Consider your product or service and prepare questions, statements, and themes about how specifically to sell to people on both sides of the spectrum of order.

Desire to Save

Nature has always favored that which saves and prepares for the future. The squirrel collects and stores nuts so that it will not go without in the winter. People who save their money are doing the same thing. They simply are using the currency of the 21st century, their money. The individual who saves is fulfilling the drive to preserve himself and his family . . . and, of course, that means their genes.

It is rare that a person can go through life without saving and live a fruitful "second half" (the last thirty to fifty years of life). If this is true, what benefits are there in being a "spender" or a "consumer?" The consumer of products and services is someone who lives in the moment. They fear not for tomorrow and they probably live with more instant gratification. They believe they should enjoy life and they feel they are deserving of the fruits of life.

Very few people can live this lifestyle and have anything left over, but It does make the early years of life more enjoyable. Unfortunately, like the animals who don't save, there will be no quality of life later.

Americans save less than 5 percent of their annual income. The Japanese save 27 percent of their annual income. That tells us that saving money is possible and that some societies are wisely preparing for their future. On the other hand, many people who live in the United States are having a better life today, whether or not they are sacrificing their future for immediate pleasures. Look at the continuum below. Are you the kind of a person who is storing money for the future when you may be less able to earn it? Do you regularly say "no" to consuming and spending and "yes" to investing and saving? If so, you fall on one side of the continuum. On the other hand, do you live for today? Do you find yourself living more richly today than others? If so, then you are on this side of the spectrum. Now, think about where most of your customers are.

DESIRE TO SAVE

Saver ——————————————— Spender

Believe themselves to be:

Conserving
Frugal   Enjoying life
Thrifty   Deserving
Planning ahead

Believe others to be:

Irresponsible	Miser
Imprudent	Money-grubber
Living for only today	Cheap
Wasteful	Self-denying
Extravagant	Penny-pincher

How do you sell the saver?

You sell securities.

✓ "Would you like me to show you how to have an even richer tomorrow?"
✓ "Would you like to really have a retirement that is filled with fun and time for what you really want to do?"
✓ "How far ahead do you want to prepare for?"

You sell real estate.

✓ "You know the best investment there is, don't you? Your home."
✓ "Can you invest too much money in your own home?"
"With your own home, every dollar works for you. Either you pay off principal or you get a tax write-off."

Exercise: Consider your product or service and prepare questions, statements, and themes about how specifically to sell to people on both sides of the spectrum of saving.

Desire for Physical Activity

In ancient times, the inactive and lazy were punished with starvation and attack by animals and enemies. It is a normal drive for people to want to be active. Not too many years ago humans spent their entire day hunting and gathering. The all-day search for food was critical to survival. No activity ultimately meant death.

Today the United States is the land of the couch potato. The majority of Americans are overweight. Not only is that not attractive, it is a harbinger of early demise. Within America there is a physical fitness movement. Many cities actually have become known as physically fit. These include cities such as Seattle and Minneapolis. People in these cities seem to have figured it out. If we keep sitting on the couch, we can have all the money we want, but it won't matter. We won't be around to spend it!

Do you find yourself full of energy? Do you enjoy vigorous activity? Are you a fitness nut? Would you call yourself athletic? If so, you fall on this side of the spectrum. On the other hand, maybe you find yourself easy going and low key. If so, you are on the other side of the spectrum.

What about your customers? Where do they tend to cluster on the spectrum of the desire for activity?

DESIRE FOR PHYSICAL ACTIVITY

Active ——————————————— **Inactive**

Believe themselves to be:

Active	Inactive
Energetic	Self-paced
Vigorous	Easy-going
Fit	Low key
Athletic	Laid back

Believe others to be:

Active	Inactive
Lazy	Jocks
Slow	Physical
Sedentary	Exhausting
Couch potato	Fast-paced

How do you sell the person who desires activity?

You sell securities.

✓ "When you have more money, what will you do with your free time?"
✓ "Will you find yourself participating in more fun activities when you see your portfolio build?"

You sell real estate.

✓ "Are you going to want a room that we can put a Nordic Track or Stairmaster in?"

Exercise: Consider your product or service and prepare questions, statements, and themes about how specifically to sell to people on both sides of the spectrum of activity.

The sixteen desires are all rooted in our instinctual evolutionary drives. These are the drives that shape human behavior. Some of the drives are obviously more important to tap into on average than others in the sales process.

Review these two chapters regularly so you can be certain that your sales and marketing messages are feeding into not only the drives but the reaction to the drives (the other side of the spectrum) as well. Are you MAPping into the right drives with the right people? That's ultimately one of the keys to scientific selling and the master key to sales success.

CHAPTER 5

Rapport!

Building rapport is one of the most powerful things that you can master to optimize your effectiveness in the selling process. It creates a subtle affinity that puts people at ease and helps them to open up to you in a way that is almost unbelievable. What rapport does is help people feel that you are similar to them, and people are attracted to people who share a similarity.

Here is an example of two salespeople, one exhibiting **rapport skills** and one using traditional "cold-call" tactics. Tom seems to have a magical touch. He could literally sell last week's newspaper and the buyer would walk away totally happy with his purchase. Jack just cannot figure out what it is that Tom has going for him.

Both of them are in computer sales, with roughly the same level of education and a similar sales-experience background. Yet for some reason Tom consistently outsells Jack month after month. When a new account is signed, the boss offers it to Tom first. Although Tom has been known to fail on occasion, he is still the first in line to be considered.

The difference between Jack's and Tom's success rate is largely due to Tom's ability to achieve **rapport** with his clients. By matching his communication patterns to the patterns of the person he is talking to, Tom is able to create an atmosphere of mutual liking, trust, and understanding with anyone he meets.

Achieving Rapport

Rapport is achieved when two people can see the other person's viewpoint, be on the same wavelength, and appreciate each other's feelings. Studies have shown that people are more inclined to buy from, agree with, and support someone they relate to than someone with whom they feel no connection.

Oftentimes we will meet someone, whether at work or a social function, that we like immediately. It is as if there is a special connection or bond between you, even though you are strangers. You start talking to this person and discover that you have a lot in common. Within half an hour, you may feel as if you have known this person all your life. That is the magic of *rapport*. It is that sense of connectedness to the other person.

When observing people who are in rapport, it has been noted that the greatest similarities were in the areas of:

- ✓ breathing
- ✓ voice tone and quality
- ✓ posture
- ✓ movement and gestures
- ✓ language content-visual/auditory/feelings and key words
- ✓ beliefs
- ✓ values

There are many nonverbal components to communication, and body language is the often the strongest and easiest to observe. Our posture, our movements, our voice patterns, and our breathing are all elements that come into play when we talk about establishing and maintaining rapport. (You will learn a great deal about body language in great detail later in this book!)

All of our lives we have been interpreting the unconscious body language of the people around us. As a salesperson you need to be able to take this knowledge and use it consciously to gain your customer's trust, to build rapport, and to guide that person towards your point of view.

If you were to sit on a bench in a mall and watch the other shoppers, you would see a wide variety of behaviors. From their walking pace, breathing rate, gestures, facial expressions, eye movements, stride, tone of voice, etc., you could gather a wealth of information about those people without ever exchanging a word.

The New Science of Selling

Imagine how successful you could be as a salesperson if you had the same kind of insight at your fingertips whenever you interacted with a customer. One of the basic premises of the new science of selling is that you already have within you all the resources that you will ever need.

You can learn how to tap these inner resources and use them to create a climate of trust and understanding with anyone you meet. You will be amazed at the results you achieve once you begin weaving the dynamics of rapport into the fabric of your personal and professional life.

A fundamental tenet, in relation to persuasive communication for sales people, is that for you to facilitate influencing, it will be much easier if you have rapport with the person or persons with whom you are communicating. This rule applies to customers, business associates, or social contacts.

The standard dictionary definition of rapport as "a relation of harmony, conformity, accord, or affinity" indicates the importance of rapport to communication. Rapport then, for our purposes, is the central organizing concept for any communication interaction.

It is important in any interaction with a customer, whether it be over the counter, on the phone, or any other sales situation, that you develop rapport. If you do not have rapport, you may lose the sale before it even began. It is vital that you build this rapport, and maintain it throughout the entire sales process. If you should notice that you have lost rapport at any point (we'll tell you how to spot this a little later in this chapter), stop, **reestablish** rapport, and then proceed.

Rapport creates an atmosphere of:

1. Trust
2. Confidence and
3. Cooperation

With these three factors set in motion, people can and will respond freely.

BENEFITS OF RAPPORT

A key benefit of rapport is the establishing of **sameness,** the moving together through time. Rapport is reduced when there is a decrease in sameness. **Difference** is the basis of poor rapport. At any given time there will be between two or more people a range of sameness and **difference, conscious** and **unconscious.**

What, then, do we do to gain rapport with people? How do we create a relationship of trust, confidence, and participation? How can we refine and extend this vital communicating skill?

In studying how to create rapport, it is helpful to notice contexts in which rapport already exists. Observe and listen to everything about you! Notice how people relate to each other in restaurants, at class reunions, theaters, church events, at birthday, cocktail, Halloween, Christmas, and New Year's Eve parties, in airports, at sporting events, any place where people are interacting. Observe that when people are in rapport, **their communication takes on a pattern of a dance.** It is rhythmical; their bodies, as well as their words, match each other smoothly and easily. When people are in rapport they unconsciously **mirror, match,** and **pace** each other.

MIRRORING

When people are mirroring each other, they adopt the same physical posture and mannerisms. Mirroring happens when you copy the behavior of others as if you were a mirror reflection of them—for instance, when they cross their left leg over their right leg, you cross your right leg over your left leg. (In the field of psychology we call this "synchronization," but that really doesn't sound like a good term for selling, so here we use the term "mirroring!")

When you are in "deep rapport" with another person, mirroring often occurs at the unconscious level. You do it without even thinking about what you are doing. Watch two people who are in love. When they mirror each other they do so smoothly and naturally. They aren't aware of it on a conscious level, but each shared gesture and mannerism strengthens the bond between them by deepening their rapport.

The same behavior can be observed when old friends sit down over a cup of coffee. One of them crosses his or her leg, and a few moments later the other person does the same thing. They will each reach for the coffee cup at the same time, and even take a sip together. They will adopt the same physical posture and mannerisms. Their silhouettes seem to reflect the same profile as they talk about their homes or their jobs or their relationships.

By the same token, it is very hard to have a conversation with someone whose body language is very different from your own. If they are standing there with arms crossed in response to your own open posture, you may find yourself at a loss for words. By using their bodies in this way, they are telling you in no uncertain terms that they do not feel a connection to you.

When you mirror someone, you are simply offering that person an unconscious reflection of himself. This simple technique has a very powerful impact because of the way people respond to their own behavior. When you reflect their behavior, they relate to it on an unconscious level and experience a sense of affinity. Nothing in life is so satisfying as the reflection of ourselves in another person. It is therefore a powerful tool you can use when you want to establish rapport with another person.

Although the terms mirroring and matching are sometimes used interchangeably, there is a real difference between the two techniques. When we mirror someone, we are offering them an exact reflection of their posture or movement or both. When we match someone, we can be much more subtle than that.

MATCHING

Matching occurs when the behavior of one person is similar to the behavior of another person. For instance, if the person you are matching crosses one leg over another, you can match the person by crossing your feet a few seconds later. The movements are enough alike for the person to feel a connection with you, but different enough that he will not feel that you are mimicking him.

Matching should flow as a natural extension of your movements as you match your actions in some way with the movements of the person you're communicating with. A person may tap his finger or a pen on the desk and you could match them by tapping your foot. The matching of the movements, their fingers and your foot, sets up an unconscious biofeedback-type of loop. The unconscious perceives your movement as a reflection of the other person's unconscious actions.

Here is an example of matching in an everyday setting. My (WH) wife swings her foot constantly. It proved to be especially distracting to me when we were driving in the car. I would point it out to her and she would stop the movement, only to start again in a few moments. I found that if I tapped my fingers on the steering wheel in a rhythmic pattern, it put us in sync and I would not become distracted by her foot movements.

(I found I could also slow down my finger tapping and her foot would match the speed of my fingers. More on this type of "leading" later.) This demonstrates how rapport can be used in all settings.

Connectedness—the Goal of Rapport

One goal of creating rapport is to connect with the unconscious mind by getting into the same mindset as the other person. Matching the physiology of another person is one of the simplest ways to do this. This means extending the process of matching beyond body posture and mannerisms to include breathing and voice patterns as well.

Some people do this on the unconscious level (without even thinking about what they are doing). Again, watch two people who are in love. When they match each other, they do so smoothly and naturally. They aren't aware of it on a conscious level, but they are matching each other's physiology. With each shared gesture and mannerism, they strengthen their rapport and feeling of connectedness.

Everyone has a unique voice, but it is possible to adjust the parameters of your voice to match someone else. People like to hear similarity in voice patterns. The similarity helps them feel more comfortable with the other person. How do you match the voice parameters of another person? Start by listening. If the person tends to speak quickly, you do the same. Listen to the volume, tone, pitch, and rhythm of his words. Match them as closely as you can.

Another subtle form of matching physiology is assuming a breathing pattern similar to that of the other person. This can be very powerful and effective because breathing is such a highly unconscious process that it usually goes undetected. Breathing is linked directly to our emotional state.

Have you ever come across a breathtaking sight along the highway? Maybe it was in the mountains or along the seashore when you were on vacation. Did you stop, get out of the car, and take a deep breath? Of course you did. We all do. Why? We do this for several reasons. First, we wanted to experience it with more than just our sense of sight. Second, taking a deep breath and letting it out relaxes us and helps us to feel good.

On the other hand, have you ever been in an extremely stressful situation? Your breathing rate starts to quicken as your heart starts to pound—both are very real signs of stress. To a large extent, breathing controls our inner state. So when someone matches our breathing, it creates a climate of trust and understanding. We start to relate to that person on an unconscious level.

Mirroring and Matching—a Dynamic Partnership

Rapport is established when there is a significant degree of **mirroring** and **matching.** Matching and mirroring can take place at one or more levels. Matching and mirroring through time is called **pacing.** Pacing can be of another person's sequence and/or process.

Whenever any of us are communicating with others, we are doing at least one of two things:

1. Behaving the **same** as the other person or
2. Behaving **differently** from them.

The more our behavior is the same as another person's, the more we will remind the other person (at the unconscious level) of him, her, or themselves, and thus the more likely we will be in rapport with such other person or persons.

The benefits of **matching** and **mirroring** are:

1. Enhancing and maintaining rapport
2. Increasing attention
3. Building expectations of your listeners
4. Building response potential by your listeners
5. Increasing credibility and trust, consciously and unconsciously
6. Establishing the basis for successful influencing/leading

NOTE: Matching and mirroring are not mimicking. Rather, it is replicating the structure of another person's ongoing processing. As indicated above, **matching** and **mirroring** the sequence of changes as the person processes is called **pacing.** Influencing the ongoing processing is **leading.** It is most important to match and mirror the structure, quality of movement, and usually not the degree, that is, the quantity of movement. Exaggerating the quantity is the basis of mimicry and will probably lead to a reduction in rapport.

Influence and Leading

Leading is the process of influencing toward a specific direction and/or outcome. It is a term that has been used by many communicators. More recent authors have shown a preference to refer to this interactive process as "influencing." The word "leading" seems to imply that it is only one influence and puts too much attention on one of the two or more persons involved in the interaction. It is therefore important to maintain the larger perspective of the repeating interaction and the many influences, both external and internal, that are involved.

FIVE THINGS TO MATCH, MIRROR, AND PACE

1. **Voice.** Listen to the pitch (how high or low the voice tone is), rate (how fast or slow and with what rhythm—including pauses—the person speaks), and volume (how softly or loudly the person speaks), and then match one or more of these components with your own speaking voice.

2. **Language.** This aspect of rapport-building has two major components. The first involves choosing words that are included in the spoken vocabulary of the person with whom you're interacting. Rapport is developed when we use the same "language" as the person with whom we are communicating. In other words, if the person's language is made up of a simpler vocabulary, **match, mirror,** and **pace** that vocabulary. Likewise, if the person is using a well-developed vocabulary, **match, mirror,** and **pace** that.

Warning: If you do not have a well-developed vocabulary, avoid attempting to match, mirror, and pace someone who does. You will only reveal yourself as a person whose vocabulary is less than well developed. Additionally, the other person may determine that you are attempting to take on "airs" and you will be seen, heard, and/or sensed as being phony. Such a perception by the other person can destroy rapport.

The second component of pacing language is to listen for and **pace** and **mirror** particular language patterns, which we call **predicates.** Predicates are **verbs, adverbs,** and **adjectives.** This type of language is selected at an unconscious level and thus reflects the underlying unconscious structures that produced them. Predicates indicate in which **sensory representational system** the person is engaged. In other words, the language of the speaker is "sensory-based" and indicates whether the speaker is thinking in pictures **(visual),** experiencing sounds and self-talk **(auditory),** or focusing on bodily sensations, touch, and feeling **(kinesthetic).** Although taste **(gustatory)** and smell **(olfactory)** are less common elements of Western language, they sometimes have a strong impact and are important.

SENSORY REPRESENTATIONAL SYSTEMS

When the speaker is in the **visual mode** the listener will hear language such as:

"**I can** clearly see how this workshop is going to help me."

"I've **looked** at it from every **perspective** and it's quite **clear** how it will fit into the big **picture** of things."

"I mean, from my **viewpoint** it is going to bring a lot of things into **focus** for me."

"I'm really **looking** forward to being there."

"I **see** what you are saying."

"It **looks** good to me."

"She was a **sight** for sore eyes."

"That makes everything perfectly **clear.**"

"Her future is surely **bright.**"

"I'm not sure he got the **picture.**"

"It's all very **hazy** to me."

"Everyone will be shocked when it is **brought to light.**"

"There are some people who you can't **show** anything."

"The workshop brought that into **focus** for me."

"He has a keen **insight** into problems."

"**Visualize** Mary Ann in a bikini, if you can."

"Tomorrow it will be my turn to **shine.**"

"They **foresee** a day when all men will be free."

"Would you please **illustrate** that for me?"

"She has a great **outlook** considering everything."

"She is a heavenly **vision.**"

"That is something you'll want to **watch for.**"

When the speaker is in the **auditory mode** the listener will hear language such as:

"This is something you will want to **hear.**"

"She couldn't help **listening** to your conversation."

"It would be helpful if we **sound** him out."

"The message was **loud** and clear."

"The boss gave the new guy the **word.**"

"It is a very **noisy** restaurant."

"That name **rings a bell** with me."

"You literally can't **tell** some people anything."
"They have no idea what she will **say** when she sees them."
"The **accent** should be on getting the work done now."
"We could solve the problem if we would just **discuss it.**"
"They can **proclaim** victory."
"If you don't mind I'd like to make a **remark** to that argument."
"Why don't we give it a **shout.**"
"The news was so bad that everyone was **speechless.**"
"She certainly is **vocal** in her praise of you."
"She had a **shrill** attitude."
"The quarterback called an **audible** at the line of scrimmage."

Kinesthetic people process most comfortably with feeling words. When the speaker is in the kinesthetic mode the listener will hear language such as:

"Jane needs to get a firm **grasp** on this information."
"I am out of **touch** with the new manager."
"She had a strange **feeling** this would happen."
"The guy is **solid.**"
"These new instructions are really **heavy.**"
"The boss feels we need to get a **handle** on things."
"This has been a really **rough** week for everyone."
"Susan really **connects** with her customers."
"This company is on the **move.**"
"We have a **contact** in Miami who will **handle** that."
"There is always a big **push** at the end of the year."
"As Shakespeare said, "Ah, there's the **rub.**"
"Christopher really is a kind, **warm** person."
"She is one **cold** fish if you ask me."
"The deficit is the major problem Clinton will have to **tackle.**"
"The whole department has been under a lot of **pressure.**"
"Boy, is she ever **sensitive.** I mean, she is really **touchy.**"
"Charles never seems to be bothered by the **stress.**"
"We need something more **tangible** than that."
"What a meeting! You could have **cut** the **tension** with a butter knife."
"He has **concrete** evidence that she stole his virtue."
"It would be helpful if you would be more **gentle** with her."
"I wish I could get **hold** of him by telephone."

"We will barely **scrape** by this winter."

"She is really **hard** to **pin** down on money matters."

"That was a really **smooth** sale."

The least common language patterns are **olfactory** and **gustatory,** smelling and tasting. A person using these verbal patterns talks about experiences that leave a **bad taste** in his/her mouth, or opportunities that she/he missed because of **rotten** luck. She/he may tell you that his/her boss has ideas which really **stink** and that she/he would like to give her a **taste** of her own medicine.

Realize that when a person leans toward one particular pattern (visual, auditory, kinesthetic, olfactory, or gustatory), it is important for you to respond back in that particular mode or style of responding because she/he is using that pattern to process thoughts and to create her/his reality.

3. **Breathing.** People who speak rapidly usually breathe high up in the chest, while those who speak more slowly usually breathe lower in the chest and abdomen. Matching breathing is a very powerful way to get rapport with others. It requires that you pay careful attention to them, and often you will come across as an "excellent listener" who is very present in conversations.

4. **Posture.** What should our posture be while listening? Well, if we want to create rapport, then, just as we do with voice, language and breathing, we will want to match and mirror the posture of the other person. Be particularly alert to notice when the other person leans forward or leans back. Be alert to notice the general relaxation or tension in the other person's body, and mirror that. By doing so, you will remind him of himself.

5. **Emotion.** In emotional pacing, we are meeting the other person where he or she is emotionally at the moment of our first interaction, and then, throughout the interaction. Emotion often is expressed in the face, posture, breathing, and in the voice. Taking note of the other person's emotional state and how it is expressed will guide your own nonverbal behavior.

IMPORTANT NOTE: Although being liked can be a by-product of rapport, it is important to remember that rapport is much more than simply being liked. To become the kind of master communicator who easily and fully establishes rapport with others, one must become an exquisite partner in the dance that is communication. To seek rapport with others is to invite them to dance, and then **influence** them smoothly and elegantly throughout the interaction, as you both **reach an outcome** that is mutually desirable.

You might find it useful to think of rapport as how responsive the other person is to you and your positive intentions. You create rapport by being responsive to the other person through pacing and mirroring that person's verbal and nonverbal behavior.

Overview of Rapport

To create rapport, it is important to mirror, match, and pace the person or persons with whom you are communicating. The elements of effective mirroring, matching, and pacing are:

1. **Physiology:** Matching (mirroring & pacing) body position, breathing, voice, gestures, etc.

2. **Movement:** Matching what a person does; the types of movement, gestures, etc.

3. **Strategies:** Matching how a person does things.

4. **Values and Beliefs:** Matching what the person believes and values.

5. **Identity:** Match the sense of identity. (In groups and organizations this becomes very influential.)

In order to mirror, match, and pace, it is important for you to open your sensory channels. Opening sensory channels is an operational skill that you can train yourself to build and refine. Opening your channels provides you with the ability to see, hear, and sense external changes (minimal cues, both verbal and nonverbal) presented by individuals with whom you are communicating. This is the first step to eliminating an internal response and mind reading.

We have talked about several things for you to match, mirror, and pace. Before you can effectively mirror, match, and pace another you have to see, hear, and sense. The following list adds to the listings we have already presented to mirror, match, and pace, and indicates in more detail the things for which you need to learn to see, hear, and sense:

1. Breathing-rate change.
2. Breathing-position change.

3. Skin-tone change.
4. Skin-color change.
5. Lip-size change.
6. Pore-size change.
7. Pupil-size change.
8. Pulse-rate change.
9. Eye-position.
10. Eye-blink rate.
11. Voice-tone change.
12. Voice-tempo change.
13. Body-temperature change.
14. Body-position change.
15. Small-gesture movements.
16. Head-tilt change.

The above list is by no means complete and can be extended to all external changes you see, hear, or sense in an individual.

By paying close attention to specific behaviors as others communicate, we can know the structure of their thoughts. We cannot tell what they are thinking, but we can know **how** they are thinking.

The Power of Rapport

The following story demonstrates just how powerful rapport can be.

Several years ago I (WH) applied for a position that I wanted. It was the regional director for the Governor's Commission for a Drug Free Indiana, and to get it I had to go in for a panel interview. I was going to be questioned by about ten people who sat on the board. Many of you have been through these types of grueling interviews yourselves.

A little background on this commission is in order. The primary responsibility of the person holding the position would be to get a group of volunteers to develop a region-wide plan to reduce alcohol and drug abuse. That person would coordinate the groups, get consensus on priorities, and release the funds to these groups. (The money was raised through added fines from the legal system for alcohol and drug offenses.) Various people wanted a slice of the pie. This included police, treatment, education, and social services. They all wanted a big slice.

Now, I have to stress the unique thing about this interview was that the panel was composed of the people who would also sit on some of the same committees that wanted the funds. (What a way to run an interview!) These people were vested deeply in wanting their type of person for the position. All candidates were given around fifteen minutes for the process.

Once I knew I was selected, I decided to use these skills in a situation that would test the true power of these techniques in a real situation. I knew the panel would be made up of some of these leaders in our area. A judge, a director of the United Way, a probation officer, a director of a detox/halfway house, a social worker, to name a few. I mistakenly thought they were the types of people who might notice what I was doing. I truly thought they would "catch me" mirroring them. I decided to do it anyway.

Once I was called in, I sat in front of the group. They opened the interview with brief pleasantries and then began the critical questioning. As each person asked his/her question, I would totally focus on that person. I would sit exactly as she/he was sitting and time my breathing to match the interviewer.

I would then repeat his/her question so we were both on the same wavelength. This would validate the interviewer and let that person know I was totally focused on him/her. I would then say, "That's a good question." I would then answer the question in such a way that I seemed to agree with that person's desired response. Any physical movements they made, I mirrored and matched completely. I did this with each person who asked me a question.

It went well enough that after about thirty minutes a knock on the door alerted the panel to the fact that this interview had extended past its allotted time frame. (I knew then that my interview had made an impact!)

I was offered the position because, as the panel director stated, I made everyone feel comfortable. I was in rapport with each of them. They translated this rapport into believing I shared the same agenda as the commission. I then used these same skills in every organizational meeting. Often times these basic rapport skills can be used in intense situations to lower stress levels.

It has to be emphasized that to master these skills takes a lot of physical practice. The more you use these skills, the more natural they will become. This is the key, being natural in your movements, following whomever you are matching. If creating rapport seems forced to you, it will be obvious to the person you wish to match. This is why you have to practice, practice, PRACTICE! Building rapport may seem such a simple action, but to become truly proficient at it, for it to become so natural that people around you are not even aware of your action, you must exercise this skill.

I must stress that your clients are not the people to sharpen your rapport skills with. Enlist the aid of friends, family, co-workers, or my favorite, go to the mall and utilize other retail salespeople.

It's probably obvious to you by now that the building and maintenance of rapport is directly correlated to your success in sales. You can certainly keep reading this book straight through but you must do these exercises to build your skills. Research is pretty clear. Reading information without taking action on the information is a waste of time. The section below is packed full of exercises to help you become a master at rapport. Start them now!

Rapport Exercises

I would suggest that you start out by taking each of the exercises and doing them several times. When you feel you are ready, add another level to your skills.

Do this until you notice that your rapport skills (mirroring, matching) become second nature.

1. Identifying Rapport Based on Body Posture

Natural rapport is very easy to spot. In the park, at a restaurant, in the mall, at the airport, in church, at the beach, anywhere people interact, you can find instances of true rapport if you look for it. For this exercise, be on the lookout for a social setting in which two people seem to be in rapport based on the body posture. Are they both sitting forward? Are they both leaning back? What is the position of their arms, hands, fingers? What is the position of their legs, feet? How do they hold their shoulders? Are their heads inclined the same way? See how many similarities you can find.

2. Identifying Rapport Based on Breathing

Matching the breathing rate (shallow, quick breaths, rhythmic breaths, or deep breaths) of another person is a very effective way to establish rapport. Sometimes people who are in deep rapport will even fall into the same breathing rhythm, taking a breath simultaneously and letting it out together. In addition, the position of the breathing (from high in the chest, from the mid-chest, or from the abdomen/low stomach) may be the same as well.

For this exercise, observe two people in a social setting who appear to be in rapport based on their breathing. Watch them as they interact and try to determine if their breathing rates are the same. Does the breathing rate stay the same throughout their interaction? Watch their breathing rhythms. Do they both take a breath at the same time? Do their breathing rhythms remain the same? What is the position of their breathing? Do they breathe from high in the chest, from the mid-chest, or from the abdomen/low stomach?

3. Identifying Voice Patterns

A social setting may provide more fluctuation of voice patterns than a business setting. Social settings are more casual and people are inclined to be freer with their emotions at these times. For this exercise, observe two people in a social setting who seem to be in rapport based on their voice patterns. Characteristics of voice patterns include speed or pace, volume (soft or loud), pitch (high or low), and tone (persuasive, consoling, angry, sad, indifferent, happy, etc.).

Are they both speaking at the same speed or pace? Is the volume of their voices the same? Is the pitch high or low? What is the tone of their voices? Are there any changes in their voice characteristics during the conversation? Do these changes affect the rapport? If so, in what way are they affected?

4. Identifying Rapport Based on Rhythm

We all have a signature rhythm, a preferred way of moving that we use unconsciously when we interact with others. This movement can take many forms. Some people gesture with their hands when they talk. Some people scratch their head or touch their nose or rest their chin in the palm of their hand. Some will touch their hair or stroke their mustache or their beard.

For this exercise, observe two people in a business setting who seem to be in rapport. Are there any changes in their movements during the interaction? Do these changes affect the rapport? If so, in what way are they affected?

5. Establishing Rapport through Mirroring Posture

Most people, initially, are somewhat awkward in their gestures and clumsy with their timing when they first begin to consciously mirror another person. That is why it's best not to start out by practicing on customers.

Body posture is the position of the body; the position of the arms, hands, and fingers; the position of the legs and feet; the inclination of the head; how the shoulders are held; and the weight distribution of the body. Now that you have had practice identifying rapport through posture, it is time to try to establish rapport by mirroring the posture of another person.

For this exercise, you will mirror the posture of someone in a social setting. Ideally, this should be someone you have just met. If that's not possible, try to choose someone you don't know well. Remember, when you mirror someone, you copy their behavior as if you were a mirror reflection of them—if they cross their right arm over their left arm, you cross your left arm over your right arm. Afterward, think about the different forms of posture you were able to mirror. When you mirrored their posture, did you notice a difference in rapport?

6. Establishing Rapport through Mirroring Movement

Now that you have had practice establishing rapport by mirroring the posture of another person, it is time to try mirroring the movements of someone else. What do we mean by movements? It could be a hand adjusting a collar, a shrug of the shoulders, a movement of the head. Watch the other person as you interact in a social setting, looking for movements that you can mirror. Does he gesture with his hands as he speaks? Does he touch part of his face? Does he adjust an item of clothing, like a tie or scarf? Does he shift his weight from one foot to another? Afterward, think about the different movements you were able to mirror. When you mirrored his movements, did you notice a difference in rapport?

7. Establishing Rapport through Mirroring Rhythm

As we noted earlier, all of us have a signature rhythm, a preferred way of moving that we use unconsciously when we interact with others. Being able to recognize and mirror another's rhythm can mean the difference between landing or losing a contract or deal. But, once again, we caution against practicing on a client or customer. For this exercise, pick a co-worker and try to mirror their movements when you interact with them.

Watch for hand gestures when they talk. Some people scratch their head or touch their nose or rest their chin in the palm of their hand. Some will touch their hair or stroke their mustache or their beard. Afterward, think about the different movements you were able to mirror. When you mirrored their movements, did you notice a difference in rapport?

8. Establishing Rapport Through Matching Posture

For this exercise, you will match the posture of someone in a social setting. This could be at a luncheon or a party or any other social setting. The goal is to adopt a similar posture, without actually mirroring him/her. For instance, imagine that you are having lunch with someone. The person sits down and clasp his/her hands on the table. You could then match the person a few seconds later by placing your hands on the table and holding your water glass in both hands. Watch carefully and make a mental note to yourself of the different ways you are able to match that person's posture. Did you find this exercise easier or harder than mirroring posture in a social setting? Which was more effective at establishing rapport? Why?

9. Establishing Rapport through Matching Breathing

Matching someone's breathing involves matching both the rhythm (shallow, quick breaths or deep, slow breaths) and position (from high in the chest, from the mid-chest, or from the abdomen/low stomach). For this exercise, you will match the breathing of someone in a social setting. Afterward, make a note of your observations. Did you find this exercise easier or harder than matching posture in this setting? Which was more effective at establishing rapport? Why?

10. Establishing Rapport through Matching Voice Patterns

When you are in rapport with another person, it is often because that person reminds you of yourself in some way. Maybe it's the way they stand, their smile, or even the sound of their voice! For today's exercise, you will match the voice patterns of another person in a social setting. You should listen for the speed or pace of his voice, the volume at which he speaks, the pitch (high or low), and the tone of his voice. Afterward, make a note of your observations. Did you find this exercise easier or harder than matching posture? Was this exercise easier or harder than matching breathing? Which was more effective at establishing rapport? Why?

11. Establishing Rapport through "Matching" Movements

For this exercise, you will be matching the movements of a co-worker in a business setting. Note that in matching you are not mimicking the person. This is just a matching in a similar manner, matching actions, not body parts. If he adjusts his tie, you can brush a piece of lint off your shoulder. If he rests his chin in the palm of his hand (usually when sitting), you can put your forearm on the table in front of you. If he crosses his arms, you can clasp your hands in front of you. If he drums his fingers, you could swing your foot. If he touches his hair, you could rub your nose.

Afterward, think about the various movements you were able to match. Did you find this exercise easier or harder than matching posture? Was this exercise easier or harder than matching breathing? What about when you matched their voice? Which was more effective at establishing rapport? Why?

12. Pacing and Leading Posture in a Social Setting

In the previous exercises, you practiced mirroring and matching another person's posture in order to establish rapport. Now it is time to take your pacing skills (mirroring and matching another person's behavior) to a new level by trying to lead the other person. When we pace (mirror and match) someone, we are telling the other person on an unconscious level that we understand them. The key to pacing and leading is a smooth transition.

Once you have established rapport through mirroring and matching the other person, you may want to wait until it is your turn to speak before you try to lead them by changing your posture. For today, you will pace (mirror and match) the posture of someone in a social setting. Then, once you think they are in rapport with you, try to lead them into mirroring and matching your posture.

13. Pacing and Leading Posture in a Family Setting

Pacing serves two purposes. First, it is a good way to test a situation and determine if you have really established rapport with someone.

Second, it allows you to lead someone's thoughts in the direction you wish them to be. This can be very effective when you are having a disagreement with someone in your family, for instance. For this exercise, you will pace (mirror and match) the posture of someone in your family. Then, once you think they are in rapport with you, try to lead them into mirroring and matching your posture.

14. Pacing and Leading Breathing with a Co-Worker

Pacing someone's breathing pattern is subtle, because breathing itself is such an extremely unconscious process. When you mirror and match another person this way, it is almost impossible to detect and is therefore an excellent way of generating rapport. Pacing breathing involves matching the rate (shallow, quick breaths, rhythmic breaths, or deep breaths). The rhythm (taking a breath and letting it out at the same time as the other person) and the position of the breathing (from high in the chest, from the mid-chest, or from the abdomen/low stomach). For this exercise, you will pace (mirror and match) the breathing of a co-worker. Then, once you think he is in rapport with you, try to lead him into mirroring and matching your breathing.

15. Pacing and Leading Breathing with a Family Member

Breathing is directly linked to a person's emotional state. People breathe differently when they are excited, compared to how they breathe when they are bored. Did you ever take a deep breath to calm down when you were stressed or angry? Of course you did. To a large degree, breathing controls our inner state. In today's exercise, you will pace (mirror and match) the breathing of someone in your family. Then, once you think they are in rapport with you, try to lead them into mirroring and matching your breathing.

16. Pacing and Leading Vocal Patterns in a Social Setting

People like to hear a similarity in vocal patterns as much as anything else. They feel more comfortable with people who speak the same way they do. They will take note of the speed or pace of someone's voice, the volume at which they speak, the pitch (high or low), and the tone of the voice. Today, you will pace (mirror and match) the voice patterns of someone in a social setting. Then, once you think he is in rapport with you, try to lead him into mirroring and matching your voice patterns.

17. Pacing and Leading Movements of a Co-Worker

Pacing takes place on many levels and within a multitude of contexts. For this exercise, you will be pacing the movements of a co-worker in a business setting. If he crosses his legs, you can cross your feet. If he drums his fingers, you could tap with your pen. If he adjusts his tie, you could straighten your collar. Then, once you think he is in rapport with you, try to lead him into mirroring and matching your movements.

Now if you really have done each of these exercises you will notice that you are becoming a true master of rapport. Remember, it is important to practice these skills until they become second nature. It is proficiency at building and maintaining rapport that creates great salespeople!

CHAPTER 6

Anchor Your Way to Success

To become an elite salesperson you need to become a master at "installing anchors." An anchor is a stimulus-response cycle that, once installed, can be used to your advantage. Think back to school when you learned about Pavlov. His experiment was to take some dogs, and every time they were exposed to food, a bell was rung. Soon just the bell's ringing caused the dogs to salivate. Pavlov linked (or anchored) the ringing of a bell (stimulus) with the salivating (response).

If you would like a visual image of how this works, picture a bell curve. As you enter into any "state" (emotional experience), it will usually start slowly and build to a peak. This is the upside (left side) of the curve. The effects of the emotional experience peak at the top of the curve and then diminish on the downside (right side) of the curve.

When an event happens, a unique stimulus is applied. Following the cycle, as you are hitting the peak of the emotion, that stimulus will cause you to enter into that same "state," or feeling. This cycle will be duplicated each time that stimulus is applied.

Stimulus-Response Cycle

An example of this stimulus-response cycle could be a conversation with a new client. The client laughs (you now begin to climb up the left side of the bell curve) and you touch his wrist as you laugh with him. (The anchor is set.) You remove your hand as the laughter dies down. (Now you are on the down side of the curve as the anchor is released.) Later in the conversation you share a story that is very amusing. You make certain that as you come to the humorous part of the story, you fire the anchor by once again

131

touching your client's wrist. (Once more, you are on the left side of the curve.) Next, you immediately release his wrist as your client laughs again.

Another example is the 1996 presidential election. We witnessed President Clinton masterfully anchor himself to the country's economic success. That election demonstrated some of the best examples of anchoring we have seen in public. It was done so subtly that very few people even noticed it. At one point in the 1996 debates, President Clinton walked to the center of the stage and proceeded to list several of the following facts about the state of the union at that time:

✓ The economy was booming.
✓ More jobs had been created in the last four years than in the previous twelve.
✓ Unemployment was at an all time low.
✓ We were at peace.

After President Clinton had listed all these wonderful things, he made the comment, "I can't take all the credit for all the good things that have happened these last few years."

It was a brilliant comment, and as he said "all the good things that have happened," he touched his tie. Each time Clinton said a positive thing about the country, he touched his tie or face. He was in essence anchoring all those positives to him.

Now this stimulus-response cycle can be used to anchor both positive and negative responses. At this point, President Clinton went on to influence public opinion further by saying, "We still have problems in this country. People are being left behind." As he said this, Bill Clinton made a gesture with his hand that pointed toward Bob Dole.

People watching the debates were using their conscious minds to track the information while their unconscious was wide open for this type of salesmanship. This could explain the great public ambivalence toward Bill Clinton. In our subconscious minds he is anchored to good things. Lest we find Clinton as the only politician guilty of anchoring, we need only to think back to the "Great Communicator" Ronald Reagan. He also was a master at anchoring positive responses.

Anchoring

In the basic process of communicating with a client, it is important that the salesperson develops a sense of rapport with the client. Rapport is the condition when two people, in this case the salesperson and client, have achieved a connectedness—the ability to see the other's viewpoint and appreciate each other's feelings.

One important fact to remember is that **rapport must be maintained.** The achieved level of rapport can diminish in the middle of the sales call! The secret technique that many successful salespeople use to quickly reestablish the initial rapport is called **anchoring.** Anchoring allows you to do this. Below are the basics about anchoring:

1. An anchor can be set in a matter of seconds. Do not fall into the trap of thinking that it takes a long period of time to establish an anchor. Repeated motivations and conditioning will reinforce an anchor.

2. Reinforcement and direct rewards are not required for an anchor's association.

3. Internal responses and experiences are significant. Although internal reactions are not measurable, they are a definitive response.

4. Anchors are "set" and "fired off." The more profound the experience when the catalyst is set, the stronger the retaliatory response.

5. Timing is crucial while establishing an anchor. It is necessary that the correct trigger sets off the desired response. The strength of the response will guide the client's mind in the necessary and desired path.

6. The more original the motivation, the easier it is to reestablish the desired rapport. The repercussions of mixed responses due to general stimuli could often be detrimental to the client as well as the relationship as a whole. By establishing unique stimuli, it allows for little margin of error and an ease for reaccessing the desired state.

7. Anchors can be established in the visual, auditory, and kinesthetic representational systems.

8. Anchors can be set and fired off both consciously and unconsciously. People regularly create anchors in everyday experiences. They may watch a news show about an incident or situation they feel strongly about (negative or positive). From that point on, any time a word comes up that brings forth the memory of that news show, it will elicit a certain response. In effect, an anchor has been "set" and "fired off."

You can imagine the power of this tool in a sales application. If you could anchor your clients (and you can) into positive emotional states, would that not help you in the relationship?

Anchoring and Sales

Below are two examples of how anchoring can be used in a sales environment:

Jeff is a car salesman in Indianapolis. He relates an occasion when he used anchoring to create a positive mental mindset in a customer who was determined to be "just looking." When the customer entered the showroom, Jeff approached the man and greeted him in his usual congenial manner. The client responded with the "just looking" response. Rather than accept the rebuff, Jeff decided to try anchoring. The client was looking at a couple of Nissan Maximas and seemed interested.

Jeff said, "Nice cars," and got a curt reply, "Yeah, but I'm just looking."

"Of course," Jeff casually agreed. "May I ask you a question? Did you ever have a car you really liked?"

The customer looked at him curiously. Jeff went on, "I mean, any car. What was your favorite? I always wonder about those things."

The client's eyes softened and he replied, "Oh, yeah. I had a sweet '68 'Cuda. Wow! That was a great car!"

Jeff immediately knew he had gained the information he needed to set a positive anchor. "Those were sweet rides (pacing)," Jeff agreed. "What did you like the best? The speed, power, handling?" Jeff asked as he touched the sport version of the Maxima.

"Oh, definitely the power and pickup," the customer replied.

"Yeah, pickup and power really make a car special. I like those things, too." Jeff said as he placed his hand on the hood of the Maxima. Now as well as anchoring the positive characteristics that the customer liked about a car to the Maxima, Jeff was also developing a rapport with the customer that would instill trust. As the conversation went on, every time the client said something positive about any car, Jeff touched the Maxima. But Jeff never overtly mentioned the Maxima, or its benefits. When the customer started to leave, Jeff casually remarked, "Yeah, when you find a sweet ride (client's trance words) you should go ahead and get it now."

The client got into his car and drove away. Jeff was wondering if his anchoring had worked and if so, when would the customer return. It was not five minutes later that the client returned, found Jeff, and asked if the Maxima came in a dark blue (the same color as his "sweet '68 'Cuda"). He was ready to buy and he had not even driven the car.

Another salesman, of pianos, found a unique way to use anchoring to sell his instruments. Eric was a terrific piano player himself, but when he first started to sell pianos his sales figures tended to be low. Eric was trying to sell others on what he thought was important—the musical quality and ease of playing. Then Eric decided to find out what was important to his clients.

Eric recalled the time he was talking to a customer and asked the customer what she thought was important about a piano. Each time she would mention something he thought was important to her, Eric would play a few notes on the piano. This client described how she felt about the elegant appearance of a piano at a friend's dinner party. As she described its appearance and the impact it had on the dinner guests, Eric would play a few notes on a piano. When she went on to say how impressive it was for someone to play the piano during a party, again Eric played a few notes.

When Eric asked her how she would feel owning her own piano, he played the same series of notes on the piano. This last stimulus brought about the desired response, as she bought the instrument.

Eric declared that once he learned to anchor the positive aspects of what the customers were looking for, to the unique series of notes he played during their conversation (obviously they enjoyed piano music), his closure rate went from very low to tops in the company.

Anchoring on a Personal Note

A former student shared the story of how he was in an ongoing dispute with his wife over one of their daughters' boyfriends. Bill's wife wanted Bill to tell the boyfriend to "get lost" but Bill felt the decision was not really one for them to make.

Bill decided it was time to end the difficult situation between his wife and himself. Bill realized that he could make use of the same anchoring skills he used at work, here in the home environment. So, while Susan was getting ready to go upstairs, he put on a record of "their song," the song they associated with when they were dating and later played at their wedding.

Bill said the strangest thing happened. As the song began to play, Susan stopped, turned around, and said, "I guess its okay for her to date this guy." Bill asked his wife what made her change her mind. She replied, "When that music came on, I remembered how much my family was against my dating you. I refused to give you up. We've been married nineteen years now, and I definitely have no regrets. So, maybe kids do need to make up their own minds," she finished with a smile.

Bill had counted on the music's firing an anchor that had been installed many years before. But that is not the end of the story.

A few months later, Bill took Susan for a getaway weekend on their anniversary. He brought out all the right anchors—flowers, champagne, the works. As soon as they had settled into the hotel room, he put on the same music mentioned above. His wife's movements suddenly stilled, and then Susan grabbed him by the shoulders, stared into his eyes, and demanded, "Promise me something. We will not talk about our daughter or her boyfriends, or anything like that."

Bill was astounded. Then he remembered that the last time he had played this music they had been involved in a turbulent emotional experience. Because that experience was over-laid on the old anchor, it recalled the last "anchored" experience.

Dynamic Tools

Anchoring is especially powerful when combined with rapport skills and representational systems.

Here is a story that puts the power of these combined tools into perspective. It is from Robert LaBrie, a retired master sergeant. He was on assignment the first time he put all these skills together. He was part of the inspection team troubleshooting the advertising and promotion section.

LaBrie explained how when he first arrived the supervisor had said, "Sergeant LaBrie, I am so glad to SEE you. I am so anxious to SHOW you how we run our advertising and promotion program."

The supervisor then spent time SHOWING LaBrie various slides, programs, and manuals he had written. He used visual terms. LaBrie knew that to please him, things had to look good."

LaBrie then related how the next officer in charge of the section approached him and said, "Sergeant LaBrie, I am so anxious to HEAR what you have to SAY." She wanted clear, detailed explanations of everything he was covering during the inspections.

Labrie commented to himself, "I remember thinking that it can't be this easy (but it is!)."

Then LaBrie met the final person involved in the advertising and promotion section. At first he couldn't make out this man's system. Then he noticed that every time LaBrie found something wrong, the person would get very emotional. He would put his hand to his chest as if LaBrie had stabbed him, exclaiming, "I can't believe that there is so much wrong here. I FEEL like it will take me forever to get this all corrected." There were definite signs of his experiencing the world through primarily kinesthetic eyes.

LaBrie had decided he would match each of their language patterns to see if they would confirm his representational system determinations. He got along with each of them, but LaBrie could SEE how they had trouble in their communications with each other.

Labrie had an eighteen-page checklist to get through and if the Kinesthetic person continued with the emotional outbursts, he would never complete it. LaBrie decided to try "anchoring" for the first time. He asked the man if he had ever been super successful in his life. He immediately said "yes."

Then LaBrie asked him to describe in detail that successful period of time. The more the man talked, the more LaBrie could SEE him get into a positive state. The man's face became flushed and he began to talk faster as he became more excited. When LaBrie thought the moment was right (just before the peak on a bell curve), he reached for the man's shoulder and tapped it lightly as he said, "See, I told you that you could easily be successful, didn't I?"

He said "yes" and they proceeded to the next question. This question also happened to relate to an area that needed improvement. When LaBrie mentioned this fact, the man became upset again. Labrie immediately tapped the man's shoulder. Before LaBrie could say a word he said, "I know, I know, I was successful before, I can be successful again."

LaBrie was flabbergasted. "Anchoring couldn't be that powerful, could it?" he thought to himself.

"I continued questioning him," LaBrie continued, "until we found another area that needed attention. Predictably, he became defensive again. Once again, all I needed to do was touch his shoulder, and he went into a positive state, declaring, 'I know, I know.'

"We continued in this manner until I had accomplished my purpose. It was not long before all I would have to do was approach him as if I was about to touch his shoulder and he would respond in the conditioned manner."

It was at that point LaBrie became a true believer in the effectiveness of the anchoring and rapport technology."

These are great examples of the many ways in which an anchor can be used—an association, a touch, a sound—to trigger a consistent response in your customer. As a salesperson, you can use anchors to tap into your customers' memory and imagination and transfer their positive feelings and associations to the present situation.

Anchors in Your Life

Think about some of the anchors you have. Do you have a certain song that causes you to feel a certain way? What happens when you see the American flag? What happens when your boss touches you on your shoulder and says "I need to see you in my office."

Now that you have become comfortable with the idea of anchoring, why not use it to your advantage?

When you master rapport, you have a jump-start on friendly anchors. You must remember to be aware to anchor any positive states in your clients to you. You want your image, in your client's mind, to bring up those positive thoughts and feelings.

Once you become anchored to a response it will last through time. This is true for people, products, or ideas. Here are some examples:

Coors Beer invented light beer years before Miller brought out Miller Lite, but Miller anchored lite. Remember "Tastes Great, Less Filling"?

There were at least five gold rock 'n' roll records before Elvis, but who is the King of rock 'n' roll?

Do you ever hear someone say, "I need to make a Xerox of this?" Then they make a copy on a different brand of copy machine.

Correct positive anchoring gives you that unique mental spot in your customers' minds. You want them to think, "I need office products. I better give George a call. I like doing business with George."

Whenever I (WH) teach a class, the first thing I start to do is anchor the group. I like to anchor humor, or laughter, to myself. Every time the group laughs, I will touch my tie or face, in a certain way. I will then anchor spots on the stage. (Elite presenters will talk about training the audience.)

In middle school I had a teacher, Mr. Stevens, who used to tutor a few of the students after class. One of his students, John, had a hard time coming up with the right answer to a question when called upon in class. Mr. Stevens began to tutor John and then, during class, when he would question the students, he would remark casually, "I know John has the answer to this question, but let's hear what Karen (or Tim or Mary, etc.) has to say." The result was that John started to believe in himself. Mr. Stevens anchored a feeling of confidence in John that was reflected in the ease with which he began volunteering to answer questions in class.

Here are some exercises to master these skills. The first one is for you to practice on yourself. We want you to first get a feel for these techniques, and then we will show you how to implement them into your daily work and personal life.

Anchoring a Resourceful State

1. **Identify a resourceful state or behavior.** Think of something that you already do well, some behavior or state that you would like to be able to access whenever you choose.

2. **Choose an anchor that is easy for you to remember and which you can use whenever you want to access this feeling.** Be sure to pick an anchor that is precise, such as placing your thumb and forefinger together as if making the "okay" sign.

3. **Now call up a memory of that behavior or state you would like to have, remembering a time when it was strong.** What was it like to be doing that behavior? It is important that you see this experience through your own eyes, and not as if you are an observer watching yourself. Take note of what you see and hear and feel as you call up the memory. What colors are there around you? Are the colors bright or are they soft, like pastels? Are they clear or are they slightly hazy and out of focus? What sounds do you hear? Are they soft or loud? Is there singing or talking or birds chirping? As you imagine this scene, allow yourself to experience being there until the feeling is strong and encompassing for you. As you do so, touch your thumb and forefinger together as if making the sign for "okay." Hold the position for as long as the feelings remain strong, and when they begin to fade return your fingers to a relaxed position. Shake your head or move in some way to bring yourself back to the present (also called "breaking state").

4. **The okay sign has just become the anchor for those feelings.** But we don't want to stop there. In order to ensure that these feelings are associated with that gesture, it is necessary to repeat the exercise a few more times. Each time you do, try to add more details to the memory. This makes it even more powerful. Use all of your senses

(seeing, hearing, feeling, smelling, tasting) with the experience, so that the connection between the memory and the anchor becomes powerful. It is important to remember that anchors should be set (installed) at the peak of the experience. The purpose of setting the anchor is to be able to call up that particular desired state when needed.

5. Test the anchor. Think of a different experience and make the okay sign as you do, the same way you did a few minutes ago. This is known as **firing the anchor.** What happened? Did you recall the memory in all its detail, complete with the feeling or state you were trying to recapture? If you didn't, keep trying. Sometimes a little practice is all that is needed. Remember, the sensations in an experience will often rise and fall, so you want to set the anchor as the experience is reaching its peak and remove it when the feeling begins to fade.

Now that you are starting to understand the power of these techniques, here are some exercises to develop your skills. Here are the states you will want to learn how to anchor in others:

Humor
Curiosity
Being positive
Self-confidence
Loyalty
How you feel when you make a GOOD decision
How you feel when you make a BAD decision
Excitement
Doubt
Patience

Eliciting States

Once you are in rapport with someone, you will find talking to him or her is rather easy. To get someone into the state you desire, you need to be able to elicit that emotional state in him or her. Now that may sound intimidating, but it is as easy as getting someone to talk about an experience that will put him or her in the state you are trying to elicit.

Here is an example that you see all the time:

Two men start talking about their favorite sports team. As they talk, you can watch them enter into several emotional states. When they describe the last win, they get excited, then it progresses to passionate, about the plays. Watch them as they describe a "bad call." They get angry. If their team lost, you will see evidence of negative feelings in their physical gestures.

In fact, watch any sporting event and you will see the athletes firing off anchors all the time. Maybe you played sports in school and you can still remember how you felt when you came off the field after a bad play and your coach gave you that "look," or the excitement after a good play and your teammates patted you on the back. (You have experienced anchoring your entire life.)

Here is another example before we move on to the anchoring exercises. Watch professional comics as they do their routines. If they are very experienced and a joke goes well, you will notice them set anchors in their audience.

If you have the opportunity, watch a performance of Rodney Dangerfield. Notice that as he says his famous "I get no respect, no respect at all" line, he always touches his tie.

Notice Jay Leno's anchors. He shrugs his shoulders on bad jokes, and when his jokes get laughs, he touches his tie.

Tim Allen's anchor was the grunting noises he made whenever he talked about power tools. The public automatically associates Tim Allen with power tools, and he used that to create a multi-million-dollar career.

How to Elicit States

The secret to eliciting a state in someone is **first you have to enter into it yourself!** So if you want someone to be excited about something, you have to get excited yourself. How do you do that? **Think about something that makes you feel the way you want to feel. This will cause you to enter into that state.** Then describe it in detail (even if just to yourself). Next get the person to **describe how that state feels to them.** If the person hesitates, or has problems, just **describe how you feel when you are in that state.**

Exercises

Every day pick a state you will practice anchoring in people. We suggest using co-workers and social situations before you tackle clients. Always start by getting into rapport with the people with whom you are communicating.

1. **Humor.** This does not mean you have to be a comic. Just get your target to talk about something he/she finds funny, or anything that made your target laugh. Start by telling something you find amusing. (I suggest you stay away from jokes, unless you're good at them.) If you are in rapport, he/she will start to smile with you. Then get your target to talk about something that the he/she found amusing. As your target describes it, and he/she smiles or laughs, **anchor that state to you by some action, touch your ear and smile, or laugh with them.** Repeat the above steps several times. Whenever you touch your ear, you are firing the anchor so that the target's response will be a smile and a lighter mood.

2. **Curiosity.** This one is easy. Think about how you feel when you are curious. As you enter that state, do you touch your chin? (This seems to be a naturally occurring anchor.) Get your target to talk about things that make him/her curious. As the target describes it, touch your chin.

3. **Being Positive.** A powerful state for a salesperson to have and use, both on yourself, your co-workers, and your clients. Think about how you feel when you are in a positive state of mind, body, and spirit. Anchor that feeling. Get your target to enter into a positive state, or if he/she is in one naturally due to their having a good day, big sale, or some great news, anchor it to you and to them. Anchor it to you by touching your chest area and maybe giving a thumbs-up sign. Anchor it to them with a pat on the shoulder.

4. **Self-Confidence.** Another winner for you and those around you. These are best when you find people in this state naturally, like after a good day, a good review at work, etc. I would anchor it with the same anchor as above.

The next ones will put you light years ahead of your competition.

---

5. **Loyalty.** This is one that will keep your clients around. Have them tell you something that they are loyal to, and how good they feel

about being loyal. As they describe it, agree with them and anchor it to you with a natural movement such as rubbing your hand through your hair. The key is **how they feel when they are loyal; that's what you want.** This is they way to ensure long-term relationships, **as long as you live up to your part of the deal.**

6. **How they feel when they have made a good decision.** You get your target to talk about a good decision they made, and as they describe the decision you agree and anchor that state to you or your product.

7. **How they felt when they made a bad decision.** As they talk about this negative experience, anchor this negative state to your competition, or at least point away from you.

8. **Excitement.** Get your target to talk about anything that gets him/her excited. Sports, kids, anything that puts your target into the excitement phase. You will use a key word to anchor this state to your voice, if possible. This will get your target to take your calls and talk to you.

9. **Doubt.** This is another winner for the salesperson. You may anchor in a state of doubt, so if your target brings up objections you may use this anchor to establish doubt regarding their objections.

10. **Patience.** This could be a deal saver if you need to get some extra time for the products or project. Have your target describe a situation in which he required patience from someone or something he was dealing with. Emphasize his appreciation of this patience. Anchor in this state appreciative patience. **The covert key here is how he felt when someone had patience with him.**

Anchoring Examples

Here are two stories that demonstrate many of these anchoring techniques in action.

I (WH) was called in to consult with someone who did hypnosis seminars who wanted to sell more products in the back of the room, mainly tapes and books. I watched his presentation and made a few minor adjustments, the most powerful change being the application of anchors.

First, I had him place the products up front so they could be seen. Then, as he talked about the great things the subconscious mind can do, I would have him place his hand next to the products. (This was the first step in anchoring.)

As he pointed out the things the subconscious mind can do, **the things you want, the things you need,** he casually would gesture to the products. This placed the focus on the products as a need.

For example, he talked about how once you learn to ride a bike, your mind will always remember this skill. You may not ride a bike for many years, but when do, your mind takes over and rides the bike for you. You want your mind to be able to free your attention to focus on other things, such as riding a bike, driving a car, etc. This is a good thing. You want this. (Point to product.) Then, when he did his "close" and talked about the products, he would say, "Some people need this, others want this, but what these do is free your mind. **It's a good thing.**" (As he said this he held up the products.) His sales went up over 20 percent at the next seminar.

Here is another instance of the power of anchoring for sales:

I (WH) was at a conference when someone approached me about buying some of my home study courses. I developed rapport by mirroring and matching him. I told him how excited I was to be at the conference. Knowing that excitement is contagious, I asked him if he was excited. As he described his excitement, I touched my tie.

I then went into how much fun it was just being there and laughing with my peers. I asked him if he was having a good time. As he described a funny event, I touched his shoulder, and again touched my tie.

I asked him what he was curious about in the courses. He told me of his curiosity and fascination with NLP (neurolinguistic psychology). I touched my chin, and readily agreed.

We then started to talk about some of the courses he had really enjoyed at the conference. (This elicited a Good Decision state.) As he was telling of his favorite, I touched the home study courses on the table that he had been looking at earlier.

I asked if he had been to any bad or unfulfilling seminars at the conference. As he described a couple, I made an outward gesture with my hand and talked about wasting time and money.

Now I had what I needed. I used my anchors while talking about the home study courses and how they were both fun and exciting. I touched my tie. (This fired the first anchor.) He smiled. I then talked about how this course answered all those questions about NLP many people in our field have. I touched my chin and his shoulder. (This fired the second anchor.)

We then talked about how it was important to take good quality courses. I emphasized the importance of getting your money's worth and the feeling of being fulfilled. I touched the videotapes and held them. I then talked about how there were other products and courses out there, and I did the outward gesture with my hand. (This fired the bad decision anchor.) **He bought all of my home study courses.** Yet another Win/Win!

As I was writing up the sale, I asked him about any special hobbies he may have had. He told me he loved to scuba dive. He then mentioned he learned to dive in the navy. I asked him if he liked his navy experience. He loved it.

As he was talking about his love for the navy and his loyalty to it, I gave him the information on our organization and told him how it feels to be on board. As he was leaving, I welcomed him aboard the NFNLP (National Federation of NeuroLinguistic Psychology) ship. (This anchored loyalty.) That weekend he brought over two other people, one of whom bought a home study course.

CHAPTER 7

Getting the Inside Information
from Your Customer

In Chapter 2 we showed you the magical questions that uncover your customers' values. Now it is time to expand your ability to gather information. In this chapter you will learn how to expand your ability to open the doors to your target's mind.

Now once you achieve rapport with your customers, you will find gathering information easier. They will want to talk to you, because they will feel a sense of connectedness. Now you can use this connectedness to help you.

To gather the correct information from your customers, however, you will need to do more than just listen to their words. You will also need to decode their meaning. You understand this from the earlier chapters. We need to now decode this information because our brains do not operate directly in the real world. We have to create models, or maps, of the world that we then use to direct our behavior. These maps or models allow us to make sense out of the world and all of our experiences. To become a top salesperson you need to be a master Map Reader.

Much like values and beliefs, these maps or models cannot be evaluated in terms of good or bad, but only in terms of their utility in helping us cope with the world. Each person has his own unique system for connecting words to his daily experience, and each person has his own set of words that connect to that experience. People are usually not conscious of the process or the words they select to represent their experience. By decoding these processes we open those doorways to clear communication.

Developing Clear Communication

Most of us create our models from the basic human language modeling

147

processes; they are deletion, addition, distortion, and generalization. These are what allow us to grow, understand, and experience the world.

The most common of these is **generalization.** This is where a person takes pieces or parts of an experience and uses them to represent the whole category from which that experience is an example. A child learns his father is a male, and he generalizes this and believes all males become daddies. This is also how you can learn quickly. For instance, when you learn how to drive a car, you can generalize what you learn about driving a car so you can drive almost any automobile.

However, generalization has some limitations. For example, when a salesperson fails in a few calls, or performs in a way he labels inadequate, he or she could generalize this into believing that they are no good at sales calls.

How can you use this information? You need to be aware that some of the comments your customers make are a result of these generalizations. When a person comes into your automobile dealership and states that "all car salesmen are slimy, you can't trust them," you will need to show him reasons to trust you, or at least start the process.

The next process is **distortion.** This is where we make shifts in how we experience our sensory data. We misrepresent reality, sometimes making it more or less important than it really is. People who do this because they are optimists are said to be looking at the world through "rose-colored" glasses. The other side of the coin, however, can present a problem, such as when someone takes a small amount of criticism from his sales manager and turns it into "He hates me and is out to get me."

It can also be a problem when someone takes a process and turns it into a thing. Love becomes something out there, to be handled and controlled, as if it were a thing.

What do we mean when we speak of deletions and additions? Well, **deletion** occurs when we selectively focus on certain parts of our experience and exclude other parts. It's something we all do to avoid being overwhelmed by the external stimuli that surrounds us.

For instance, someone in a room full of people can play a video game while another person is watching television and three other people are playing a board game. Each person in that room is deleting a portion of the total experience in order to engage in his selected activity.

How does deletion occur when we are with a customer? Imagine that you have just asked your customer a question about his computer software preference. The customer replies, describing his use of certain software and his inability to get technical help when he needs it.

As a computer salesperson with a background in programming, you have never experienced his level of frustration. You focus on the software he mentioned and talk about how versatile these applications can be. You have unconsciously deleted his technical help problems without even realizing that you did so.

Addition occurs when we add something to a representation based on our own experience. Take the above example. This time the salesperson recalls a time when he called for technical help with a software application and spoke with a troubleshooter who gave him some insightful tips about the application. He misses the frustration being expressed by his customer because he is concentrating on his own memory and recalling how knowledgeable the technical helper was and how he was able to use the tips to greatly increase his expertise with the software application.

The original representation of the customer, that his use of certain software programs led to seeking technical help that was less than helpful, is distorted by the salesperson's own experience.

Many of you have heard some of these statements:

You sell cars.

"New cars are a waste of money."
"No one ever really gets a good deal on a car."
"These cars are over-rated."

You sell investments.

"All stocks are so risky."
"The only safe place for my money is the bank."
"All brokers churn accounts."

You sell multi-level products.

"These are all a scam."
"No one ever makes money on these MLMs."
"You have to bother your friends for these to work."

You sell jewelry.

"Are these real?"
You always try to oversell what we need."
"These are too flashy."

Once you become aware that these processes are occurring commonly in your customers, you can now be prepared to use them as openings to gather more information.

Clear information gathering involves a set of questions that allows you to collect information clarifying someone's experience and giving you a full and detailed representation of that experience. The goal of clear information gathering is to create maximum understanding and learning from any specific communication.

There are six questions in English: What?, How?, Who?, When?, Where?, and Why?.

Clear information-gathering questions and responses help recover deleted, distorted, generalized, and added material and assists the information gatherer in breaking the code, or map, of the speaker and in recovering the actual, complete experience. This can be the most important part of a sales call—gathering the correct information.

The Short Method

Now that you have an idea of how we use language to make sense out of the world, and how we can lose the true meaning in these processes, let us show you a short cut.

The thing to bear in mind is to get your customer (or anyone else you are communicating with) to be as specific as possible. You want to pull them into information that is as sensory specific as possible. Things you can SEE, HEAR, or TOUCH. When you do this you will be communicating in a way that makes understanding much easier. The words you want to start to use a lot are **specifically, exactly, precisely,** and **detailed.**

Now, when you first start this process, some people may be upset by your nailing them down to specifics, but you will also become known as a clear communicator. As a culture we have lost clear communication and replaced it with the vague reference.

Here is a list of the key questions to learn to ask in almost any situation in which you want to gather clear information.

The Key Questions

1) What do you want?
   Specific—Sensory Based—What will you See-Hear—Feel?
2) What will that do for you (specifically)?
3) How will you know when you have it?
4) How will this affect other aspects (or people) of your life?
5) What stops you from having this already?
6) What resources do you already have that will help you obtain your outcome?
7) What additional resources do you need to obtain it?
8) How are you going to get there?

The easiest way to master clear information-gathering techniques, like most of the other skills you need, is to practice, practice, and practice. Once you see the effectiveness of these tools, you will want them as part of your daily skills, so here are some exercises that will put you into the elite of communicators.

Again we stress that you start in non-sales situations before you leap into the real world of customer interactions. In fact, these techniques work best in social interactions. Once you do these exercises you will be able to integrate these skills naturally into to your work life.

Here are the five exercises that will propel you into true understanding of these tools.

Exercise 1. Co-Worker, Casual

Pick a time where you can start a conversation with a co-worker in a friendly manner. Start by using your now natural rapport skills, then move on to the clear communication questions. Make sure they are as specific as possible. The key is to keep the rapport going as you challenge them into answering the questions.

NOTE: DO NOT GIVE ADVICE; ASK ALL THE QUESTIONS!

You will usually be surprised at how the answers to the questions themselves become the outline for what the person needs to do.

Exercise 2. Social, Acquaintance

In a social situation, pick a casual acquaintance and again start with your masterful rapport skills. Then pick a rather intimate subject, like what do you want from life? Then gently go through all the clear communication questions.

Again, do not give advice, just lead them through the questions. Do not be surprised when this person thinks you are a true genius later that day. You are probably the first person who has taken the time to ask the right questions, without giving advice, and listened to the answers.

Exercise 3. Social, Stranger

In a true social situation where strangers interact— a bar after work, or a coffee shop—start by acquiring your target (pick the person you want to work with), and begin your mirroring and matching before you start talking to them. (This is a powerful covert technique.) Then start your conversation, focusing on your rapport skills. Remember to anchor positives to yourself as the interaction goes on. As you get deeper rapport, move into a deeper subject area, like what does the person want in a career or a partner, and then go into your questions.

You will be pleasantly surprised at how well the interaction will flow and the answers you will get. Caution: you may make a friend for life or a person who seeks your guidance afterward.

Exercise 4. Co-Worker Problem Solving

Now you are ready for a real world situation. When a co-worker has a problem, sit with them, and as always start with your rapport skills. Then move on to the questions. You will find it much easier to ask all the questions before even starting to look at solutions at this point.

Much like in any complex situation, the answers may take you into new areas that need to be explored. The answer may become clear to the person as you are guiding him through the questions. Again, you will seem like a genius because you took the time to gather the correct information.

Exercise 5. Family

We purposely left family for last. Sometimes the hardest place to use your skills is in the home environment, but once you can do it here you are on your way to being a true master at information gathering.

Pick a situation with a family member who is stuck in some problem. Focus on your rapport skills (yes you need them also), and then start in on the questions. Sometimes with family members it is very difficult to not give advice, but stay focused on your goal, GATHERING INFORMATION, and guiding them in finding their own answers.

You may notice your family coming to you for advice, and better yet, listening when you do give guidance.

Now that you are comfortable with the process you are ready to try this with your customers. Remember that correct information is the answer to getting and maintaining happy customers. You will know what they really want and how to give it to them.

Putting It All Together

Now that you are comfortable with gathering clear information, you are ready to start to tie it into the information you learned in the first few chapters, the sixteen desires that power your customers' basic drives. In fact, you will hear these desires in some of the deletions, additions, generalizations, and distortions that people use every day.

The next step is to tie this information with how your customers decide to buy something from you. How do they decide to purchase something? What are the processes they go through to get to the point where they will say yes.

Discover Your Clients' Buying Strategies

Strategy has been defined as the science of planning and directing of military operations. *Webster's New World Dictionary* also defines strategy as "skill in managing or planning, especially by using stratagems." Obviously, strategy is both a science and a skill, and it is definitely a vital component for dynamic, successful salesmanship.

Strategy has always been the foundation of any successful business. When Ron made the decision to start a martial arts school, he realized he was entering a very competitive business. Most karate schools fail in the first year, and very few schools make enough profit for the owner not to require a second income.

Ron decided that the first thing he needed to do was find some schools where the owner was making a good living at teaching martial arts. (This is a strategy in itself. Find someone who has accomplished what you wish to accomplish and follow his example. Follow the same steps he did in building his business. This is called modeling.) So Ron took some time and began Information Gathering by visiting a few schools that had a booming business.

The first thing Ron noticed was that the schools that registered a large number of students seemed to fit their selling style to the clients' needs and wants, rather than to the head teacher's agenda.

For example, a young man comes in interested in martial art classes. The first thing the successful people did was to find out what specifically the person was looking for in the martial arts. If this person were looking for self-esteem, they would discuss how the martial arts would build self-esteem. If the client were focused on physical fitness, they would talk up the workout part and the flexibility he would acquire. Was self-defense the goal? The teacher would talk up how one would be able to defend himself in the future. If the prospect mentioned self-discipline, Ron noticed that these successful people would point out that self-discipline is the core of the martial arts training.

This is finding out what specifically the client is looking for: clear information-gathering question #1. What is your goal?

Ron then noticed that if a parent brought in a child, the teacher would address the objectives of each. He would talk up with the parents the points they were interested in. Then he would focus on what was important to the child. The master information gather collects information from everyone involved.

Ron took special note of how the teacher would ask each prospective client how they would know that they had found a school that fit their needs the best. The teacher would listen intently, taking note of what each said, such as the prospect who commented, "Well, I will see that the students have respect, that they have done well in competition, and probably I would want a free class or two."

After some more general talk about the martial arts, the teacher showed the prospective student some of the trophies won at recent events. He then asked a current student about the school's attitudes. The student discussed several, and when he mentioned RESPECT, the teacher stopped him and told the prospective client, "Respect is important here." He then invited the student for a free trial workout.

This is clear information question #2. How will you know when you have identified the goal?

Ron was amazed. He knew this technology, and had just watched this teacher get into rapport, match the client, get his strategy, find out which of the sixteen core desires were most important (accomplishment, belonging, and value), and then feed it back to the client. The client signed up before he left that evening!

Ron then watched as the teacher did the same to a mother and son. The mother wanted self-discipline and physical fitness; the son wanted to learn how to defend himself. The teacher repeated the benefits that each wanted and how his martial arts school was the answer.

The teacher then asked the mother how would she know she had found the place for her son. She stated the place had to be clean, well run, and friendly. Of course, the teacher pointed out how clean this operation was, that the classes started on time and finished on time, and that the school was like a big family. Students' family members were welcomed to watch classes. The mother signed her son up that day.

Ron got the information he needed. But as added confirmation he went to a couple of other, less successful schools. Here the teacher proceeded to tell him why his school was the best but never once asked any questions. Ron saw why the school run by the person who asked questions was growing by leaps and bounds while at the unsuccessful schools—where no one asked questions—the teachers had to hold other jobs to live.

The above was an example of strategies, how people put together how they think (the visual, auditory, and kinesthetic) with the sixteen basic desires to come up with an unconscious process of deciding how to decide. You get this information by using the clear information-gathering techniques.

SENSORY PERCEPTUAL STRATEGIES

Every person has his own sensory perceptual strategy program that he uses when he communicates. These strategies are the primary, secondary, and tertiary representational styles of the communicator. For example, a person can be a V-A-K, which means their strategy is visual-auditory-kinesthetic. When you communicate with that person, you want to use the processor words that pertain to the V-A-K strategy. The same is true for all the other representational strategies.

Theoretically there can be an infinite number of possible strategies.

These are the six most common:

    V-A-K   Visual—Auditory—Kinesthetic
    V-K-A   Visual—Kinesthetic—Auditory
    K-V-A   Kinesthetic—Visual—Auditory
    K-A-V   Kinesthetic—Auditory—Visual
    A-V-K   Auditory—Visual—Kinesthetic
    A-K-V   Auditory—Kinesthetic—Visual

How You Decide What You Do

Have you ever seen someone at a restaurant trying to decide what he or she is going to order? They may look up, pause, look down, lick their lips, touch their stomach, then order something; or they may repeat the options to themselves (in their heads, or some times aloud, "a quarter-pounder with cheese, hum").

They may even ask someone else, "What's good?" (hoping your tastes are similar). Whatever they do, they are running some type of strategy, and most, if not all, of it is preconscious. We are not aware of how we do it. We just do it.

Psychology tells us that it is a learned behavior; which it is. But once learned, it is put out of our conscious awareness. Even a Pavlovian response can be considered a learned strategy. Think about the classical Pavlov training. A dog is presented with food and paired with a bell repeatedly until the bell alone will elicit a saliva response in the dog. Somewhere in that dog's brain it is learning: bell = food = eat, or food = bell = eat. So it is with humans. We learn a strategy and then we use it over and over again, until we replace it or change it.

The problems begin to take place when our strategies are no longer working, or when we use an inappropriate strategy. This can be seen when you see someone use a strategy that works in business (profit and loss), in his/her personal relationships. They get out at the first hint of effort.

To make this easy to learn, think about what you ate the last time you went to a restaurant. How did you decide what to have? Did you look at the menu (visual), then mentally taste the food (gustatory or kinesthetic)? Possibly you said something to yourself (auditory) when you found some-thing you wished to order. Then you exited the program. One reason it is hard for some people to order food when they are really hungry is that they get stuck in their program. They keep playing options. (That sounds good, that looks good, I always like that. . . .)

You have a strategy for EVERYTHING that you do, and a lot of the strategies overlap. You may use the same style of strategy in different contexts. This may or may not be problematic.

I worked with a man who used his business strategy (which made him rich) to find a wife. He found his prospect (business venture), did his research (dating), found he wanted to acquire this property, and was willing to pay the asking rate (marriage). So they got married.

He then took a hands-off approach. He paid the price, bought the house and cars, and basically ignored his wife, unless there was a problem (the way he would run a business). He needed a romantic strategy. The good part is you can change, install, or remove a strategy. You need to know someone's buying strategy to be a successful salesperson.

People have their own strategy for everything they do. They will use these strategies when they communicate. These strategies are the primary (or lead), secondary, and tertiary representational systems of the person. For example, a person can use a VISUAL, AUDITORY, or KINESTHETIC strategy for buying a car. SEE a car you really like, hear good things about the car, drive the car and it FEELS good, buy the car, and then rationalize the costs.

Internal and External Cues

There are a lot of nuances to strategies. There are internal and external cues as well as links to the sixteen basic desires. These are strategies that you use in every situation, and you use them to develop other strategies. We will get into those later. But I want to show you how you can use this information today in your work.

First, when new clients call, ask them what they need to help them make a decision about your services. Then listen to what, and how they say it. Do they need to hear from others that your services/products worked for them? Do they want to see something in print about you? Do they want to feel comfortable with you?

Repeat what they say, and then give them what they want, or tell them you will supply them with what they need when you meet. Once they agree to a meeting, the odds are they will become clients if you have used what you have learned thus far.

It is very easy to learn another person's sensory perceptual style, or representational strategy. All you have to do is UNPACK it. Unpacking a strategy is very simple. Just ask them to remember a time when they were very happy with a decision. Then ask them to tell you what it was about that experience that made them that way.

Keep asking them to tell you again and listen for the processor words. They will tell you it was things they saw, felt, or heard. When they have told you three times, you have their basic strategy. Now all you have to do to communicate effectively with them and to develop deep rapport is to PLAY BACK their strategy.

Strategy playback involves communicating with another person in their modalities of reality. You use the same order or representation, such as V-A-K, but you use it in a different context. Basically, you feed back your information (like our karate teacher) using the appropriate processor words. When the listeners experience this through their sensory perceptual style, they will develop a deeper rapport with you and communication will be easy. You will find that more people will enjoy being with you and doing things with you simply because you can now communicate effectively with them.

Strategies are used in sales situations. If you can identify a person's buying strategy and customize your sales pitch to his program, you will increase your sales dramatically. The problem seems to be that salespeople try to get people to fit *their* selling strategy.

Anyone who has had to sit through a network marketing presentation knows what I mean. The presenter hopes that his/her hot buttons (strategies) are yours. Freedom from work, easy money, etc. are common strategies. If, however, you do not find these things exciting (they do not fit your strategy), you are not interested. This could be why people who love what they do are usually not interested in a multi-level marketing idea

Strategy and Sales

Several years ago I (WH) wanted to buy a new car, I had looked around and pretty much decided what type of car I wanted. By the time I started to go the show rooms, I had it narrowed down to a couple of choices. All I wanted to do was drive the cars and decide. In fact, my main requirement was that I wanted my next car not to lose power when I turned the air conditioner on. I had found the car that looked the way I wanted it to. Now I just had to buy the car.

Unfortunately, the first car dealer I went to did not listen to a word I said. All I wanted to do was drive the car and see if it fit me (fit my strategy). The salesperson, however, insisted on showing me the motor and going through his SELLING strategy. I left and went to another dealer of the same brand, and the same thing happened.

Finally, I went to the last dealership of that brand in my area. When I walked in, the salesperson met me and started the small talk. I told him what I was looking for and what was important to me—turning the air conditioner on and not losing power. He nodded and said, "We have a demo here with 15,000 miles on it. Drive this, get it on the highway, and turn on the air conditioner, full blast. You will love it."

He gave me the keys and let me go.

I ordered the car as soon as I got back, and picked it up a couple of days later. After I got the car I learned it was *Motor Trend* magazine's Import of the Year, and its motor was rated in the top ten of the 1990s. I stress this because a lot of people will buy something, then rationalize it later.

The moral here is forget your selling strategy, get the customer's buying strategy, and tie that into the basic desires.

Strategy at Work

I (WH) had a student tell me about the time he was working for an office supply company. He had learned the techniques we have talked about and was a top producer. In fact, he was known as One Call Joe, because he would get an order on the first sales call (or two), as opposed to four or five calls for the rest of the sales staff. The owner brought in a new sales manager who implemented a hardcore features and benefits approach and a step by step check list on what to do on each call, until you got the sale—an average of five calls.

Well, Joe was still leading but he very rarely did any features and benefits. He would get into rapport, and get the customer's buying strategy and criteria. If they had the right product fit, he would play back the customer's strategy and he would get a sale.

One day the sales manager went out with Joe on a cold call. Joe noticed the manager did not say a word as Joe got into rapport, did his clear information gathering, and found this customer's needs and his buying strategy. Then Joe played back this client's criteria and fit it into a product they had; this client was now ready for a demo. The manager at that point started to talk about the features and benefits, and the client interrupted saying, "I don't think that's important now. I am sure Joe will take care of us."

Even though they pretty much had the sale, the manager was livid over the fact that Joe did not follow their selling strategy.

"All you did was make small talk," he fumed, "and it looked like you guys were a mirror. He'd move, and you'd move. You never once talked about features or benefits. You went right for the sale. And what kind of close was that? You did not do any conditional closes!"

"I got the demo, and I will get the sale," Joe responded.

"Maybe I will give this account to Bill," the manager shouted. "At least he does sales calls the proper way."

"Bill is a nice guy, but he is near the bottom on the sales chart," Joe casually replied.

"At least he does it my way," the manager insisted.

"So doing it your way is more important than getting the sale? I want to get the sale and to keep the customers happy," Joe said quietly.

Well, Joe got the account, but it was with another company that had the insight to let a talented salesperson fly. He was a sales manager himself last I heard, and he was teaching his methods to his salespeople.

Strategies in a Clinical Setting

The following example is how I (WH) use strategies in a clinical setting. It will show you the power of a strategy, and how unconscious this use has become.

I had a client that had been using hypnosis as a form of therapy. The client had tried hypnosis for weight loss with limited success. Now she was stuck. She would do very well at work and through the main part of the day. She would have a small piece of fruit in the morning and a light lunch if she were hungry. Sometimes she would walk after work without stopping for a snack.

She was making notable progress. She would, however, start eating at night and would overeat. Since she had used hypnosis with some success, I thought we would see what her strategy was for eating at night.

I asked her what happened when she got home. At first she just said, "It seems like I walk in and start eating."

"So you have a refrigerator by your door?" I asked. "Tell me what happens as you walk inside the doorway of your home."

"Well, I open the door and I see an empty apartment." She was divorced, and her youngest child was in college. "Then what?" I prompted.

"I hear a voice that says a woman is not supposed to be alone."

"Whose voice?" I asked.

"My mother's."

"Then what happens?" I countered.

"I feel bad, like a little girl, a bad little girl," she replied softly.

"Then what?" I asked.

"I hear another voice and it says "EAT SOMETHING, YOU'LL FEEL BETTER." (Her mother again.)

"Then what do you do?" I prompted.

"I eat something, and I feel a little better. Then I feel guilty because I'm trying to lose weight."

"Anything else?" I ask.

"I hear her voice again. 'EAT SOMETHING YOU'LL FEEL BETTER.'" (Her mother again.)

"Then what do you do?" I prompted.

"I eat something, and I feel a little better. Then I feel guilty because I'm trying to lose weight."

"Anything else?" I ask.

"I hear her voice again. 'EAT SOMETHING YOU'LL FEEL BETTER.'"

And so she was off on a binge.

The Power of Strategies

This shows you the power of these strategies. (FYI: The technique I decided to use was to bypass the whole mess. When she was opening the door she would say to herself that it was so nice to choose to live alone. She would also make plans to do things she had put off for years—dance class, movies, etc. She did quite well.)

This shows how deep these strategies can run. How can you use this information?

Say you sell cars, and your client's strategy is that he must visit a dealer three times before he will buy your car. What if you have the person imagine what it would be like to have this be their third visit? Sounds simple, but it is highly effective.

What if you sell securities and your prospect states that he can tell if a broker is honest if the broker is willing to give him (the customer) bad news. You should make a point to tell this client some bad news.

If you sell insurance and your soon-to-be client states that he hates to be up-sold before he is comfortable with the current product, you should get this client's time frame for feeling comfortable before you offer him more insurance.

Here are some fast, simple exercises that will help you put together information gathering with strategies.

Exercise 1. Restaurant

PART ONE: The next time you go to a restaurant, take the time to think about how you decide to order the food you want. HOW do you know you want this certain item? Do you see it in your mind's eye? Do you taste it mentally? Do you find something that sounds good to you? Do you ask someone else what he or she is having? What is your strategy for this process?

PART TWO: Watch people at a fast food restaurant and notice the processes they go through before they order. You will see them access their strategy. Many will look up, lick their lips (taste), and then order. Some will ask about the food. Others will order what their friends are having. You may notice a few just walk up and order. Their strategy is no choice. They will choose only pre-selected items.

Exercise 2. Co-worker

The next time a co-worker mentions that he has bought a big ticket item such as an appliance or automobile, ask him the process he went through in making this major decision.

What was the signal it was time to buy this?

How did he decide to focus on this model or brand?

Did he read about it? Talk to others about it? See one somewhere?

What, specifically, let him know this was the one?

When did he decide to purchase, and what was the deciding factor?

Exercise 3. Friend

The next time you are with a friend ask him or her about their career.

How did they decide to do this as a profession? What was their process for this choice?

Did they read about this profession, or see someone do it?

Did someone talk to them about this career choice?

What, specifically, keeps them in this career?

Exercise 4. Client

Now you are ready for the real world. You are ready to take this into your sales world. Start with one of your clients with whom you are in great rapport. Ask these questions in regard to a product or service other than your own.

Ask how do they know they have a good relationship with another company?

What, specifically, do they look for in this type of ongoing relationship?

How do they know when it's time to find a new supplier?

Have your client think of the best relationship they have had with a supplier. How did they know it was the best? What did this business do differently from all the others?

We know that you can see the many applications of this information in your daily life. The key is to work this into your conversations naturally. It will come rapidly as you notice the great results.

You are beginning to know the secret of communicating with other people on both a conscious and a subconscious level. This is a powerful gift. You are now a black belt in communications.

You know what drives your clients (and all people). You can get into rapport at will. You can anchor in specific feelings in others when you wish. Now you know how to ask the questions that unlock people's subconscious thought strategies. We ask that you also use these skills not just to increase your sales but to help others when you can. You have the power to influence like few others. Use this technology in all areas of your life.

CHAPTER 8

Sales Success without Words:
Mastering Body Language

It was early in the morning on a cold winter day. The phone rang. I was still in bed after a hard day's night of writing a chapter in a book. I rolled over and grabbed for the phone.

"Kevin Hogan." Trying to sound like I was awake.

"Is this Doctuh Hogan?" New Jersey accent. No doubt trying to sell me something.

"Yes, I am very busy." Almost ready to hang up the phone.

"This is Rita Delfiner with the *New Yoke Post.*"

I bet she means New York. Isn't that the tabloid? The *National Enquirer* of newspapers? I live in Minnesota. She's not trying to sell me something. I sit up.

"Doctuh Hogan, we understand you are a body language exput." *Why don't they have "r"'s in New Jersey?*

"Yes, that's right. How can I help you, Rita?"

"The president of the United States is going to give a press briefing in a few minutes saying that he didn't have an affair with an office intern. We'd like you to watch it and give us your point of view as to whether he is lying or telling the truth."

"O.K. Call me when it's over. I'll turn on CNN now."

Why the heck would Bill Clinton deny an affair? Kennedy had Monroe. That's something you can write home about. If I were married to Hillary Clinton, I mean, the man is only human . . . but the *New York Post* . . . yeah, yeah, yeah . . . where is my robe. Ah, there it is. CNN. There is Bernie Shaw. Doesn't he ever sleep?

President Clinton appears on the screen.

He raises the index finger on his right hand. He is visibly shaken. I would be too if I had to deny an affair. It's one of those things that doesn't matter if you did it or not. You're guilty because some moron says you did.

". . . I did not have sexual relations with that woman Monica Lewinsky."

He rested his hands on the front of the podium, fingers placed over the front. There's Gore in the background. He could be president but who knows if he can even talk. Hillary is over there on the other side. She looks annoyed but supportive. Why did he put those fingers on the front of the podium? He's never done that before. He looks like he has seen a ghost.

(RING.)

"This is Kevin Hogan."

"Hi, Doctuh Hogan, this is Rita Delfiner with the *New Yoke Post.* Did he do it?"

Did he do it? I just watched the same thing you did, for goodness sake. How the heck do I know? I can't read the guy's mind, for heaven's sake.

"Rita, I'd like to watch it a few more times and then get back to you." Click.

I rewind my tape in the VCR and push play.

"I did not have sexual relations with that woman Monica Lewinsky." Rewind. Play.

"I did not have sexual relations with that woman Monica Lewinsky." Rewind. Play. Rewind. Play. Rewind. Play.

I stand up and I raise my right index finger into the air. I say out loud. "I did not have sex with Monica Lewinsky." Who is Monica Lewinsky anyway? I stand in the exact same position as Clinton. I am denying that I had sex with Monica.

Then it hit me.

I switch hands. I raise my LEFT index finger and wag it at my TV. "I did not have relations with Monica Lewinsky." Oh my! I did. Holy smokes, I did have sex with Monica. Whoa! Mr. President, you little dickens you. Tell no one, but I couldn't be happier for you.

(RING.)

"City of Bloomington." (It's my wife's voice.)

"Hey, did you just watch the president?"

"No, I'm working." (That's what all government employees are instructed to say when approached about working.)

I want you to raise your left hand, wag your finger at the camera, and say, "I did not have sexual relations with that woman Monica Lewinsky."

"What?"

"Just like Clinton just did."

"I told you I haven't been watching TV."

"Oh." (I explain the events of the morning.)

". . . so now, raise your left hand, wag your finger at the camera, and say, 'I didn't have sexual relations with that woman Monica Lewinsky.'"

She does so as I listen.

"Now switch to your right hand. Do the same thing."

She does so as I listen.

"Which hand do you believe?"

"Huh?"

"Which hand is certain it didn't have sex?"

"My right hand."

"Me too."

"But you said Clinton used is his right hand, so he didn't do it, right?"

"Clinton is a southpaw."

Click.

OK. Let's think about this. I rewind the VCR again and push play. I stand and do everything Clinton does. He did it. No wonder he's always smiling. Little dickens. Good for you, Mr. President.

(RING.)

"Hello this is Rita Delfiner with the *New Yoke Post* again. What do you think, Doctuh Hogan?"

"Rita, you can say, that Kevin Hogan, author of *The Psychology of Persuasion,* says that the president of the United States had some kind of sexual relationship with Monica Lewinsky."

"How did you determine that, Doctuh?"

I explain the whole process to her. She asks a few more questions but she has her headline. I'm the first person in the United States to say that Bill Clinton had sexual relations with Monica Lewinsky.

Boy, I hope I'm right.

By the end of the week, I was interviewed by dozens of radio stations all over the United States. Over and over and over. The same questions, the same analysis of the body language, and the dead giveaway in impotent denial.

Worst part was I like the president. Best part, this is going to sell some books. Clinton will understand. That's how you become president.

As a rule a person's body language should be similar to or congruent with his or her verbal communication. You should know that I could have been wrong about the president. I've analyzed the former president's body for his entire term in office. I have hours of the president speaking on video. (He happens to be the finest speaker as president we have ever had, and that includes Ronald Reagan, who was also a brilliant speaker.)

Had Clinton denied his indiscretion with his left hand I would have been less inclined to authoritatively state that he "did it." You can never be absolutely certain about what another person is thinking based upon his body language, but there are definitely clues in the cues that you see. This was a big one. Now, before we go on, I want you to take your right hand (or your left hand if you are left-handed) and say, "I did not have sexual relations with Monica Lewinsky." Now take your other hand/finger and do the same. Do you feel the difference?

Now that you have one specific behavior understood, let's look at some of the critical body language events in meeting with your customer.

It's Not Fair But It's True: Your Physical Appearance Matters

Your body language and your physical appearance will boost you to the top or keep you among the majority of people in the middle and bottom. You have less than ten seconds and realistically closer to four seconds to make a good first impression on those you come into contact with. There is a world of research that clearly indicates that you will be judged professionally and personally in the first few seconds of your meeting someone for the first time.

In fact, your first impression is recorded and is used as a yardstick for all future communication by those you meet. Whatever that first impression is going to be on your part, you want it to be intentional.

Before going any further in discussing verbal communication we had better take a look at how to really be perceived as attractive with your body language. Most people are completely unaware of just how much their body says and how it often contradicts what the words are saying!

There are numerous elements of what we call body language. They include your physical features, both changeable and unchangeable, your gestures and signals that you send to others at the conscious and unconscious level, and the space that you use when communicating with others. In this chapter we will touch on all of these important areas of body language.

WHAT YOU LOOK LIKE REALLY TALKS

Let's begin with our physical appearance. Here are some astounding facts that will give you pause for thought when you consider how important appearance is in attraction.

Your perceived level of attractiveness by other people will be a significant benefit or detriment in your sales career and your life. It isn't fair but it is true. People who are not considered attractive learn how to deal with less than perfect physical features and work with what they can. Before we consider just how to increase your face value in the next chapter, look at the results of some fascinating studies about physical appearance.

THE POWER OF PHYSICAL APPEARANCE

Did you know that in university settings, professors who are considered physically attractive by students are considered to be better teachers on the whole than unattractive professors? Attractive professors are also more likely to be asked for help on problems. These same attractive professors also tend to receive positive recommendations from other students to take their classes and also are less likely to receive the blame when a student receives a failing grade! (Romano and Bordieri, 1989)

Did you know that marriage and dating decisions are often made with great weight placed on physical attractiveness? A wide variety of research indicates that men will often reject women who are lacking (in their opinion) in positive physical features. Women, on the other hand, place less significance on a man's physical attractiveness in considering him for a date or marriage. (studies by R.E. Baber)

Did you know that in studies done on college campuses, it has been proven that attractive females (attraction as perceived by the professors) receive significantly higher grades than male students or relatively unattractive females? (studies by J.E. Singer)

There is more evidence that shows you must make the most of what you have physically.

Among strangers, individuals perceived as unattractive in physical appearance are generally undesirable for any interpersonal relationship! (studies by D. Byrne, O. London, K. Reeves)

In one significant study of fifty-eight unacquainted men and women in a social setting, we learned that after a first date 89 percent of the people who wanted a second date decided to do so because of attractiveness of the partner! (Brislin and Lewis)

In the persuasion process, attractive females are far more convincing than females perceived as unattractive. (Mills and Aronson)

Among American women, the size of a woman's bust is significant to how both American men and women perceive the woman. Women with a "medium-sized" bust are considered to be more likable and have greater personal appeal than women with a large or small bust. Women with a small bust are perceived as more intelligent, competent, and moral. Women with a large bust are generally perceived as less intelligent and less competent. (Kleinke, Staneski, 1980)

In yet another study, we find that young men who are obese are generally considered to be slothful and lazy. Both men and women who are obese are generally perceived to have personality characteristics that place them at a disadvantage in social and business settings. (Worsley, 1981)

CAN YOU CHANGE YOUR APPEARANCE?

Study after study reveals that how you look is critical to someone's first impression of you. So what can you do to change how you look? You can't change everything about your physical appearance but you can definitely make changes that will give you a booster shot.

Research studies tell us that the "exposure principle" increases our "face value." Specifically, the exposure principle says that the more often you are seen by someone the more attractive and intelligent you appear to them. If you weren't gifted with a Cindy Crawford or Tom Cruise face then it's time for you to take advantage of the exposure principle.

If you don't have the advantage of being "seen" time after time by a person or a group, then you must make the most of what you have. In other words, you want to look as good as you possibly can on every given day. Because of the significance of body image and weight you must do what you can to keep your body weight down and your body in shape for your overall image to be as good as it can be.

Your teeth will tell a tale as well. If your teeth are yellow and look like you just ate, your face value is obviously greatly reduced. Do everything you can to keep your teeth pearly white and you will be perceived as more attractive. (You've already seen the benefits of the perception of attractiveness.) When you watch the news tonight on TV, look at the teeth of every news anchor, weather person, and sports announcer. They all have beautiful white teeth. There's a reason for that, and that is positive impression management.

WHERE YOU SIT CAN CHANGE
HOW PEOPLE LOOK AT YOU!

Standing in someone's office is a problem that will need an immediate solution. As soon as pleasantries are exchanged, you and your customer should be seated. If you are both standing for an extended period of time and your customer doesn't have the forethought to offer you a chair, then you can ask, "Should we sit down and be comfortable?" Unless you are in a retail environment, sales are not made and deals are not negotiated standing up.

You may have an option of considering where to sit. If so, you are in luck. Scientific research is on your side in telling you exactly where to sit. Seating options normally occur on lunch or dinner dates at a restaurant and in meeting rooms. If you are in a restaurant, quickly search out (with your eyes) a location that allows you to sit facing the majority of the people in the restaurant so your customer is obligated to sit facing you, away from the clientele and staff of the restaurant. This is ideal for booth seating.

Your customer's attention should be on you, not the waitress, bus boy, and the dozens of other people in the restaurant. Your seat selection will assure you his attention. Once you have the attention of your customer, only you can make your presentation or engage in conversation.

HOW DO YOU SELECT SEATING?

Ideally you can create a seating arrangement that is most likely to facilitate the communication process. Here are the key rules in seating selection.

1) As a rule, if you have already met your customer once and you know he is right-handed, attempt to sit to his right. If she is left-handed sit to her left.

2) If you are a woman attempting to communicate effectively with another woman, sitting opposite each other is as good or better than sitting at a right angle.

3) If you are a woman attempting to persuade a man to your way of thinking, the best option is to be at a right angle if at all possible.

4) If you are a man attempting to persuade a man, you should be seated across from each other in the booth setting if possible.

5) If you are a man attempting to communicate well with a female in business or in a social setting, you should be seated across from her at a smaller, more intimate table.

WHAT DO YOU DO ONCE YOU ARE SEATED?

Waiting for the waitress to come can be awkward if you do not know your customer very well. If you are meeting your customer in her office, you will immediately get down to business after brief pleasantries. (It should be noted that sometimes pleasantries do NOT have to be brief. Many of my biggest and best presentations were made in the last two minutes of meetings that would extend to two hours with discussions of everything from baseball to sex to religion. The level of rapport and quality of mutual interests will ultimately be your guide.)

Once seated, keep your hands away from your face and hair. There is nothing good that your fingers can do above your neck while you are meeting with a customer. The best salespeople in the world have wonderful and intentional control of their gestures. They know, for example that when their hands are further from their body than their elbows they are going to be perceived in a more flamboyant manner.

While you are seated, if you are unfamiliar with your customer, it is best that you keep both feet on the floor. This helps you maintain control and good body posture. People that are constantly crossing and uncrossing their feet and legs are perceived as less credible, and people who keep one foot on their other knee when talking have a tendency to shake the free foot, creating a silly-looking distraction. Feet belong on the floor.

Meanwhile, your hands will say a great deal about your comfort level. If you are picking at the fingers of one hand, you are pulling negative mindstrings that show fear or discomfort. This is picked up by the unconscious mind of the customer and makes her feel uncomfortable. If you don't know what to do with your hands and you are female, cup your right hand face down into your left hand, which is face up. Don't squeeze your hands. Simply let them lie together in your lap.

For men, the best thing to do is to keep your hands separate unless you begin to fidget, at which point you will follow the advice of your female counterpart, noted above.

HOW CLOSE IS TOO CLOSE?

Every four years the two (or three) presidential candidates square off in three debates so Americans can get a clear view of the issues that face the nation. Americans get to see the candidates in an up-close and personal way. I've watched for years. In 2000, the British Broadcasting Corporation asked me to analyze the body language of then-Vice

President Al Gore and Governor of Texas George Bush. Specifically, they wanted to know what the candidates' bodies were saying. Then, as part of a suspenseful ploy, they asked me to predict the election. But we would wait until after the third debate to do so.

The nonverbal communication of the debate revealed a somewhat uncomfortable George Bush. He was usually ill at ease and appeared to be guarding his responses. Al Gore appeared overly confident, arrogant, and even a bit cocky. Gore was completely comfortable, at ease, and in total control of the first debate.

After the first debate, Gore was so overwhelming that his handlers coached him to be kinder and gentler in the second debate. Then, after getting "beaten" in the second meeting, Gore took off the gloves and came out forcefully in the final confrontation, which was a stand-up debate in a town meeting-type forum.

At the beginning of the first debate, Gore walked toward Bush and into his personal space as Bush was speaking. This threw Bush completely off, and Gore appeared to be a lion ready to eat his prey. Unfortunately for Gore, his behavior came off as being rude, arrogant, and too aggressive for someone who was going to be the president of the entire United States and not of just those who watch the World Wrestling Federation.

I told the BBC that this ploy on the part of Al Gore would backfire. American's don't like jerks and the people on "the fence" would swing to Bush and away from Gore just because of this one ten-second incident on television. It was now apparent to me that George Bush would win the election, though I told the BBC, "George Bush will win, but this election is going to be very, very close."

I had no idea how prophetic that would be.

Had I been advising and coaching Al Gore, I never would have let him approach George Bush in any way other than a friendly, warm manner. People like friendliness and feel comfortable around people who are kind. Almost all people feel threatened when their space is entered, especially when the perpetrator is physically larger than they are.

When you look at the tape of the debate, Bush clearly felt threatened and the viewer feels queasy as we see Bush approached. Gore's intention is uncertain, and because of this moment he lost thousands of votes.

What is the lesson?

Whether seated or standing, you should stay out of your customer's "intimate space." Intimate space is normally defined as an eighteen-inch bubble around the entire body of your customer. Entering this space is done so at your own risk. This doesn't mean that you can't share a secret with your customer. This doesn't mean you can't touch your customer. It does mean that if you enter into "intimate space," you are doing so strategically and with a specific intention. There can be great rewards when entering intimate space but there are also great risks, so be thoughtful about your customer's space.

Similarly, if you leave the "casual-personal" space of a customer, which is nineteen inches to four feet, you also stand at risk of losing the focus of attention of the customer. Ideally, most of your communication with a new customer should be at the two-to-four-feet distance, measuring nose to nose. This is appropriate and generally you begin communication at the four-foot perimeter of space and slowly move closer as you build rapport with your customer.

WHAT IS EFFECTIVE EYE CONTACT?

Eye contact is critical in any face-to-face meeting. As a rule of thumb, you should maintain eye contact with your customer two-thirds of the time. This doesn't mean that you look at her eyes for twenty minutes, then away for ten minutes. It does mean that you keep in touch for about seven seconds then away for about three seconds, or in touch for about fourteen seconds and away for about six seconds.

Eye contact doesn't mean just gazing into the eyes. Eye contact is considered any contact in the "eye-nose" triangle. If you create a triangle from the two eyes to the nose of the customer, you create the "eye-nose" triangle. This is the area that you want 65-70 percent of eye contact.

Should you sense that your customer is uncomfortable at this level, reduce your eye contact. Many Americans who were born and raised in the Eastern countries (Japan, for example) are not accustomed to the degree of eye contact that other Americans are.

Eyes are a fascinating part of the human body. When a person finds someone or something very appealing to them, their pupil size (the black part of the eyes) grows significantly larger. This is one of the few parts of body language that is absolutely uncontrollable by the conscious mind. You simply cannot control your pupil size. If you are interested in someone else, your pupil size will grow dramatically. If someone else is interested in you, their pupils will grow larger when looking at you and there is nothing they can do about it. This is one of the powerful predictors of liking in nonverbal communication.

It should be noted that pupil size will also get larger in situations of extreme fear and when a setting is dark. Pupils expand to let more light in and, like a camera, when the setting is very well lit the pupils will contract to the size of a very tiny little dot.

If you follow the tips in this chapter for improving your appearance, being careful about appropriate dress, and are careful with your use of space, you will be perceived as more attractive in personal relationships and in business.

There are two other telling behaviors relating to the eyes.

First, if someone is blinking far more rapidly than they normally do, that is usually an indicator of annoying lighting in the setting or of anxiety and/or lying on the part of the person.

In 1998 President Clinton gave a short speech offering his reasons for having an illicit affair with Monica Lewinsky. During this speech his eyes blinked a momentous 120 times per minute. Two days later he gave a speech about a U.S. bombing raid on a terrorist group overseas. In this speech his eye blinks were about thirty-five per minute.

The difference is extremely important in evaluating the comfort level and honesty of the president in each situation. If someone is blinking far more often than normal (and you do have to know what normal is for each person you meet and adjust for lighting), you know they are very probably extremely anxious and very possibly lying.

> *When your customer's eyes blink rapidly, he may be anxious or he may be attempting to deceive you.*

Second, if you are in conversation with someone and their eyes are easily distracted by the goings on in the environment, this is usually a good indicator that you haven't earned the interest of your listener. In general, it is a very wise strategy for you to keep your eyes trained on your customer in distracting environments.

To constantly look around at the environment when you are with someone else is perceived as rude. To keep eye contact with another person instead of being distracted by extraneous activity is considered flattering and complimentary, especially by women.

> *Always sit at a table so your customer is not distracted. Your customer should see you and only you.*

So, there you have it! You don't have to look perfect and own Trump Towers to be incredibly attractive to the multitudes! However, you want to take advantage of every aspect of your attractiveness that you can. Later in this book you will discover specifically what to do to really bring your best you forward!

THE EYES HAVE IT

Did you know that you are able to get a pretty good idea of how people feel about you by looking at their eyes? You get even more information about how someone feels about you when you put that "look" into the context of their facial expression and their body language.

How you look at someone can be perceived as seductive, frightening, caring, loving, bored, secretive, or even condescending. The eyes reveal a great deal about what is going on inside of us. If you can learn how to look and send the right message at the right time with your eyes, you will be perceived as more attractive by more people.

There are six basic emotions in the human experience, and the eyes capture them all. There are many more than six different emotions, but most of the emotions we experience are a combination of the six basic emotions. By simply looking at a person's eyes we can tell what they are experiencing.

Six Basic Human Emotions

Happiness
Surprise
Disgust
Fear
Anger
Sadness

Think about that. Across the world people are the same in this respect. We all show the six basic emotions in the same fashion. The eyes are amazing windows to the emotions we all experience. By paying close attention to the eyes we can learn a great deal about our customers and, in particular, those we wish to sell to today.

It is a true statement that most people will judge other people in the first two or three seconds after their first meeting. Therefore, doesn't it make sense to have them hypnotized by your eyes and your understanding of their wants and needs? How do you do this? You use your eyes in simple yet powerful ways to build rapport and create feelings of arousal in the person you are attempting to attract. To do this you need only to apply the key ideas you will learn in this chapter.

I (KH) recently had laser surgery on my eyes to improve my vision without glasses. In the screening process, I learned that some people shouldn't have the surgery because their pupils dilate (get bigger and blacker!) to a size that is abnormally large. Everyone's pupils dilate when it is darker in the environment and they contract when it is lighter. When the sun is shining brightly in your eyes, your pupils will be at their smallest. When you walk into a dark room, your pupils will be at their largest. The pupils get larger to gather more light. This helps the eyes see more of what is in the environment.

Your pupils will also get larger when you are terrified. There is an evolutionary response in your body that helps you collect more information about an experience that is frightening. The senses all sharpen in moments of great fear. Your hearing becomes more acute, your sense of touch is enhanced, and you can even taste fear. The pupils in your eyes get larger. This helps bring more light in even if the environment is already well lit. Your brain needs that information to help you escape and to protect you from danger.

Everyone's pupils dilate to a different maximum size, and everyone's pupils have a slightly different normal state. However, there is one amazing fact about those eyes: When someone looks at you and their pupils get big and black, they are either scared to death of you, or they like you!

It's almost impossible to control the increase in pupil size that occurs when we see something we like. This expansion is also an evolutionary process that happens to take in more of something that is very dear to the person. Unfortunately for the observing person, it is an uncontrollable response.

> *Look at your customer's eyes and you will know whether they like you.*

Recent research into pupil dilation has proven quite interesting to attraction. Showing pictures of a baby to women results in pupil dilation in the majority of women. Women viewing pictures of a baby with the mother elicits an even greater pupil dilation response. The same women viewing a beautiful landscape experience an enlarging pupil size as well.

Interestingly, women viewing a picture of an attractive man, on average, don't experience quite the size of pupil dilation noted in the above scenarios! Women can be impressed by a man's appearance but at least at an evolutionary or biological level, physical appearance isn't going to turn on every woman who passes. (Just what does turn women "on" will be discussed later in this book!)

These same researchers took the picture of that same beautiful baby and showed it to men. The men's response was a non-event. Their pupils, on average, didn't dilate. When viewing the baby with the mother there was again a non-event. Generally speaking, nothing happened. When the men were shown pictures of a beautiful landscape, again nothing happened. As soon as a man was shown a photo of a beautiful woman, the pupils, on average, dilated to a big and black orb. A man, it would appear, is very much turned on by the sight of the beautiful woman, even a picture of one.

Pupil dilation by women, when in the presence of real-live men, is another matter. Women typically are not visually aroused by photographs in the same way that men are. Women are very stimulated by some men in some contexts. When women are sitting across from men who arouse them, their pupils do dilate. To the observant witness, it is obvious. Most people are oblivious to the enhanced pupil size and yet it is one of the most telling signals of attraction.

As a public speaker, I (KH) have talked to hundreds and hundreds of audiences all over the world. As I speak, I am aware of the women whose eyes are big and black, and I always address my presentation to them, making eye contact with those who appear to be aroused or attracted to me. They don't know this is why I selected them to make eye contact with (at least they didn't until now).

Part of my job is to excite and inspire an audience when I speak. Therefore I need to gain as much rapport with the audience as I can. By making contact with the people who like me the most, I am able to gain agreement from those people. They nod their heads, lean forward, show interest, and smile, and everyone in the audience sees how much fun they are having. In groups, head nods are like a virus. Once one person nods his head almost everyone else does!

I receive all of this positive feedback, in part, because I don't just look at faces in an audience. It is because I look at the eyes of dozens of people in the audience and find the biggest pupils I can locate! These searches are like a treasure hunt that always has a pot of gold at the end. If I can do this with an audience of 50 or 100, can you imagine how easy this is to do in a smaller group at a party or in a public place? Start paying attention to the eyes that are looking at you.

You may wonder, "What if you are wrong? What if those eyes are just big because they are among the women whose eyes are normally large? Then aren't you just fooling yourself into believing that all of those women are attracted to you? My response is, "Of course." When you hallucinate, it should always be something that increases your self-esteem and self-confidence! We'll talk about how your beliefs and self-confidence effect your attractiveness elsewhere in this book!

A little while back there was a fascinating study which revealed that when you show two pictures of the same woman to a man, the man will perceive the picture of the woman with the biggest pupils to be significantly more attractive. Many magazine cover editors know this and actually touch up the cover picture.

Obviously, in the bright light of a photographer's studio the subject's pupils would be very small. Because of the importance of pupil size and attraction, the models' pupils are enlarged to be much larger than they possibly could be. This makes the final picture irresistible to the magazine purchaser. We simply love people with big eyes!

Men desperately want eye contact with women. Men gauge the interest of a woman by her eye contact. Men are very competitive and territorial when it comes to women looking at other men. They see this as a sign that the woman is no longer interested in them, or that the interest is fading. Therefore, if a woman wants to continue to make a good impression with her male customer, the woman needs to maintain steadfast eye contact. A man's self-esteem will crumble if a woman begins to observe all the other males in the environment.

On the other hand, we can safely predict that if we have the full attention of the one we are with, he or she holds us in esteem to some degree. There is no other indicator that is as powerful as eye contact that can show interest in another person. Our eyes unconsciously and automatically move toward that which interests or arouses us. We all know that and we all judge our value in some part by the response we receive from other people. The eye contact we give and receive is just the beginning of the sales process.

It's interesting to note that people with blue eyes are more demanding of eye contact than people with brown eyes. It is quite easy for us to look at a person with blue eyes and see the size of their pupils. When they expand and contract it is evident. The person with blue eyes is used to people looking at them for an extended amount of time, in part because of the contrast between their blue eyes and black pupils. The contrast can be striking at an unconscious level.

People with brown eyes, on the other hand, are used to other people looking away more rapidly because at the unconscious level it appears that the person with brown eyes is not as interested in them! The brown eyes present a weaker contrast to the black pupils. It often appears at the unconscious level that those brown eyes are not interested in us! Therefore we tend to look away from the person with brown eyes when in fact they may have been very interested in us!

When the person you are attracted to has brown eyes, you must pay more attention to their eyes to see the contrast between the black and the brown. What seemed to be an uninterested person may be someone who is actually quite excited about you!

Confirming our beliefs about the value of eye contact in selling yourself is an attraction study that was done some years ago. People watched films of a couple that communicated with each other in two distinct ways. The first film showed a couple that had eye contact during 80 percent of their communication. The second film showed a couple that had eye contact 15 percent of the time. The observers of the films rated the couples that had eye contact 15 percent of the time as cold, cautious, submissive, evasive, defensive, and immature (among others). The observers of the films whose couples had eye contact 80 percent of the time described the people in the film as mature, friendly, self-confident, sincere, and natural.

Gazing into someone's eyes is much more than just something special for the two engaging in the eye behavior. It is a clear signal to the rest of the world. These people like each other!

THE EYES DON'T LIE

Whenever you are in a situation where attraction takes place there is plenty of room for deception! People have been known to stretch the truth about their age and income, their intentions, and even their degree of love for another. The eyes act as a leading indicator of truth and deception.

In 1997 and 1998 I was heard on hundreds of radio shows talking about the body language of President Clinton, Monica Lewinsky, Kathleen Willey, Hillary Clinton, and numerous other key players in the White House scandal that led to the president's impeachment. The interviewers wanted to know who was telling the truth, who was lying, and what the facts were based on the body language cues I was reading.

Having carefully watched the president for almost seven years, I was familiar with his every facial expression and body posture. President Clinton certainly was the most charismatic president since John Kennedy. His ability to excite an audience and win over people who disagreed with him is legendary. He is an outstanding speaker who thrives on being in the limelight.

There were, however, two speeches and the famous grand jury testimony where the president was not his usual charismatic self. On these three occasions he was uncomfortable about his deception. The first was when he shook his right finger at the world and said, "I did not have sex with that woman Monica Lewinsky."

The next was during the grand jury testimony where he was videotaped from the White House. The third was the speech he gave that very evening, after the grand jury testimony, when he offered his regret for being involved in the situation.

On these three occasions, his eyes gave him away as being deceptive. The one speech that I want to share information with you about is the speech in which he apologized for his behavior.

For seven years I had watched the president communicate with the country, and even though he has been called "Slick Willie," his body language has rarely indicated any internal discomfort with what he communicated to the public. In this particular "apology speech," however, his anxiety, fear, and deception cues were very high.

When I watch people to see if they are being deceptive, I look to the eyes for important cues. I want to especially know how many eye blinks per minute a person experiences in contrast to when they are telling the truth. President Clinton's eye blink pattern was about seven to twelve blinks per minute. That is very normal. During the "apology speech," however, his eye blinking was recorded at seventy per minute! What that means is that on some level the president was being deceptive in his communication.

Once eye irritants such as contact lenses and allergies are ruled out, the only internal experience that will cause eyes to blink at that pace is the experience of anxiety normally associated with deception.

You should know that some people have eyes that never blink, and a small number of people have eye tics that just won't stop blinking. On average, though, a person will blink from seven to fifteen times per minute. When a person is being deceptive their eyes will blink five to twelve times that pace.

Like pupil dilation, controlling eye blinks is very difficult if not impossible. Take a moment right here and now. Simply try and keep your eyes open for thirty seconds without blinking. It's not easy is it? Now here's another experiment for you to do. Stare at a friend for thirty seconds. No blinking is allowed.

It is very difficult to stop your eyes from blinking! If you are in conversation and suddenly you notice a big jump in the number of eye blinks per minute, you can safely bet there is some deceptive behavior going on somewhere in what they are saying!

The eyes may or may not be the windows to the soul, but they certainly are strongly linked to the emotions and the entire makeup of the brain's responses to other people.

SOUND BYTES FROM SCIENTIFIC RESEARCH

✓ Generally speaking, the longer the eye contact between two people, the greater the intimacy that is felt inside
✓ Attraction increases as mutual gazing increases.
✓ Others rarely interrupt two people engaged in a conversation if they have consistent eye contact.
✓ Pupils also enlarge when people are talking about things that bring them joy or happiness. They often contract when discussing issues that bring them sadness.
✓ Women are better nonverbal communicators than men. Men can improve, though. One reason men aren't as good in reading body language is that men often communicate sitting or standing side by side and don't see as much nonverbal communication as women do.
✓ Women engage in more eye contact than men do.
✓ Eye contact has been shown to be a significant factor in the persuasion process.

- ✓ When women are engaged in a great degree of eye contact, they tend to be more self-disclosing about personal subjects.
- ✓ When eye contact decreases, men tend to disclose more and women tend to disclose less!
- ✓ The longer your eye contact, the more self-esteem you are perceived to have.
- ✓ The more eye contact you can maintain with others, the higher self-esteem you rate yourself!

SIMPLY IRRESISTIBLE EYES

Given what we know about the eyes and attraction, we can summarize the experiences of millions of people into a few key ideas for irresistible attraction.

- ✓ Start with your eyes. Are they clear or are they bloodshot? People who look at you will notice, and the clearer your eyes the more attractive people will perceive you to be.
- ✓ If you wear sunglasses, get ready to take them off. People want to see what they are getting. They want to see your eyes.
- ✓ If you wear glasses, consider contacts or other alternatives. People need to be able to see your eyes!
- ✓ If you want to be attractive to someone, look at them. Look at them again and again. And smile!
- ✓ Look at a man from head to toe on the initial contact. He will be flattered. Look at the woman from the shoulders up and she will think you have depth and possibilities.
- ✓ Look at the person you are attracted to about 70 percent of the time when you are communicating with them.
- ✓ Avoid looking at others for any length of time when you are with someone who may be special. Make the person feel as if they are the only one in the room that could possibly catch your eye.

Scary Fact: The Customer Often Says "Yes" or "No" before You Shake Hands and Say Hello

What you wear, your makeup, your jewelry, your watch, your socks, your shoes, your coat, your glasses, and everything else about how you look can make or break a sale before you ever open your mouth. Have you ever heard of love at first sight? Two sales were made before two people ever spoke. Both people decided that they wanted what they saw, heard, smelled, and felt inside. Sales are made and broken every day in the same manner.

In this chapter you will learn how to help your customer fall in love with you *and* your products and services before you even say a word. Nonverbal communication is almost always unconscious communication. Most people have no idea what is going on at the sub-language level of communication. This chapter will help you master this most critical process of communication.

Many self-proclaimed experts of influence have misquoted a brilliant study by Albert Mehrabian to the effect that 93 percent of all communication is nonverbal. That wasn't what Mehrabian concluded at all. However, Mehrabian and most of the best psychological researchers do agree that nonverbal communication is between 50 and 80 percent of the impact of a communication. The same is true for the selling climate.

The first element of nonverbal communication you want to learn about is that of space. The space you occupy while in the sales process makes a great deal of difference as to the result of the process. Imagine that you are making your sale at a kitchen table. Would it matter if it were yours or your client's kitchen? Imagine that you were closing a deal in a restaurant and then contrast that with closing the same deal in a nightclub. Different?

Now imagine that you are in an office setting and that your customer is sitting directly across from you. Next, imagine that your customer is sitting to the right of you. Imagine you are standing in a retail store next to your client. Now, imagine that you are seated and your customer is seated. How are each of these different to you? Each of these images creates different feelings and probabilities of selling your customer.

Is Your Scent Making a Statement about You?

If you are going to be spending most of your day meeting with men and you are wearing a cologne or perfume, you have already lost valuable percentage points on your selling probabilities for the day. If you are a woman and are going to be selling to women, you can be lightly scented. Whether you are a man or a woman, if you are seeing men, have no scent but that of a clean body. If you are a man selling to women, you should have no scent.

> *In general, all of our studies show that colognes and perfumes are a biological turnoff to the opposite sex. There are minor exceptions, but there are no scents that you can wear to enhance sales compliance.*

Scents are powerful in the selling process, and if you have customers coming to your office you should contact the authors for a special consultation. The science of aromachology has revealed that certain scents cause people to spend more money, take more time in stores, relax, feel more erotic, and experience a plethora of behavioral changes from arousal to helping attitudes. In the sales process outside your home office, you, the sales professional, need to be scentless. If you wear deodorant, buy one that is scentless.

Twenty Tips to Look Perfect for Your Customer

Both female and male sales professionals make many mistakes that cost some salespeople far more than ten thousand dollars in income per year. It is interesting that our research indicates that women will far outsell men of the same skill and knowledge level IF their appearance is perceptually correct. Women make far more mistakes with their appearance than men do in selling.

Physical attractiveness is important to how many sales you make and how much those sales are for. We know that in personal relationships people tend to choose their spouses based on two factors: money, or potential income, and physical attractiveness. Women value money as the number one characteristic in a spouse and physical attractiveness as second. For men, it is the opposite. Both find physical attractiveness very important. In selling, the same holds true. Physical attractiveness matters.

In order to begin to understand how important physical appearance is, let's look at some research that has been done in the area of interpersonal relationships. Study after study shows that physical attractiveness is very important in one person's perception of another person. 89 percent of all people on their first date decided "yes" or "no" to a second date based on the physical attractiveness of the other person.

> *People judge others positively or negatively in large part on their physical attractiveness. Enhance your attractiveness to increase sales.*

Numerous studies show that men will reject women based on what they perceive as deficiencies in the women's appearance. (In the realm of inter-personal relations, women are more interested in money than men, show-ing some practicality, but continuing the thread of superficiality in this Mind Access Point!)

Many elements of your physical appearance are genetic and are not going to change. You can't grow two more inches and you can't change the shape of your face. There is, however, much you can do to enhance your perceived physical attractiveness. Here are the keys to your appearance for both men and women. Follow these twenty tips and you won't be pulling the negative response Mind Access strings in your customer's mind.

1) Women: Never dress suggestively. Research shows that you will get a longer interview but you will make fewer sales. Dressing suggestively pulls out an entirely different set of Mind Access strings to be pulled. Low-cut blouses and shirts are out. Mini-skirts are out.

2) Women: If your wedding ring is large and you are going to be see-ing women, take it off and put on your band instead. A large wedding ring reduces sales. Women outwardly express their excitement about a large wedding ring but it is perceived as a negative for numerous reasons. Your sales will go down if your wedding ring is significantly larger than that of your customer.

3) Women: If your fingernails are more than one-half-inch long, cut them and you will increase your sales. Long fingernails are perceived negatively by men and women in the sales process.

4) Men and Women: If your fingernails are anything but clean and well-rounded, get a manicure. Your fingers are the one area that can turn off both men and women. A sales professional has nice-looking hands.

5) Men and Women: If you wear glasses, normally smaller glasses are appropriate. You are normally better off making sales presentations wearing contact lenses if they do not irritate your eyes too much. Glasses rarely make sales and often break them.

6) Men and Women: Your weight will make or break sales. If you are

more than 20 percent over normal, you lose credibility in the sales process. Begin a program of eating right and activity to reduce your waist-line. Thinner salespeople sell more. Period.

7) Men: Facial hair reduces sales in almost all cases. If you are a man and have a beard you should cut it now. There are no men with beards in the top 100 sales professionals. If you have a mustache, ask men and women for their opinion. Some men appear to look better with a mustache, but in general all facial hair reduces sales.

8) Men and Women: Ear and nose hair can create feelings of disgust in many of your customers. If you look in the mirror and you see ear or nose hair, cut it and keep it cut.

9) Women: Makeup that is lightly applied is not distracting. If your makeup is heavy, you will lose sales. The closer to "natural" you appear, the better.

10) Men and Women: Teeth. Teeth should be white, flossed, and clean before you meet any customer. If your teeth are stained, get them cleaned. Yellowed teeth lose sales.

11) Men: Hair Length. If your hair length goes beyond covering the back of your neck you will lose sales. Long hair can feel good and even look good, but it isn't taken seriously. Decide whether you want to make all the sales you want to or whether you need your hair long.

12) Men and Women: Dress like your customers dress . . . plus 10 percent. If you see conservative clients, dress very conservatively. If you are selling to casual clients, you will dress "dressy casual."

13) Men and Women: When wearing suit coats, nothing goes in the outer pocket except a spotless and perfectly fitted handkerchief. No pens, no calculators. Nothing else goes in the suit coat outer pocket.

14) Men and Women: Your shoes should be shiny and looking new.

15) Men and Women: Jewelry. Men should wear nothing other than a

watch and a wedding band. Women should wear nothing more than a watch, a wedding ring or band, a thin necklace, and a pin. Earrings that are small for women are acceptable but they should not distract. Earrings for men are always out. No earrings are permissible for men. You will lose sales.

16) Men and Women: You should be showered every morning and have your hair conservatively and neatly in place before every sales call.

17) Men: Your briefcase should be no larger than is necessary to hold two copies of *The Encyclopedia Britannica*.

18) Women: A large purse is out. Never bring a large purse on a sales call. If you do, you will look disorganized. Bring a trim purse with whatever essentials you need during the day. Everything else can stay in the car or in your desk at the office.

19) Men: Your suit should fit properly. With your coat buttoned, take your fist and place it between your belly button and the coat. It should comfortably touch both. If you can't squeeze your fist comfortably between your stomach and your coat, your coat is too small.

20) Men: Your pants should touch the bridge on your shoes. They should not run on the ground or be raised high on your socks. If they don't touch your shoes get them altered. Anything unusual costs you sales, and that means you lose money.

Saying Hello and Shaking Hands

What should be the most natural thing in the world has become one of the most difficult. How do you say hello to your client?

Walk into the office with excellent posture taking medium-length strides and say, "Hi, I'm Kevin Hogan, the author of *The Psychology of Persuasion.* You're John, right? Nice to meet you."

On the word *John,* you shake hands. If you walk into the office and your customer takes the lead by introducing himself, simply follow his lead and shake hands as he extends his.

Hold his hand for two or three beats and gently release it. Assuming you shake hands with your right hand, your left hand should NOT take part in this ritual. Here are the ten keys to shaking hands properly.

TEN DO'S AND DON'TS OF SHAKING HANDS

✓ Always maintain eye contact when shaking hands.
✓ Do not use the infamous two-hand handshake.
✓ Do not grab his elbow with your left hand.
✓ Do not hold his hand for more than two seconds.
✓ Do not squeeze to crush his hand.
✓ Do not try to get a better grip than your customer.
✓ Do not have a limp handshake.
✓ Your hand should be firm but under control.
✓ Your hands should be dry and warm.

Do I Walk Funny?

Many people do. When I (KH) moved from the Chicago area to a small rural town in Minnesota in my senior year of high school, I learned this lesson the hard way. I had won a role in a play called *The Crucible* as the Reverend Hale. It was a wonderful role for the young person that I was. Unfortunately, I didn't walk "normally" and my posture was terrible. I had a bit of a swagger and my shoulders bounced as I walked. It was cute to some, but it was a sign of bad posture and needed correcting.

The drama's director, John Fogarty, needed his reverend to walk with an air of confidence and not a "Chicago shuffle." He decided he would tie five-pound weights to each of my ankles. Now that may not seem like a lot of weight but imagine a half gallon of milk tied to each of your ankles. It slows you down and straightens you up. I had to wear these weights all day for six weeks. At the end of the six weeks I walked upright and not like the Cro-Magnon man I had once resembled.

In life we all play roles. We play the roles of parents and spouses. We play the roles of volunteers and business people. As a salesperson, you play the most important role of all. You play the role of a person who literally helps the world go around.

When you are walking, you should be walking as if a big hand were scooting you along by putting pressure on your butt to go forward. This is an important first step to improved posture. Practice walking around the house in that manner. That will help you with your walk and your posture. The alternative is the weights . . . and that is a lot of work.

How Do I Make Presentations to Groups?

Everything you have read up until this point still applies, of course. Presentations simply offer a few more challenges and a few greater rewards.

If you are presenting to a group, you already know that you have something important enough to say to get the attention of the group. No one in the group showed up by accident.

Know what you are going to say in advance. You don't have to write out your presentation. In fact, unless you are the president of the United States, no one will listen if you do.

There are a few keys to speaking before groups. One is seat selection. If you are the key speaker and will be speaking from the one and only table, you want to sit on an end or in the middle of one of the two sides.

If you have any known detractors of your product or service, you should have them sit to your immediate left or immediate right. These are the least powerful positions on the table. Notice that in presidential press conferences where members of both parties are present at a seated table, President Clinton always had the Republican leaders seated immediately next to him. These positions have no focal attention and rarely speak with any credibility.

If you have to speak before a group and you have a podium, you have an opportunity to make or break a sale by a strategy that I discovered by watching television evangelists. This strategy takes some time to master but is remarkably effective.

Strategic Movement?

The most powerful nonverbal process you can use with an audience that must determine as a group to "buy" or "not buy" your products or services is that of strategic movement. Other sales trainers call similar strategies spatial anchoring. Both are applicable and here is what strategic movement is all about.

Do you remember Johnny Carson? He was the host of "The Tonight Show" for almost thirty years before Jay Leno took over in the 1990s. Each night when Johnny came out, he stood on a small star that marked exactly where he was supposed to stand. It was the best spot on the entire stage for camera angles and connecting with the audience. Because of the curtain backdrop, we knew without seeing Johnny's face that he was there—not a guest host, who would stand on a different star.

The only thing Johnny ever did from this specific location was make people laugh. He didn't wander around the stage and tell his jokes. He stood right there and made people laugh. There were many nights when Johnny literally could just stand on his star and people would laugh. That is spatial anchoring. Audience laughter was anchored (conditioned to) Johnny's standing on his star.

When I (KH) first visited NBC in 1984, I thought it was fascinating that only Johnny stood on that star. At the time I thought it was an ego trip or some bit of arrogance on the part of Carson. How wrong I was. I knew nothing at that time of spatial anchoring and strategic movement.

When you are called on to make your sales presentation in front of a group, you are on stage. You are the star. You will want to select three specific points on the stage, or in the meeting room, from which to speak. Each of these points is a specific location and not an approximate area. Point "A" is your podium. Podiums and lecterns are used by teachers and preachers. Therefore *the podium (point "A") will always be used only to relay factual information to your audience.*

You will choose a point to your left about four feet from your podium from which you will deliver all of the bad news discussed in your presentation. (You can't make many sales without painting a vivid picture about how bad things will get if the corporation doesn't hire you.) The bad news point is point "B," and from that spot you will only talk about problems and anything that is going to be perceived as "bad" by your audience. *Point "B" will be approximately four feet to the left of the podium.*

Point "C" will be approximately two and a half feet to the right of the podium, and you will always paint uplifting, positive, exciting, motivating pictures from this location. Everything we want the audience to agree with will be discussed from this point after we establish this as the "good news point."

Imagine that you are giving your presentation and you need to be very persuasive. My favorite example here is that of fund-raising for a charity. Your job? Get a big check for your favorite charity.

You place your folder or notes on the podium and immediately walk to point "B." You tell a story about a hurting child or a suffering individual. You then explain how this one incidence is far from isolated. You move to the podium. You expound the facts and figures about the problem that you are asking the group to help solve by making a big donation.

Now you move to point "C," where you will become excited about how the charitable organization is currently solving the problems and helping the suffering you talked about at "B." Everything that is good and wonderful you will "anchor" into point "C."

As you conclude your speech you will have a path that you have laid. You have moved from A to B to C to B to A, several times. *You conclude on point "C" because it is the good news point and offers each person a chance to participate in healing the wounds you opened at "B."*

The truly unique tactic in strategic movement is the ability to subtly answer questions at the unconscious level without saying anything significant on the conscious level. Imagine that the audience is given the opportunity for questions and answers with you. An individual in the audience tells you the group is consideratiing donating to a competing charitable organization.

"Well, of course, you know that charity is a good charity and there would be nothing wrong with that, of course . . . (walking to point "C"). By taking advantage of the plan that we have, we can accomplish all of the goals that you want to have accomplished in the community. I'm sure you realize it is up to you to make it happen. We can only help those who need it if you make a decision tonight."

Discussing the other charity in a neutral or slightly positive manner from point "B" allows you to unconsciously associate all of the negative feelings to your "competitor" and you solve the problem as you move to the "C" point. *If you find this manipulative, then you are working for the wrong charity. If anyone else is more qualified to help a group, sells a better product, or offers a better service, you should be working for them!*

There is no more powerful manner of utilizing space than that of spatial anchoring combined with strategic movement. The next time you watch a great speaker, notice how he or she utilizes strategic movement. If he stays at the podium, notice how all the good news is given while gesturing with hand "A" and all the bad news is discussed when gesturing with the other hand. The greatest speakers are masters of spatial anchoring and strategic movement.

Body Language:
29 Points to Make Sales Soar

✓ The right side is where you make the best impression.

✓ Pupils dilate when they are interested in what they see.

✓ Rapid eye blinks often mean anxiety and deception.

✓ Forward leaning is a sign of liking.

✓ Eye contact when it isn't necessary is almost always a good sign.

✓ 70 percent eye contact is just about right in the United States.

✓ Your body weight sends a message.

✓ Your hairstyle speaks volumes.

✓ Hairpieces usually indicate insecurity.

✓ Rapport begins by matching physiology.

✓ Women feel comfortable when men are just a bit below eye level.

✓ Women feel comfortable when you are straight across from them.

✓ Men feel comfortable when you are at a 90-degree angle from them.

✓ Touch is a sign of liking.

✓ Nod your head. It unconsciously affirms your customer.

✓ Look out for leakage, a sure sign of nervousness.

✓ The nose usually engorges when the person is deceptive.

✓ Dress appropriately to the situation.

✓ Radical dress means the person is making a statement. What?

✓ Spatial anchoring is a powerful nonverbal communication tool.

✓ The person sitting next to the person standing has no power.

✓ People in rapport tend to synchronize together.

✓ Physical attractiveness means more than we wish it would.

✓ Blue-eyed people expect to be looked at more than others.

✓ Scents of vanilla are considered positive in the United States.

✓ Our face value goes up with each exposure!

✓ Negative emotions are usually triggered on the right side of the brain.

✓ Smile. It's tough to resist a sincere smile.

CHAPTER 9

Tuning into Your Clients'
Most Unconscious Communication

As we move into this area, it is important that we stress the importance of taking your skills to the next level. Have you ever been to a seminar, read a book such as this, or attended some type of training that at its conclusion you felt terrific? You felt ready to take on the world? Then, over time, the excitement faded and the training seemed a distant memory, and you returned to your old behavior.

Sales managers are always looking for ways to improve their sales staff. Dr. Hogan and myself are the experts at rapidly installing long-lasting change. We pointed out at the start we were going to make you black belts in the sales arena. Now it's time for you to give us a little of your time, and we will reward you with permanent new skills.

One of the most expensive mistakes people make is to think that because they understand something, they can do it without the practice necessary required to really understand the new skill.

The key to this permanent change is simple. Do not confuse complexity with competence. These simple ideas will change your life, but you have to do the steps.

The human mind understands one thing, and that is results. Once you learn how to do something, that behavior will stay until it is replaced with a more effective behavior. When your mind sees the results in a new behavior, it will do it again and again and then it will take this successful behavior into other areas and apply it. Your early success here will reap you huge rewards in all areas of your life.

Any martial artist can do a knockout with sheer force, but a true master understands how to do a knockout with a minimum of power. We want you to become the master of these knockout communication skills.

My focus here is to bring you practical ways to do this.

To begin to understand and communicate with another person's unconscious mind, it's necessary to review the fundamentals of rapport and look a little more deeply at how the human mind (at least in theory) works. Once you understand this, you can begin to see how great salespeople are able to bypass the "critical thinking" of the mind.

The first thing you need to do to sharpen your skills is to learn how to focus on your customer's communication style. You need to learn how to calibrate your customers or anyone else you may be communicating with.

Memorial Day, 2000. I (WH) had the opportunity to sharpen my skills in communication. I had been on my way from Chicago to Newark to speak at a conference. I arrived at the airport only to find I had missed my plane. It was completely my fault. When I had purchased the tickets, I had not checked the times closely. I had thought the plane was scheduled to leave at 1:11 P.M.

When I arrived at the gate I was surprised to find the plane had left at 11:11 A.M. I checked the ticket and sure enough, it had been printed, however lightly, with the correct 11:11 A.M. departure time. I had misread the ticket.

I had walked toward the ticket counter and found a long line, caused by some weather problems. I got in line and was thinking about how to get to the conference. My first reaction was to go on the offensive with the airline personnel, faulting their equipment's light printing. In fact, I had been experiencing self-anger, and was externally focusing it on the situation.

As I got closer to the head of the line, I could see the anger that the airline agents were being subjected to. Naturally the airline personnel were on the defensive. I realized that I needed another strategy to achieve my goal of getting to the conference without paying a huge ticket price. As I stepped to the front of the line, I heard the overhead speaker announcing that all flights of this airline were now full.

As my turn arrived, I took a calming breath and approached the next agent. I immediately made eye contact and realized she was mentally and physically exhausted. Unconsciously, I immediately began to model her. My shoulders were rounded and I slumped as if I, too, had had a rough day.

"Looks like you're having a rough day," I said very tiredly.

"You would not believe it," she replied.

I looked at the line as she said this and agreed, "Yeah, but do you work this weekend?"

She replied with a note of relief in her voice, "No, a couple of hours and I am out of here for the holiday."

"Well, keep that picture in your mind and it may help you get through the rest of the day. Got any special plans?" I asked trying to get her to pull out of the situation and get into a better mood. I deliberately added energy to my voice, and pulled my shoulders back.

"Yes, I can't wait," she said smiling for the first time.

I took the ticket out of my pocket and handed it to the agent saying, "Well, I hate to admit this, but I really screwed up." I handed her my ticket as I continued, "I hate to show you how silly I was." I paused and then added, "Did you ever make a stupid mistake?" I had hoped she would respond to the appeal in my tone.

"Oh, all the time," she replied. "Let me see. I bet I have fouled up worse," she said as she took my ticket.

"Keep thinking of this weekend," I said as I handed her the ticket. I deliberately anchored a positive response emotion.

"So you misread the ticket?" she asked.

"Yeah, it was silly," I replied.

"Well, it was hard to read," she remarked. "All of our flights are full.

Not giving up hope, I explained, "I was going to a conference this weekend. I'm scheduled to speak to a group of therapists and hypnotists. I guess I will miss it now."

I sighed, looked down, and became the image of disappointed acceptance. I quickly looked back up at her and added, "Well you keep thinking of how much fun you will have this holiday weekend."

A look of curious interest appeared on the airline agent's face. She said, "Hypnosis? That sounds interesting. Let's not give up yet. Let's see what we can do."

She spent a couple of minutes on her computer, then looked up and declared, "Hurry and get to the next terminal. I have put you on a business flight on another airline." She smiled as she handed me the new ticket. "Enjoy your conference."

"You keep your eyes on the weekend," I said as left the counter.

By pacing and calibrating to the ticket agent's state, I was able to get into rapport with her, and led her into a more positive state. In this state I was able get her to want to help me.

This skill is a must for any elite salesperson.

CALIBRATION SKILLS

You experience the world by collecting information through your five senses and processing it internally. The five primary senses are visual, auditory, kinesthetic, gustatory (taste), and olfactory (smell). These five senses send input to your brain for processing, which is then translated into corresponding internal representations, or *maps,* that create a likeness of the real world.

So through your eyes, ears, sense of touch, taste, and smell, you make contact with the world. This contact is what we term **reality.** However, it isn't so much what is out there, the things you see, hear, touch, taste, and smell, that fill your everyday experience. It is the maps of reality **inside your head.** These maps are your beliefs, values, and biases; your experiences of the past; dreams, hopes, fears, and expectations of the future. These maps also include immediate, short-term, and long-term wants and needs. The maps, which fill your thoughts and feelings, are the major portions of the **reality** to which you respond. The same is **true for each person you encounter.**

What is important to remember is that your perceptions and "realities" are different from those of someone else because your central nervous system selectively "filters" the information as it is received by your brain.

For instance, have you ever watched the news and heard several eyewitness accounts of a plane crash? If you have, you probably noticed that the accounts differed in subtle ways. One person starts off by describing the noise of the aircraft as it crashed. Another person begins by describing the sight of the plane hitting the ground and bursting into flames. Still another person relates the sick feeling that came over him when he realized the plane was going to crash.

Every minute of the day your representational systems are bombarded with an incredible amount of information. Your central nervous system selectively sifts through this information, allowing only a portion of it to reach your conscious attention. These filtering processes are called deletion, distortion, and generalization. Without these filters you would be engulfed by an incessant stream of information.

Each person has his or her own unique perception of the world. Your family, friends, co-workers, neighbors, and colleagues view the world through different sets of filters than you do. What you say, what you think, and what you do may mean something totally different to each of them.

Your representational systems influence your thinking and over time you gradually develop preferences in the way you use them. The three primary representational systems are visual, auditory, and kinesthetic. The olfactory (smell) and gustatory (taste) systems are usually used as triggers for the other systems.

Most people will use one system more than the other two. This results in the preferred system's being the one by which fine distinctions are made. For instance, people who are influenced more by what they see are said to be **visual.** Other people rely more on what they hear, and they are said to be **auditory.** For others, their favorite method of focusing is through feelings and sensations and they are known as **kinesthetic.**

Those people with a preference for the visual representational system think primarily in pictures. If you asked them, "Do you know John?" they would very likely reply, "Is he the tall man with the thin mustache who drives that dark blue Mustang?" They would not mention his accent or how they feel about him. Their visual descriptions would be more detailed than those of an auditory or kinesthetic person.

By contrast, auditory people will tend to make finer distinctions in sound than in images or feelings. After a presentation, they will often remember the exact words that a person used, but might not be able to recall as quickly the color of the speaker's dress or how they felt during the presentation. They would be more likely to remember that John had a Southern drawl. Auditory people can be easily distracted by background noise and often prefer to work in places where they have a soothing background.

People who prefer the kinesthetic system rely heavily on their feelings. They would rather "get a feel" for something than look at a picture or hear about it. They would tell you that John is thick-skinned, but also has a level head on his shoulders. Kinesthetics generally make good counselors and negotiators, because they can be extremely sensitive to other people's feelings.

Although most people have a preferred representational system, that does not mean that our other senses or representational systems are dormant. Rather, we use the other senses to complement what our preferred representational system communicates to us. In this way we get a more complete picture of what is going on around us.

When you know what a person's modality is, which representational system that person primarily processes in, you will know one of the most important aspects of his personality—how he perceives the world around him. This is a major factor in communication. It is a common denominator in which some people are alike and others different.

A person's preferred representational system is often expressed in his choice of words. A visual person will "see the potential" of a new strategy or idea, while an auditory person will "like the way that sounds." A kinesthetic person will tell you, "I've got a good feeling about that." By paying close attention to your customers' words, you can determine how they structure their thoughts. You won't be able to tell *what* they are thinking (this is not a mind reading course!), but you can tell "how" **they are thinking.**

Recognizing a change in another person's state and noticing a specific condition of body posture, breathing, vocal qualities, or movement is called **calibration.** A person's state is constantly changing, although sometimes the change can be as subtle as an increase in the breathing rate. At other times, the change in state is obvious—a baby who was crying suddenly has a smile on its face.

Calibration is a useful tool because it requires you to step outside of yourself and direct your attention to the people around you. When you do that, you can identify consciously the physiological communication that is usually taken in and processed on an unconscious level.

For instance, can you remember when you were a child and your mother would get angry with you? Sometimes she didn't even have to say anything. She would get that look in her eye, and her lips would press tightly together, as if she didn't trust herself to speak. When she put her hands on her hips and squared her shoulders, then you knew you were in *real* trouble.

By effectively calibrating nonverbal behavior, you can begin to understand human thinking and behavior. You can do this by directing your conscious efforts to seeing, hearing, and sensing the other person's internal representations through their external manifestation of it. What you are actually doing is noting the other person's "BMIRs" (Behavioral Manifestations of Internal Representations). This is one of the most obvious Mental Access Points, or MAPS.

For instance, if I know that you are making pictures internally (visual), then I can establish deep rapport with you by entering your world using visual language. Or, if I know that you are talking to yourself internally (auditory), my rapport-building behavior will involve auditory language.

Likewise, if I am aware that your experience is centering on kinesthetic awareness, then my language will be oriented toward touch and feelings.

The following information covers five physiological clues you can observe to determine "how" your customer is thinking. Not **what** the person is thinking, but **how** the person is thinking.

1. BODY POSTURE: People often assume systematic, habitual postures when deep in thought, and talking. These postures can indicate a great deal about the sensory representational system the person is using. The following are some typical examples:

> Visual: Leaning back with head and shoulders up or rounded. Chin tends to be pointed up.

> Auditory: Body leaning forward, head cocked (as though listening), shoulders back, arms folded.

> Kinesthetic: Head and shoulders down. Body leaning slightly to the person's right.

EXERCISE—IDENTIFYING BODY POSTURE CUES— POLITICAL INTERVIEW

1. PHYSIOLOGY: Watching a political interview on television offers an excellent opportunity to practice the skill of identifying body posture cues. These programs often depict real people responding to questions subconsciously (as opposed to a political debate, where the responses are often scripted). For this exercise you will practice identifying body posture cues by watching a political interview show such as "Meet the Press" or "Politically Incorrect."

First, we recommend that you tape the show (but don't watch it while you are taping it). Then, when you are ready to begin this exercise, rewind the tape to the beginning. Now you are ready to begin the exercise. Turn off the sound so that you will be able to give your full attention to the non-verbal cues used by each person. Observe the body postures of the host and guest at the beginning of the show and describe it in the space provided below.

As the show progresses, note any changes you observe in body postures. At the conclusion of the interview, look over your notes and write down what you believe is the representational systems of the guest and the host, based on your observations of their body postures. Then watch the interview again, this time with the sound on. Did their words confirm the representational system you selected? Why or why not? The following are the cues to look for.

Visual: Leaning back with head and shoulders up or rounded. Chin tends to be pointed up.

Auditory: Body leaning forward, head cocked (as though listening), shoulders back, arms folded.

Kinesthetic: Head and shoulders down. Body leaning slightly to the person's right.

Now review the tape and notice:

Beginning body posture, interviewer
Beginning body posture, guest
Changes in body posture, interviewer
Changes in body posture, guest

What is the interviewer's preferred representational system, based on body posture?

What is the guest's preferred representational system, based on body posture?

2. ACCESSING CUES: When people are thinking and speaking, they cue or trigger certain types of sensory representations in a number of different ways, including breathing rate, "grunts and groans," facial expressions, snapping their fingers, scratching their heads, and so on. Some of these are unique to the individual and need to be noticed and "calibrated" to the particular person performing the behaviors. Many of these cues, however, are associated with particular sensory processes and can be generalized across individuals. The following are some typical examples:

Visual: High (in the chest), shallow breathing, squinting eyes, voice of higher pitch and faster tempo.

Auditory: Diaphragmatic breathing, knitted brow, fluctuating voice tone, and tempo.

Kinesthetic: Deep abdominal breathing, deep, breathy voice in lower tempo.

EXERCISE—BREATHING, TONE, AND TEMPO—SOCIAL SETTING

The easiest way to master the skill of identifying breathing patterns is practice, practice, and more practice. For this exercise you will observe the breathing, vocal tone, and tempo of people in a social setting. These may be people you have just met or people you have known a long time. As you do this, note the situation also. Can you identify their preferred representational system based on their breathing, vocal tone, and tempo?

Visual: High (in the chest), shallow breathing, squinting eyes, voice of higher pitch and faster tempo.

Auditory: Diaphragmatic breathing, knitted brow, fluctuating voice tone, and tempo.

Kinesthetic: Deep abdominal breathing, deep, breathy voice in lower tempo.

Name:

How long have you known this person?

Describe the social setting:

What is their breathing, vocal tone, and tempo?

What is their preferred representational system?

3. GESTURES: People will often touch, point to, or use gestures indicating the sensory organ they are using. Some typical examples include:

Visual: Touching or pointing to the eyes; gestures made at or above eye level.

Auditory: Pointing toward and gesturing near the ears; touching the mouth or jaw. Stroking the chin thoughtfully.

Kinesthetic: Touching the chest and stomach area; gestures made below the neck.

4. EYE MOVEMENTS: Automatic, unconscious eye movements usually accompany a particular thought process, indicating that the person is accessing one or more of the sensory representational systems. This theory has not been proven, and there is some debate as to its foundation, but to this author it appears to be useful in understanding the next level of communications and sales.

When people are thinking and talking, they move their eyes in what are known as eye-scanning patterns. These movements appear to be symptomatic of their attempts to gain access to internally stored or internally generated information in their central nervous system. This information is encoded in the speaker's mind in one or more of the representational systems. When a person "goes inside" to retrieve a memory or to create a new thought, the person "makes pictures," and/or "talks to himself/herself," and/or "has feelings and kinesthetic sensations."

With a little bit of practice, eye-scanning patterns are easily observable behavior. When you see people talking and thinking, you can notice their eyes are constantly in motion, darting back and forth, up and down, occasionally glancing at objects and people, but just as often "focused" on inner experiences. As previously mentioned, these movements are symptomatic of the way they are thinking. That is, during the moment of information retrieval, people are generally not conscious of external visual stimuli. Rather, they are concentrating on internally stored or generated images, sounds, words, and feelings.

BODY POSTURE EXERCISES

Body Posture-Workplace

Today you will observe the body postures of the various people in your workplace. As you do this, note the situation also. For instance, you might observe people in the course of a company meeting, with a client, a chance meeting in the hall, etc. See if you can determine their preferred representational system based on their body posture.

Visual: Body Posture Cues: Person leans back, with head and shoulders up or rounded. There is also a tendency to hold the chin up.

Auditory: Body Posture Cues: Person leans forward, with the head cocked (as though listening), shoulders back, and arms folded.

Kinesthetic: Body Posture Cues: Person has head and shoulders down, with the body leaning slightly to the person's right.

Name:

Job Description:

Situation:

Body Posture Cues:

Preferred Representational System:

REPRESENTATIONAL SYSTEMS

Seeing (Visual)

Eyes: These people might look up to their right or left or their eyes may appear unfocused.

Gestures: Their gestures are quick and angular, and include pointing.

Breathing & Speech: High, shallow, and quick.

Words: The words that capture their attention include: see, look, imagine, perspective, reveal.

Presentations: They prefer pictures, diagrams, and movies.

Hearing (Auditory)

Eyes: These people might look down to the left and may appear "shifty-eyed."

Gestures: Their gestures are rhythmic, touching one's face (i.e. rubbing the chin).

Breathing and Speech: Mid-chest, rhythmic.

Words: The words that capture their attention include: hear, listen, ask, tell, clicks, in-tune.

Presentations: They prefer list, summarize, quote, read.

Feeling (Kinesthetic)

Eyes: These people might look down to the right.

Gestures: Their gestures are rhythmic, touching chest.

Breathing and Speech: Deep, slow with pauses.

Words: The words that capture their attention include: feel, touch, grasp, catch on, contact.

Presentations: They prefer hands-on, do-it demonstrations, test drive.

IDENTIFYING YOUR REPRESENTATIONAL SYSTEM

For each of the following questions, think about the person, place, or object described and circle the first answer that comes into your mind. Check your responses with the assessment key provided.

1. When you think of coffee, what comes to mind first?

a. An image, e.g. a cup filled to the brim with rich, dark coffee?

b. A sound, e.g. coffee dripping into the glass carafe?

c. A touch, e.g. the warmth of the cup filled with coffee?

d. A smell, e.g. the aroma of coffee as you lift the cup to your mouth?

e. A taste, e.g. the rich taste as you take your first sip?

2. When you think back to what you did on your last birthday, what is the first thing you remember?

a. A taste, e.g. something you ate?

b. A sound, e.g. a song you heard on the radio?

c. A smell, e.g. of your environment?

d. A touch, sensation, or emotion?

e. An image or picture, e.g. some place that you went?

3. When you think about your favorite restaurant, what do you think of first?

   a. What you see, e.g. the decor or the people you are with?
   b. An emotion or touch, e.g. how you felt when you were there?
   c. Something you hear, e.g. the conversation, the music?
   d. A taste, e.g. your favorite dish?
   e. A smell, e.g. the aroma from the kitchen?

4. When you think of your childhood and the house that you grew up in, which of these come to mind first?

   a. A smell, e.g. mom baking cookies in the kitchen?
   b. A sound, e.g. conversation as the family gathered together?
   c. A taste, e.g. your mom's macaroni and cheese casserole?
   d. An emotion or touch, e.g. a feeling of security or the smooth wood banister you held onto as you came down the stairs?
   e. An image, e.g. the way the house looked after the first snowfall?

5. When you think about something humorous, do you first think about

   a. An emotion, e.g. someone tickling your feet?
   b. A sound, e.g. a joke you heard?
   c. An image, e.g. a favorite pet playing with a toy?
   d. A smell?
   e. A taste?

6. When you think about your workplace, what is the first thing that you think about?

   a. A touch or an emotion, e.g. how you feel about the work you do?
   b. A sound, e.g. of machinery or other people's voices?
   c. A taste?
   d. A picture, e.g. what you do while at work?
   e. A smell, e.g. of the environment?

7. When you think about something you do that is physically challenging, what do you think about first?

   a. A sound or conversation you have with yourself?
   b. A touch or emotion?
   c. An image or picture?
   d. A taste?
   e. A smell?

8. When you think about your closest family member (mother, father, sister, brother), what do you think about first?

   a. An image, e.g. what they looked like the last time you saw them?
   b. A smell, e.g. the favorite cologne or perfume they like to wear?
   c. A sound, e.g. their voice?
   d. An emotion, e.g. your feelings for them?
   e. A taste, e.g. a meal you shared together?

9. When you think about your favorite thing to do on the weekend, what comes into your mind first?

   a. A taste, e.g. a favorite food, such as barbecued ribs?
   b. A sound associated with doing this, e.g. the sharp crack of a base-ball bat connecting with a ball?
   c. An emotion or touch, e.g. how you feel when you think of spending your time this way?
   d. A smell from the environment, e.g. the flowers at your favorite park?
   e. An image, who you would do this with or where you would be?

10. When you think about a major disappointment in your life (e.g. a promotion or job you didn't get or a test you failed), what do you think of first?

   a. A taste?
   b. A touch, e.g. the feel of something, or emotion, e.g. what you felt when you heard the news?
   c. An image or picture, e.g. where you were?
   d. A sound, e.g. what you heard or what you said to yourself?
   e. A smell?

11. When you think about something physical that you don't like to do, e.g. taking out the garbage or weeding the garden, what comes to mind first?

   a. A touch, e.g. the feel of the weed as you pull it from the ground, or an emotion, e.g. how you feel about doing this task?
   b. A taste?
   c. A smell, e.g. the smell of the garbage as you carry it to the trash can?
   d. An image, e.g. the weeds against the dark earth?
   e. A sound, e.g. the crickets chirping near the garden or the rustle of the garbage bag?

12. When you think about taking a vacation in the Bahamas, what do you think of first?

   a. A sound, e.g. the laughter of children as they play in the surf?

      b. An image, e.g. palm trees swaying in the breeze against a brilliant blue sky?

      c. A smell, e.g. the salty air from the ocean?

      d. A taste, e.g. a cool, refreshing drink?

      e. A touch, e.g. the feel of the warm sun as you relax on the hotel deck?

Circle the letter that corresponds to your choice for each question. Add up the total number of letters circled in each representational system. The one with the highest totals are an indication of your preferred representational system. The system with the highest score is most likely your preferred representational system.

Note: You will need to focus on the representational systems that you are the weakest in. Pick the one you used the least, and for the next few days use those words as much as possible. Then go to the second weakest. This will build added flexibility in you communication. It will also allow you to cross reference much easier.

Each representational system has sensory-based words called *predicates* (verbs, adverbs, and adjectives). This is useful because sometimes your initial contact with someone will be over the phone. To determine his preferred representational system, listen to the words he selects and notice which predicates are used most often:

Visual	Auditory	Kinesthetic	Unspecified	Olfactory/ Gustatory
See	Sound	Feel	Think	Smell
Picture	Hear	Relax	Decide	Fragrant
Perceive	Discuss	Grasp	Understand	Stink
Notice	Listen	Handle	Know	Reek
Look	Talk	Stress	Develop	Aroma
Show	Call on	Pressure	Prepare	Pungent
Appear	Quiet	Smooth	Activate	Sour
Clear	Inquire	Clumsy	Manage	Sweet
Pretty	Noisy	Rough	Repeat	Acrid
Colorful	Loud	Hard	Advise	Musty

Visual	Auditory	Kinesthetic	Unspecified	Olfactory/ Gustatory
Hazy	Outspoken	Grip	Indicate	Fresh
Observe	Articulate	Warm	Consider	Bland
Flash	Scream	Rush	Motivate	Stale
Focus	Pronounce	Firm	Plan	Fresh
Bright	Remark	Euphoric	Anticipate	Bitter
Scene	Resonate	Clammy	Create	Salty
Perspective	Harmony	Touch	Generate	Nutty
Imagine	Shrill	Calm	Deduce	Delicious
View	Oral	Dull	Direct	Salivate
Vista	Whimper	Burning	Achieve	Spoiled
Horizon	Mention	Stinging	Accomplish	Sniff
Make a scene	Tongue-tied	Get the drift	Initiate	Smokey
Tunnel vision	Ring a bell	Boils down to	Conclude	Bitter pill
Plainly see	Loud and clear	Hang in there	New knowledge	Fish notion
See eye-to-eye	Idle talk	Sharp as a tack	Creative option	
Mind's eye	To tell the truth	Slipped my mind	Aware of	
Bird's eye view	Word for word	Pull some strings	Intensify	
Catch a glimpse	Rap session	Moment of panic	Incorporate	
Bright future	Unheard of	Smooth operator	Differentiate	
In light of	Call on	Get the drift	Represent	

Once you become familiar with the language of the different modalities, you can then choose words that will literally "make more sense" to the people with whom you want to develop rapport.

Now practice with a co-worker:

IDENTIFYING PREDICATES—CO-WORKER

All of us use predicates that indicate our preferred representational systems, and your co-workers are no exceptions. For today, listen to the predicates used by a co-worker with whom you spend a lot of time. Note the area which seems to be his/her preferred representational system.

Listen for the predicates from the above table. Which area do they fall under?

Visual
Auditory
Kinesthetic
Olfactory/Gustatory

Now repeat the above for:

Friend
Stranger
Selling situation where you are the customer
Family member

CHAPTER 10

The Psychology of Selling: The Ten Unconscious Laws of Persuasion

You drive down the street. You have to stop at signs, yield to oncoming traffic, and even slow to 55 m.p.h. (at least when you see a highway patrolman!). These are all simple laws. Laws created by society for the safety and betterment of the masses aren't necessarily perfect, nor are they absolute. Laws of society don't always work.

On the other hand, universal laws such as the law of gravity always work. If you drop 10,000 baseballs off the top of the Sears Tower in Chicago, the balls will all fall to the street below, probably doing major damage. None of the balls will rise toward the atmosphere as you drop them from the Sears Tower. These are universal laws that never change.

If you try to break a universal law, normally you won't get a second chance to make things right! Legislated laws are different. If you follow them, you probably will live longer and pay fewer traffic tickets. The laws of persuasion aren't quite like the laws of society or the laws of the universe. In fact, most people aren't even aware of the laws of persuasion. They simply tend to act in accordance with the laws at a completely unconscious level.

There are major prices to pay when the laws of persuasion are broken. The problem is that most people aren't aware of the laws in the first place. If people unconsciously follow the rules, they will be happier and communicate well with others. If people don't follow the rules, they will run into lots of problems, have broken relationships, receive less income, be more readily downsized in corporations that are cutting back, and . . . well, you get the idea.

There is nothing you do that is more important than communication with others. There are very specific laws that govern not only the communication process but also the sales process. Sometimes when you drive past the highway patrolman at 75 m.p.h. you don't get a ticket. Sometimes you don't yield to oncoming traffic and you don't get in a car accident. Every now and then you run the stop sign and you don't hit a pedestrian.

The laws exist, though, and when they are followed they tend to work in the favor of the law-abiding citizens. When they are broken, the chances that something will go wrong are dramatically increased. The same is true for the laws of persuasion.

How can there be laws of selling? How can something like sales or communication have laws?

As our species has evolved over millions of years, we have discovered that we tend to need the cooperation of others to succeed. Gaining the cooperation and compliance of other people is absolutely critical to the persuasion process and the continuance of society as we know it.

The remainder of this chapter will deal with the Ten Unconscious Laws of Persuasion. Following each of these laws is important in gaining compliance from others. In most situations on most days of your sales career, if you follow each law you will find selling to be a fairly simple experience. What's better? If you utilize these ten laws in all of your communication, you will find that your sales career is fun, sometimes challenging, and always rewarding.

Law of Reciprocity: When someone gives you something of perceived value, you immediately respond with the desire to give something back.

It's December 24 and the mail has just arrived. You open a Christmas card from someone you had taken off of your Christmas list! This is a crisis! "Honey, are there any more Christmas cards left?"

"Yeah, in the drawer."

"Thank God."

You go to the drawer and, sure enough, there is a card there but there are no envelopes to fit the card. You search and search, finally deciding to use an envelope that isn't quite large enough. You have to use something!

You sign the card and yes, you personalize it! You write something special just for the sender! You stuff the card into the envelope that is still too small. You slide in a picture of the family and you even find a leftover "family newsletter" that tells everyone what your family has been up to all year.

"I'll be back in a while," you announce. "I have to go to the post office and mail this letter."

Why do you have to go to the post office?

You have to go because the letter must have a postmark before Christmas! December 24 will show that you cared. December 26 will show that these people were an afterthought in your mind, not worthy of sending a card before Christmas. You race off to the post office . . . and you have just discovered the power of reciprocity.

You were taught to share your toys and your snacks and your space and your time with all those around you. You were scolded when you were selfish and you were rewarded with kind smiles and pats on the head when you shared. The law of reciprocity was instilled at a very early age.

The world's greatest salespeople and marketing mavens give something to their customers, and I don't mean a business card.

✓ Have you ever received a bar of soap in the mail?
✓ Have you ever received a box of cereal in the mail?
✓ Have you ever received return address labels from a charity in the mail?
✓ Have you ever received a handful of greeting cards from a charity in the mail?
✓ Have you ever received a sample-size shampoo bottle in the mail?

These are all examples of what we call "inducing reciprocity." The practice is very simple, yet absolutely brilliant. If your product is top quality and it is something that everyone can use, send everyone a small sample of it and they will be more likely to buy it the next time they go to the store. There are two reasons:

1) We will recognize it as something we have used. The brain picks up on what is familiar. (Have you ever noticed how many cars there are like yours on the road? What happened to all the rest?!)

2) Reciprocity has been induced when someone gives you something and you give them something back. Reciprocity has also been induced when someone gives you something and you feel compelled to give something back. Kellogg's was nice enough to send us their free box of cereal

and because it tasted good we should at least buy their cereal this one time. We return the favor.

Reciprocity, based on scientific research, appears to be the single most powerful law of selling persuasion there is, but is there a problem?

✓ If you sell life insurance, you can't give away $10,000 of free coverage.
✓ If you sell real estate, you can't give away bathrooms.
✓ If you sell speaking services, you can't give away free speeches.
✓ If you are a stockbroker, you can't give away 100 shares of Microsoft.

What do you do if you don't have sample-size products and services? How do you take advantage of this powerful law of share and share alike?

> *Give away something of perceived value to someone and others will feel compelled to do likewise.*

You do not have to give away free samples to utilize reciprocity. You MUST give away something that has perceived value. My favorite method of inducing reciprocity is taking someone to lunch or sharing a valuable tip related to building their business or income in some way. (I like these approaches because they are measurable and the person knows that you really helped them when they follow through on your suggestion.)

Taking someone to lunch is usually an inexpensive way to induce reciprocity, and you have the added benefit of meeting one of your customer's sixteen basic desires (his desire to eat). Sharing helpful secrets that are truly specialized knowledge is also an elegant way to induce reciprocity. One simple idea can often help someone earn hundreds or thousands of dollars per year more in income.

Can I share a secret with you?

I keep some of my money in the Strong Funds Money Market account. It pays a lot more interest than a bank does and the money is safe. You can write checks on your account, just like a checking account, and if you just knew that secret to make more money, I'd be happy that I shared that with you.

Can I share another secret with you? The Strong Advantage Fund is even better! It pays about 1 to 3 percent more interest than the Strong Money Market Fund, and you can write checks on that account, too. If you only took $10,000 out of the bank or C.D. and put it into the Strong Advantage Fund, you would earn 2 to 3 percent more per year on that money than you do in the bank or C.D.

Now, granted that only comes to about $300 per year, but how many free copies of this book can you give away to your friends in return for that one $300 gift? How will your friends feel about you when you give them a gift that gives them the most cutting-edge selling power ever put into one book?

Here are a few creative ideas for salespeople to use as inexpensive giveaway items to your prospects.

Life insurance and financial product salespeople: Give away a report that lists all of the top performing investments for the last three years. (Even if it contains information that is positive about your competitors!) Give away a handy chart that people can place on the refrigerator that shows the ten questions to ask telemarketers to determine the legitimacy of investment opportunities and charitable donations.

Real estate salespeople: Estimate the amount of the loan the customer will take out and run several amortization tables showing how small extra payments each month will cut years off the life of the loan, save the customer tens of thousands of dollars, and create long-term financial freedom. If the customer is already putting every penny toward the thirty-year mortgage, give away a handy booklet that shows how to do simple maintenance on the house, how to find good service people to work on the home in the future, and also tips on keeping the home in top-dollar condition should they decide to sell.

Automobile salespeople: If you sell a great car, give away a recent *Consumer Reports* article to all of your prospects comparing your car with others in its class. If you sell a car that is a good car, but not listed as one of the best, give away a list of the top ten strategies to keep the car running cheaply and its resale value high.

The message to you is that everyone can give something away with nothing expected in return. It is a scientific fact that reciprocity is effective. The key is that what you give away must have perceived value on the part of the customer. Traditional promotional items such as personalized pens and datebooks may be useful or they may not be. You can test them to see if they assist in making sales. It doesn't matter what your giveaway actually costs you. What matters is the value the customer places on the item, report, or product.

Law of Time: Changing someone's time perspective helps them to make different decisions. When people change their time perspective, they change how they feel about something and the decisions they make in regard to it.

Time is the subtle equalizer in life. No matter how rich or poor you are, time is the one commodity that is the same for everyone. Everyone has this moment of experience only. What happens in this moment is normally not a matter of conscious choice or thought.

Quite often when you walk into a customer's office or you contact them in some other way, they will immediately equate you, at the unconscious level, with all of the other salespeople they have ever met. In all probability they have more negative experiences than positive experiences with salespeople.

Two things need to happen. You must distinguish yourself from all the other salespeople they've known, and you need to move their time filter from the past to the present or future. People have emotional responses that are attached to various stimuli. You are a stimulus. You trigger positive and negative experiences in all of your customers' minds whether or not each customer knows it.

What's more interesting is that this response isn't necessarily linked to YOU! Most people see you as a SALESMAN and they have a negative emotional response to ALL salespeople. Therefore, in most cases, you are a BAD SALESMAN when you walk in the door. You haven't opened your mouth or asked any questions and you are already a BAD SALESMAN. Ready for more?

When you walk out the door, your customer is going to think differently of you, but by the next time you talk with your customer his brain will be back in BAD SALESMAN mode for two reasons. First, he will confront many other IDIOTS posing as salespeople between now and then. Second, his past emotional memories are not going to be wiped away by a fun one-hour meeting with you!

Therefore you must become an expert at altering time. You MUST become a master of moving people through time so that they are not effected by their past programming and emotions. You must be able to get them to look at your product and service from a completely different perspective! And you can.

Time plays a big role in people's decision-making process. There are three fundamental ways that people experience time: past, present, and future.

Past: Some people live in the past or use the past as their guidepost for all decisions they will make in the present and future. These people are often cynical and depressed. They also make fewer bad decisions than other people. Their guard is up and they will make fewer errors because of this. They will also miss out on opportunities because of their experiences. You will need to remember this!

✓ I was ripped off once while doing this.
✓ I ate at a place like this once and it was terrible.
✓ I got conned the last time I bought a car.
✓ I never get a good deal.
✓ The stock market always goes down when I invest.

These are all common experiences for people who process all information through "filters" of the past.

Present: Some people live in the present moment. These people tend to have much less stress and tend to give little thought to the past or future. They tend to be lousy planners and seek instant gratification. Usually their credit cards are maxed out because they have sacrificed a future they cannot see for the pleasure of the moment. They think like this:

✓ I know it's right when I feel it.
✓ I do what feels good.
✓ I just wanted to have fun.
✓ It looks fun so I'm going to do it.
✓ I never thought I'd get pregnant.
✓ Who'd have thought I'd lose all my money?

Future: Some people filter most of their thoughts by the future. They tend to live in the future, delay instant gratification, and have determined that the past, for better or worse, isn't that relevant for them.

People who live in the future are constantly planning, organizing, preparing, and sacrificing. They sacrifice the moment for a brighter tomorrow. They think like this:

✓ I could buy a car now but that money is better off invested.
✓ I'll wait for retirement.
✓ I could buy that now but I'd like to watch that money build up over time.
✓ I better not do that because I might get pregnant.

Once you know how a person generally filters their information, you can have them look at different events in the past, present, or future, OR you can change the perspective from which they are looking.

You can change someone's time perspective with some linguistic maneuvers that rival the martial arts.

To get your customer out of the mistakes of the past, get him to see things from a future perspective.

Customer: "Look what happened to the market this last year. It went to hell. Dropped by 50 percent. Why would I want to invest in your mutual funds?"

Salesperson: "You might *not* want to. But the next time the market doubles or triples, wouldn't you want just a little piece of that for your future?"

Customer: "My experience is that I listen to a salesperson and I get ripped off."

Salesperson: "When you go out 10 years into the future and look back, what do you do right to correct that?"

Customer: "Last time I bought a big Yellow Page ad I lost my butt."

Salesperson: "Understand. If we can create an ad that will pull in the future will you be up for that?"

Customer: "I tried hypnosis before and it doesn't work."

Salesperson: "So you had someone who didn't know what they were doing. If you were to work with someone who was adept at his art that knew how to help you, would you be willing to do that?"

Law of Contrast: When two things, people, or places that are

relatively different from each other are placed near to each other in time, space, or thought, we will see them as more different, and it is easier to distinguish which one we want most.

There is a wonderful piece of television history from the archives of "The Tonight Show" with Johnny Carson. One night, Johnny had the number one Girl Scout cookie salesman in the country on. He asked her the secret of her success.

She said, "I just went to everyone's house and said, 'Can I have a $30,000 donation for the Girl Scouts?' When they said 'no,' I said, 'Would you at least buy a box of Girl Scout cookies?'"

The audience couldn't stop laughing and neither could Johnny. The little girl had mastered the contrast principle, at age eight.

Have you ever walked through a grocery store and watched people, especially women, take two competing products and put one of them in each hand then look at them side by side, literally weighing which one they should buy? The principle that guides people in this product choice is called the Law of Contrast.

Psychological studies have shown that salespeople can use the Law of Contrast in a very specific and pre-designed fashion. If you can show your expensive product or service first, then show what you would like to sell (what you think creates the best win/win with your customer) second, the customer is very likely to purchase the second item.

When you were a child you would go into a store with one of your parents and as Mom shopped, so did you. You may have picked up two or three items to propose to your mother for possible purchase. Time after time your mom programmed into you either one of two themes:

1) It's too expensive, you can't have either of them.

2) You can have the little (cheapest) one.

You soon learned that the best method of selling Mom was to note how little the item cost. "Mom, it's only a dollar," your voice would resonate in a pleading fashion. With the proper eye contact and pitiful face, the strategy regularly worked.

The Law Of Contrast doesn't say that you will always sell the least expensive of two products. It does say that if you put two products or services close together in space, in time, or in a person's mind, the person will begin to clearly see the differences, and their programming will help them choose "which" instead of "whether or not to."

Price is the most common programming installed into children, but there definitely are many parents who programmed the theme "it's junk, don't buy garbage" into their children. These adult customers now buy higher-quality items when possible. The Law of Contrast acts within each of us to help us choose which of a number of items to buy.

> *Show your customer the product you believe is their best option and/or least expensive last. The customer is compelled to own something and normally will take the last, or the least expensive item if it is shown last.*

Real estate salespeople: Show your client a home that they will dislike first, then show them a home that meets all of their buying criteria second. People tend to buy what they are shown or experience second.

Financial product salespeople: Tell your client you have two products to show her. The best financial fit for your client is to own a diversified portfolio of mutual funds. You first show her an expensive annuity product and then follow with a brief explanation of another option, that of owning mutual funds that require a smaller investment and offer an easier "out" should she need her money. The better product and lower price both come second in this case, creating a compelling unconscious urge to invest in the funds.

Clothing salespeople: Once the customer has agreed to buy the suit or dress, present a tie, a scarf, a new pair of shoes, or a nice necklace as an absolute must. If the customer has purchased a $400 suit, isn't a $37 tie a necessary purchase?

Electronics salespeople: Your customer has said yes to the computer. Now you can show him the extended service plan, a piece of useful or fun software, or an extra battery for emergencies. These $100 items contrast nicely to the $2,000 he just spent on the computer and almost seem irrelevant in contrast.

> *Let your prospect buy one of several necessary items first, then let them buy the add-ons or accessories second. In contrast to the large investment, they seem small and a good value for the price.*

A useful rule to remember in any sales situation is that when someone mentions that your product or service is "too expensive" or "costs too much," you respond with a gentle, "Compared to what?" "Compared to what" is a question that puts your clients' thoughts into perspective and allows them to re-think their apparent "no" response. If your client was heading toward a "no" response, "compared to what" may often bring him back to the "yes" response.

Law of Friends: *When someone asks you to do something and you perceive that the person has your best interests in mind, and/or you would like him/her to have your best interests in mind, you are strongly motivated to fulfill the request.*

How many times have you experienced someone knocking on your front door and asking you to donate money for some cause? Compare the number of times you donated to the cause when you knew the person who asked you to donate, in contrast to how often you donated when you didn't know the person who asked you to donate.

If you are like most people, you donated more often when your neighbor came to the door asking you to donate. You felt empathy for the person you know who is possibly being put "out" by this charitable requesting. The people who solicited from you received donations less regularly because they didn't have that same empathy or trust. We tend to say "yes" when we know someone or perceive he is our friend.

In a similar context, most people would never go to a meeting for multi-level marketing if their friends or acquaintances didn't ask them to look at this business opportunity. The greatest strategy a multi-level marketing corporation can utilize is the "listing of friends and family" strategy as the first contacts in the MLMer's early days in his new business. These friends and family are the most likely to actually go to a meeting.

As salespeople develop relationships with their customers, they become friends. Friendships grow and become special, and future sales are all but assured with the ongoing relationship.

Help people see you as their friend and someone who cares about them, and you will dramatically increase the probability of their compliance.

An extremely powerful persuasion tool that few salespeople ever use is that of **pointing out the negative aspects of your products and services.** Psychological research backs up our assertion. One of the most effective ways to influence people is to argue against your own point of view or argue against your own self-interest so that it appears that you are being unbiased in your proposals.

One group of researchers had a heroin addict tell people that there should be stricter courts and more severe sentences. The researchers found the heroin addict to be more credible than others presenting similar points of view. This was one of the few instances in which people believed someone who was not perceived as physically attractive.

When the message conflicts with the expectations of your buyer, you'll be perceived as more serious. This is a powerful Mind Access Point. When you utilize it with a careful skill, you will regularly bring out any minor negative aspects of your products and services.

Be eager to point out any negative aspects of your proposal. This accomplishes two important things. First, it makes you appear far more trustworthy, and second, it allows your customer to be set at ease because you are doing his job of finding the drawbacks of the proposal.

Financial product salespeople: Tell your customer a story of how you recently helped your family members with their finances in the same manner that you are going to help your customer. When they understand that they are going to be treated exactly like family, they perceive you also have their best interests in mind.

Real estate salespeople: Share with your customer why you would NOT buy a specific house. If it is clear that your customer is NOT interested in the house, and you don't like it either, explain why this house is not something you would recommend your friends buy and then explain in detail why. This strengthens the bond between you and your clients.

Law of Expectancy: When someone you respect and/or believe in expects you to perform a task or produce a certain result, you will tend to fulfill his expectation whether positive or negative.

There is a famous study from the 1970s by psychologist Dr. Rosenthal that reveals that the expectation of one person can radically alter, both positively and negatively, the actual results of how people will perform. The study divided students into what teachers were told were bright and dull groups. The students were told nothing. The group that was made up of supposed high-IQ students performed at an average of an "A" level after eight months.

The group that was made up of supposed low-IQ students performed at an average of a "D" level after eight months in their school work. In reality, there was no difference in the IQs of the students. They were randomly divided into the groups, and the only variable in the study, which was immediately discontinued, was the expectation of the teachers involved.

The behaviors you expect of yourself and others are more likely to be manifested in reality. If you believe that your customer will most certainly buy from you, they probably will.

In psychology, the placebo effect is a well-documented and scientifically measurable response on the part of the body to be healthier (or in the case of a nocebo, to be sicker) based upon expectancy, suggestion, and belief. In the Korean War, there were thousands of casualties and not enough morphine to relieve the pain of the suffering soldiers. Medics and doctors were forced to give sugar pills with the suggestion that the soldiers would shortly be out of pain. Approximately 25 percent of all soldiers taking the placebo had their severe pain relieved.

This same level of expectancy is necessary as a belief in yourself about your abilities to be successful and also about your ability to win your customers to your products and services.

Exercise: How can you utilize the Law of Expectancy when selling your products or services?

Law of Association: We tend to like products, services, or ideas that are endorsed by people we like or respect.

Tell me, what is it that Michael Jordan knows about underwear that I don't? Didn't Michael sign a $40,000,000 deal with Calvin Klein to do a few commercials about underwear? Now, it's my opinion that I know as much about underwear as Michael Jordan, and I would have shot those commercials for HALF what he got!

BUT Kevin Hogan is a name known in the field of selling. Michael Jordan is a name known throughout the world. Michael Jordan was really paid two cents for every person on earth that knew his name. If I were paid two cents for every person that knew my name, I'd get paid about $7,000. That is why Michael Jordan got paid $40,000,000.

Calvin Klein paid $40,000,000 to link one of the world's most loved and best known people to its product. Underwear. That is what the law of association is all about.

When your products and your services are linked to credible, likable, positive-image people, your customer will tend to like the products or services.

For years authors have known that the best way to sell a book is to get people to write favorable backmatter and frontmatter for the book. This adds credibility to the book because we respect the person who wrote the quotes.

The power of a testimonial or of someone famous using your products or services can be the key that turns the locks of the doors of the unconscious mind. If you cannot have the famous endorse your products or service, ask other people who are using your service to write you a short letter testifying to the fact that your product or service has helped them change their life or their business or made some significant difference that they didn't have before.

The testimonial speaks volumes about you so you don't have to.

> *Allow people to see you and your products or services linked to the respected, the famous, or the experienced, and your probability of the "yes" response is heightened dramatically.*

Exercise: How can you utilize the Law of Association in selling your products and services?

Law of Consistency: When an individual announces in writing (or verbally, to a lesser degree) that he is taking a position on any issue or point of view, he will strongly tend to defend that belief regardless of its accuracy even in the face of overwhelming evidence to the contrary.

Your customers' past decisions and public proclamations dramatically influence their beliefs and attitudes. Once a person has publicly said, "I'll never X," they normally never do. Many people make public statements that they have not thought out, that often turn into beliefs and permanent attitudes. The reason is simple. We are taught that our word is our bond. When we say something, you can count on us.

Former President Bill Clinton has been on both sides of this law. In 1994 his continual changing of his publicly stated positions cost his party House and Senate seats, creating a Republican majority in both houses of Congress for the first time in decades. In 1998 his adamant stand against talking about the Monica Lewinsky affair helped him build the highest popularity rating by a president in years. When he consistently stated, "I'm going to just do my job," the country began to believe in Bill Clinton again and stood behind him as their president.

Did you know that 70 percent of all people are the same religion they were when they were raised as children? This is the law of consistency in real life in action! The following table will illustrate the power of various religious sects to hold members over a lifetime. Maintaining consistency is at the core of loyalty.

PERCENT OF CURRENT MEMBERS RAISED IN SAME FAITH

Source: Adapted from American Demographics Research

Fundamentalists	52%
Southern Baptists	86%
Misc. Protestants	40%
Other Baptists	77%
Lutherans	75%
Methodists	72%
Inter/non-denom.	27%
Liberals	49%
Presbyterians	59%
Episcopalians	54%
Catholics	89%
Jewish	83%
All Religions	70%

Americans respect consistency and predictability.

A recent research study had subjects make decisions among various choices.

Group A was asked to "remember their decision."

Group B was asked to "write their decisions on a magic slate and then pull the sheet up, 'erasing' their decision."

Group C was asked to write their decisions on paper with ink and hand them in to the researchers.

Which group stuck with their decisions? Right. Group C stuck with their decisions over three-fourths of the time. Group B kept their decisions half the time and Group A tended to change their minds. The lesson is to get your client to write things down as he participates in the sales process. He could write down anything from goals for the coming year to what he would really like in a car, a house, a stock portfolio, or a vacation time-share package. The key is to get a pen in the customer's hand and have him write!

> *Never ask a question that will pin the customer down to a permanent "no" response.*

Exercise: How can you utilize the Law of Consistency in selling your products and services?

Law of Scarcity: When a person perceives that something he might want is limited in quantity, he believes the value of what he might want to be greater than if it were available in abundance.

What the public finds valuable never ceases to amaze us. Remember the Christmas season of 1996? This was when advertisers promoted Tickle Me Elmo dolls to children and then, to drive the price up, simply refused to produce the dolls in quantity. The prices of the dolls grew to outrageous levels. Stores sold out of the dolls after creating huge demand and over-pricing them. Within weeks, the *Minneapolis Star-Tribune* printed six or seven columns of classified ads of people offering to sell their Tickle Me Elmo's for anywhere from $300 to $695! Imagine this: A child goes into the store when the dolls first come out and Mom buys her child a doll for $30. Eventually the media promotes these dolls to the point where stores and shopping centers are flooded with people trying to find Tickle Me Elmos. Many were forced to settle for other products in the store for their children's Christmas presents. The marketing campaign was a bonanza for Tickle Me Elmo, radio station giveaways, and retailers, and it was all induced by intentional marketing scarcity.

Which of the following should you use as an indication of scarcity?

1. Act now!
2. Limited Supplies!
3. One Day Only!

All of those are common themes in advertising and marketing. Which works best? "Act now" is third most effective. "One Day Only!" is an effective theme but doesn't even compare to "Limited Supplies." If you can show that there are only a few of your products or services available, that is going to increase your product's perceived value!

The limited-supply frame almost always goes back to your client's childhood. There were one or two pieces of cake left, and when your customer was four years old, he knew that if someone else got that piece of cake there would be none for her. It was imperative to attempt to get one of the last pieces of cake. Scarcity was installed at an early age and has been reinforced throughout our adult life. The strings wound into scarcity are very powerful indeed, and you should begin to devise methods to use the principle of scarcity in your daily sales meetings.

> *Your customer must be made aware that something about you or your services or your product is scarce. (Scarcity can include quantity of product, the time you have to spend with someone, or a number of specific products at a special low price.)*

Real estate salespeople: In the state of Minnesota in the year 2001, many homes are selling in literally days. It is completely ethical to tell your clients that "The average house in Minnesota is selling in eleven days. If you want this house, put an offer on paper, now."

Automobile salespeople: There are only three cars like this on the lot. I suspect they will sell out by Monday. That doesn't mean you can't get a car like this again, but it does mean you could wait weeks or months to get a factory-delivered car with all of these options. It's up to you.

Financial product salespeople: You can never predict the future, but what happens if this January is like most Januarys and the market goes up 4 percent while you are deciding whether this is the time to open your IRA?

> *What is it that your customer loses if he doesn't buy from you? That is your scarcity point.*

Law of Conformity: Most people tend to agree to proposals, products, or services that will be perceived as acceptable by the majority of people or a majority of the individual's peer groups.

Everyone wants to be accepted. "What will people think" is something that we all think about at the unconscious level. We all want to be liked, and we all want people to look at what we buy and do with respect and admiration. When your customer thinks about how his peers will view his purchase, the sale can be made or broken without going any further. *Therefore it is important to assure your customer, at the unconscious level, that his buying your product and service is an outstanding idea.*

Conformity is related to consistency in some ways. Conformity is being consistent with your peer group's acceptance. Consistency is being perceived as predictable and ethical within your peer group and even within yourself.

Non-conformists and "rebels" even tend to conform to their groups that are known to be rebellious against society. Consider that Greenpeace activists are very much non-conformists in the eyes of the public, but among their own group they conform to the non-conformist standard.

Jehovah's Witnesses and Latter Day Saints are both Christian sects who are considered apart from Christianity by other denominations. They are non-conformists and are proud and honored to be. However, within their own groups, they have clear-cut and definite standards that must be conformed to. Your understanding of your customer's conforming standards can make or break your sales.

> *Allow your client to see his future after purchasing your product and services as one where his peers and family not only approve but are excited about his purchase.*

"Imagine how your wife will respond when she sees that you have gone out and bought her and really your whole family a brand new car."

"Imagine how your husband will feel when you show him that you took the initiative to invest in your retirement so his life will be easier . . . essentially not having to work until he is seventy-seven."

Law of Power: People have power over other people to the degree that they are perceived as having greater authority, strength, or expertise in contrast to others.

Power comes with authority and charisma. Power is the ability to change. Power is both real and a perception. Your customers will perceive you as more powerful if you act with confidence but not conceit, comfort but not disregard, and certainty but not knowing it all. Power is something that exists within you and must be brought out. Once people perceive you as competent, caring, knowledgeable, confident, and certain, then their confidence level in you goes up.

If you attempt to use power *over* other people, instead of *with* other people, then you will lose sales and lose friends. Power with people is perceived by most as strength and is often called "charisma." Power over others is normally resented and people are less likely to conform if they think you are trying to control them.

One recent study that discussed power and authority revealed that 95 percent of all nurses were willing to dispense drugs to patients, after being authorized by physicians, that they knew would indeed likely kill the patient. That's power.

> *When you are selling a product, it is assumed you are the expert. If you know everything there is to know about your product, you become the go-to guy. Subtly make sure your customer knows you are the best or among the best in your company. People like to deal with the guy at the top.*

Auto mechanics may not have a high recognition value for power, but when your car breaks down, they become the most powerful people in the world, don't they? They have the solution to your problem. If they made the solution appear easy they would have no power. The simple fact that most people are ignorant of how to utilize power is why most salespeople are perceived as beggars or nuisances.

Exercise: What are three subtle ways you can let your customer know you are among the top salespeople as far as knowledge, customer service, and/or sales in the company? How can you show your customer that you are not "just another salesman?"

CHAPTER 11

The Secret Ingredients of Selling

"It's only words . . ."

The following conversation happened so often to all of us in child-hood that we all recognize it immediately before coming to the "punch line."

Child: "Mom can I go to the neighbors'?"
Mom: "No, Honey."
Child: "C'mon, Mom, can I go to the neighbors' to play?"
Mom: "I said NO."
Child: "But why?"
Mom: **"Because** I said so."

The word *"because"* is the first "Word MAP" you can use every day with every customer you meet. This simple word is the perfect example of a MAP (a stimulus/response mechanism) that was installed early in your customer's life. Early in childhood, the word "because" was condi-tioned as the absolute answer and reason for questions that we asked Mom and Dad. Today we respond the same way to the word "because" as we did when we were children. "Because" is typical of a MAP easily entered. Like magic, you utter the word and people comply.

> *Use the word "because" as part of your verbal reasoning for almost any question asked of you and you will find your customers begging to comply with your requests.*

Does this sound too amazing to be true? Is unconscious communication really this simple? Does just uttering the word "because" in a sentence really cause an instant reaction for compliance in your customers? What evidence exists for such a claim?

Dr. Ellen Langer, a Harvard social psychologist and editor of *Psychology Today* magazine, wanted to know the answer as well. In a study where Dr. Langer was considering the impact of asking for "favors," she contrasted the use of inquiries with the word "because" (a reason for having something done) and without the word "because." The study, which is now almost a part of persuasion folklore, went like this:

People were waiting in line to use a copy machine in the school library. Someone would ask one of three questions.

(A) Excuse me, I have five pages. May I use the Xerox machine because I have to make some copies.

(B) Excuse me, I have five pages. May I use the Xerox machine because I'm in a rush.

(C) Excuse me, I have five pages. May I use the Xerox machine?

Before going any further, take a moment and imagine the scenarios and predict what the results were.

Ready?

When option (C) was used an amazing 60 percent of people agreed to let the person make copies, just for asking.

When option (B) was used an astounding 94 percent of people agreed to let the person make the copies.

Finally, option (A), which was used as a control to contrast with option (B), found that 93 percent of the people complied with the requests.

At least one and maybe two MAPs are immediately displayed in this simple but brilliant study:

> *Asking for a favor can be an effective tool in gaining compliance.*

The second point is to remember that the word "because" is a MAP. It is a stimulus-response mechanism in most people.

> *Use the word "because" in response to "why?" questions because it triggers compliance at over 50 percent the normal response rate in many situations.*

There are a number of words and phrases that are MAPs that are easy to enter. You have learned how to utilize words that are MAPs earlier in this book. You can easily understand how simply and innocently word-strings are programmed into our thinking.

In *The Psychology of Persuasion*, I wrote about seven of the most powerful words in the English language and how to use them in communication. Through some prodding from my partner we have decided to publish the complete master list of magic words and terms. These are the words we use when we sell and write. In the next few pages you will find the magical building blocks of selling: the words you use.

First, we have listed the magic words of selling. These are 150 of the most attention-commanding terms in the English language. When you prepare your message for your customers, make sure that these words are peppered throughout! These words seem to have equal effectiveness in interpersonal communication and in text.

Later in the chapter you will read phrases and sentences that have a proven track record of selling in face-to-face communication. Begin practicing today so you develop the nuts and bolts skills of selling. Nothing you read here can take the place of actually writing out sentences and headlines for your services. Nothing you read here can take the place of adopting these words into your vocabulary.

Acclaimed	Boosts	Deserve	Experience (d)
Advancement	Breakthrough	Discount	Expert
Amazing	Challenge	Discover	Extraordinary
Announcing	Change	Discovery	Fast
Appealing	Choice	Distinguished	Free
At last	Classic	Easy (ily)	Fresh
Attention	Comfortable	Effective	Fun
Authentic	Compare	Energy	Guarantee
Aware	Complete	Exceptional	Heal
Bargain	Convenient	Exciting	Help
Because	Delivers	Exclusive	Honest

How to	Now	Reliable	Stimulating
Hurry	Offer	Relief (ve)	Striking
Imagine	Original	Remarkable	Stylish
Important	Overcome	Research	Superior
Improved	Peace of mind	Results	Sure-fire
Indispensable	Perfect	Risk free	Surprising
Incredible	Please	Revolutionary	Thank you
Informative	Pleasure	Romantic	Timely
Instantly	Plus	Safety	The truth about
Intimate	Popular	Sale	Traditional
Introducing	Power (ful)	Satisfaction	Trusted
Irresistible	Practical	Save	Ultimate
Last chance	Prevents	Scientific	Unlimited
Love	Price reduction	Secret	Unusual
Luxurious	Profitable	Security	Useful
Magic	Promise	Sensational	Valuable
Miracle	Proven	Service	Wanted
Money	Quickly	Simplifies	Warning
Money-making	Realize	Soothe	You
Money-saving	Recommended	Special offer	Yours
Natural (ly)	Refreshing	Status	
New	Relax	Stop	

Exercise: Create at least twenty-five sentences using this instruction: Utilize two or more of the magic words in sentences that pertain to your product or service. Create several possible uses for the magic words and weave them into phrases and sentences that will help you sell. Reading this book will help you sell. Utilizing the tools in this book will ensure you success.

(Example: This scientifically **proven** program includes three **easy**-to-use techniques that will **change** your life forever.)

Hypnotic Language Patterns

People who study hypnosis learn that there are many ways to get a person into a specific frame of mind and then get them to think about anything the hypnotist desires. Our goal in hypnosis is to get people to imagine something, or a specific outcome. Imagining something is often the first step to getting it, or avoiding it. In the case of selling, we want people to focus their attention on our products and services. Then we want them to tell us how they will go about buying our products and services.

People will not give you these secret codes to their thinking just because you ask, however. You need to use scientifically proven techniques in a very artful manner. There are specific words and phrases that yield amazing results in gaining compliance. Below are some of the phrases that have been shown to lead a person to a conclusion that is all but predetermined.

You will notice that the hypnotic language patterns are in bold face, and we assume that whatever follows the pattern will be acted upon. In the first example, the hypnotic command is to **"buy this car . . . that's your decision."** It follows the hypnotic sentence fragment **"I wouldn't tell you to . . ."**

All of the commands are written in regular type below and the hypnotic language is in bold. A command is the specific action we want the customer to take. Most of these patterns are not what would be considered "good English" or "grammatically correct." **However, these patterns are very powerful, and we recommend caution when using them. Some brief but important comments follow in parentheses.**

I wouldn't tell you to buy this car. That's your decision.

I wouldn't tell you to invest more money in stocks. You need to figure that out on your own.

(I wouldn't tell you, but notice that the command is still coming!)

How do you go about deciding to buy a new car?

How do you go about deciding how much you are going to invest?

When you ask how they go about deciding, you learn specifically how they decide and then they give you the specific instructions on how to sell them!

You might want to . . . now; join the club for only one year then renew.

You might want to . . . now; buy this beautiful or car.

(You don't **have** to; you just might!)

What is it that helps you know whether you should buy an X or a Y?

What is it that helps you know whether you want to upgrade **now** or wait awhile?

(Again, you are really asking for their specific decision strategy.)

You don't have to decide **now.**

You don't have to invest in several funds; one or two is just fine.

("I will if I want to!")

Why is it that some people just don't see the value of owning a quality car?

Why is it that some people just see greatness and it eludes others?

(Not you, Mr. Customer, but some people . . .)

I don't know if signing up **now** is what you want to do.

I don't know if deciding **now** is absolutely necessary so you don't lose out.

(Actually I do know but I'm being very gentle.)

Would you like to see a bigger house?

Would you like to see this in blue?

Would you like to see our customer service people call you regularly?

(You are asking for specific features and benefits that they might want . . . or not.)

Some people are investing a great deal of money right **now.**

Some people are snapping up houses like they are going out of style.

(Some people . . . are your customers.)

If you could have a perfect car, what would it be like?

If you could have the perfect speaker for your function, what would he be like?

"If you could have . . ." = **"imagine"**

It goes straight to the unconscious mind and goes to work like a mind virus.

If you could choose any mutual fund, what qualities would you want it to have?

If you could choose a better insurance company, what would be most important to you?

(He can choose and his brain will tell him so now!)

Have you ever seen a truly amazing sales trainer?

Have you ever seen a speaker that motivates the day AFTER they leave?

(Again, this is the same as "imagine." It's a no-pressure question that darts through the brain at high speeds causing a "yes, I want it" response.)

Would you be surprised if I told you that most people aren't as astute as you are?

Would you be surprised if I told you that this car gets thirty miles per gallon?

("Would you be surprised if I told you" implies you have the shocking truth.)

Imagine what would happen if your portfolio averaged 12 percent per year!

Imagine what would happen if you lived in a house that you could really be proud of!

(Once again, we have "imagine" lighting up the brain like a Christmas tree.)

Are you interested in making more money short term or long term?

Are you interested in making the online experience for your customers easy and fun?

(He knows he should be interested, and now he has to say yes or pick which is best for him.)

If I could show you a way to make more money, **would you** hire our firm?

If I could show you a way to literally look ten years younger, would you do it?

(This is a perfect pre-closing question. You wouldn't ask it unless you COULD show him, so now you get the "yes" response and then you close after you show him.)

What would it be like if you had an extra $25,000 per year in income?

What would it be like if you had a body that people would be magnetized to?

(Imagine that . . .)

You may not know that this is going to be fun.

You may not know that we are going to be working together for a long time!

(He'll know right after you say, "You may not know . . .)

Can I show you seven ways to increase your personal sales?

Can I show you how to work out in such a way that you will be stronger and look better?

(Getting permission to sell your customer is kind and effective.)

I'm wondering if deciding today will make you feel comfortable inside.

I'm wondering if investing today is going to make you the most money long term.

(I'm wondering while you imagine.)

Don't you think that it's time for a new president to lead our country?

Don't you think that a mutual fund that has a proven track record is better than . . . ?

(It's hard to say no to anything that follows "Don't you think that . . .")

Don't you feel that you are happier when you have someone do your taxes for you?

Don't you feel that you are better off with a new car than an old one?

(Same as previous comment.)

Exercise: Use each of the language patterns above and fill in commands for your customers to respond how you want them to respond to you. Do this exercise before going on!

Sometimes, hypnotic language patterns don't translate particularly well from language to language (English to Polish, for example) or from real life to the textual environment of a book. Words and phrases need to be stressed and articulated in very specific ways to be most effective.

THE MASTERS FORMULA TO FIND YOUR MAGIC WORDS

What are the most powerful phrases in your specific industry? Is there a way to know what words are changing minds for your competitors? Here's the formula that will allow you to finally get the inside information:

1) Find the most successful products in your category. If you sell aspirin to retail stores you will select Advil, Tylenol, Bayer, etc.

2) Rank the products first by total gross sales. Assign the bestselling a product value of 10. The next best a value of 9 and so on. You will weigh each word based upon the value assigned to it. A company's advertising that sold 10 bottles of aspirin doesn't receive as much weight as a company that sold 1,000,000 bottles.

3) Write out each word that appears on the label of the product on a sheet of paper. (Ignore ingredients and consumer warnings in this specific case.) In the case of Tylenol, there are several hundred words on the label of the box I'm holding. Here are some of the words that are in the biggest and boldest fonts:

A) Easy	G) Fever
B) Swallow	H) Reducer
C) Extra	I) Geltabs
D) Strength	J) Exclusive
E) Pain	K) Gelkote
F) Reliever	L) Process

(Of course, no one cares about the "Gelkote process," but the marketing big shots at Johnson & Johnson will figure this out and replace those words at a later date. Aside from this error, the people who make Tylenol are using the magic words and hitting all the hot buttons.)

4) After all of the words have been cataloged, move to your next competitor and write down all of the words on its packaging.

5) Put a check mark by each word on a master sheet that lists all the words on all the packages of all of your competitors, so you can count the frequency of the word in all of your top competitors'

packaging. For example: If Gelkote is listed on all of your top competitors' packaging, you know that it belongs on yours. However, it's not there so don't put it on yours! Instead, you will be using PAIN, RELIEVER, FEVER, REDUCER, EXTRA, PRESCRIPTION, and STRENGTH. These are the words that are going to be on all the top products in the analgesic group.

6) Therefore you will model the success of the 10s, 9s, 8s, and 7s in your industry! It would have taken you MILLIONS of dollars to find out this information in test marketing. However, you are getting it for the price of two hours work.

But what if you don't sell a product? What if you sell a service or own a restaurant or sell mutual funds? Find the advertising from all of your top competitors, the boys at the top of the totem pole, and do the exact same thing. Find out the frequency of words and phrases that all the companies at the top are using. These then become the words and phrases you want to model for your written communication with your customers.

Of course, knowing that these are the words that got your customers to buy your competitors' products gives you some pretty amazing intelligence, doesn't it?!

CHAPTER 12

Samurai Selling:
Turning Fear into Power

Mike, a seasoned professional salesman, sits in his car dreading knocking on the next door. The last few sales calls have not gone well. He takes a deep breath and tries to relax but his mind keeps replaying the earlier rejections. Mike is in a major sales slump. Intellectually, Mike knows this is just a phase that will pass but, emotionally, it fills him with fear. The more he tries to ignore it, the worse it gets.

The new salesperson, Linda, sits at her desk staring at the list of calls she has to make. Her mind is filled with all the horror stories she's heard about cold calls. Her stomach is in knots and she even feels a little nauseous. Picking up the telephone is like trying to lift a 1,000-pound weight. Beads of sweat form on Linda's brow as fear takes over.

Your heart races and you have trouble catching your breath. Your hands shake, your vision narrows, your hearing shuts down, and your mind races with negative thoughts. You "naturally" interpret these sensations as fear. "Why am I afraid?" you ask yourself.

This state of fear can visit anyone, but it becomes a salesperson's greatest obstacle to success. It is so easy to let the fear overwhelm you, dominant you. To overcome this, let's take a page from the techniques I use to teach martial artists how to turn fear into an ally. Use fear to propel yourself to greater success.

Mind Training 101:
Become a Sales Warrior

To do this you must first be able to realize the difference between an "adrenal push" with its physical effects and the psychological state we label as fear— and make friends with them both. It is inevitable that they both will occur, so let's put them to good use and help you become a sales warrior.

Lets look at the psycho-biological stages of this state we call fear. To do this, we must separate the physical responses from the psychological interpretations of them. This is the first step to overcoming them.

Fear is defined as a strong, often unpleasant emotional and physical response to real or **perceived** danger.

Physical

Adrenaline is a natural hormone secreted by the adrenal glands, nature's response to stressful environmental triggers. Its only job is to prepare the body for action, fight, or flight. It should be your ally. It comes in basically four steps:

1. "Pre-Event," Slow Release of Adrenaline. This state occurs often. Many people refer to it as a stress reaction. You're tense, slightly nervous, and on edge. If this state is prolonged it can exhaust you. (This is why high-stress jobs "burn" you out.) This state is intended to put you on alert, physically and mentally. It also releases neuro-transmitters for heightened mental focus. Fear of fear can increase this.

2. The Event Rush or Adrenal Dump. This occurs rapidly and very intensely. It is when your adrenal glands "dump" large amounts of the hormone into your system. This is to prepare you for major physical activity. Fight or flight. The effects of adrenaline are varied, but it is important to remember that this state is the ultimate survival tool. Adrenaline can cause:

✓ Tightening of your muscles in preparation for trauma.
✓ Visual Exclusion. Narrowing of vision. This causes you to lose your peripheral vision, creating tunnel vision.
✓ Auditory Exclusion. You lose a high percentage of your hearing. (It's why you can't hear the crowd noise during an athletic event.)
✓ Speeding up of the heart rate.
✓ Release of ATP to give extra physical strength, causing rapid exhaustion. (It gives you the shakes.)
✓ Rapid cognitive activity. You get an overload of thoughts flooding

your mind, usually negative. It can make you feel overwhelmed.

✓ Increased breathing.

Remember that none of these things, in and of themselves, are bad, and should not be feared. They prepare your body for action. People that channel this into productive use excel in tense/stressful situations. These are the people who do better on rank tests and other events when most people go down a notch.

3. "In-Event" Adrenaline. This is a second dump that increases the effects of the above as well as:

✓ Blocks pain

✓ Gives a secondary rush of energy

✓ Creates extra negative thoughts—fighting doubts

This state is intended to give you that "second wind," extra physical endurance, strength, and power to finish an "event" (flight-flight, etc.). This state explains why some people get better as a game (or fight) goes on. This is why some football players go out of their way to hit or get hit a few times in order to get into the flow of the game.

4. "Post-Event" Adrenaline Drip. After an event, the adrenal glands secrete small amounts of adrenaline. This causes slightly higher physical tension and leads to mentally repeating the event—reliving the fight. This state is much like the first and is intended to help your body readjust to the effects of the stressful event. This leads to physical and mental exhaustion.

Now that you can understand that the physical states are intended to help you, you can see the importance of not labeling these as good or bad. Just accept that these states *are,* and then let the mind take over and channel this extra energy from adrenaline to good use. Insight and knowledge are only the first steps.

How to Channel Fear into Power

To learn to harness this process, as stated above, the first step is to recognize that it is normal. Insight and knowledge open the door, and now we can learn to channel this wonderful, power-packed state to give you an edge in hostile situations.

1. The first step is to find and identify the first feelings of "fear"—the pre-event adrenaline release.

✓ How do you feel?
✓ Where do you feel it? (stomach, chest, shoulders, back, etc.)
✓ How is your state of mind?

To do this exercise, think of something that makes you fearful (that cold call, the new prospect, confrontation with your boss, I.R.S. audit, etc.). Really relive it and notice the above sensations. Now label this FEAR and store this info.

2. Develop a "Circle of Power or Excellence."

Think of a time when you were at your very best. You were in control. You were physically and mentally alert. It could be a great sales call, an interview you did well at, or another event, maybe golf or a sporting event. You were focused and sharp. Now imagine a circle on the floor and it is *your* "Circle of Excellence and Power."

✓ What color is it?
✓ Does it have a sound?
✓ What else do you notice?

3. Think of the event from above and step into your "Circle." Breathe in deeply. Pull the "Circle" into you. Throw your shoulders back. Feel the focus and power. Repeat this twice.

4. Step out of the "Circle" and reaccess the fearful state. As you begin to feel the fear (adrenaline state), step into the circle and breathe in. Do this five times. **Fear into Power!!**

5. Search in vain for that old fearful state. As you start to access fear, you will naturally go into a state of power.

Now that we have a basis for blocking the old fear response, you can take it to the next level to excel. Once you have channeled fear into power, you can face it as Tsunetomo Yamamoto, an 18th-century samurai did. Consider his famous writing Hagakure (which translates to "hidden among the leaves") that says,

> The realization of certain death should be renewed every morning. Each morning, you must prepare yourself for every kind of death with composure of mind. Imagine yourself broken by bows, guns, spears, swords, carried off by floods, leaping into a huge fire, struck by lightning, torn apart by earthquake, plunging from a cliff, as a disease-ridden corpse.

Every day you have to vividly imagine your greatest fear, Fear of Failure. Once we master this, what else can stand in our way?

What does this mean to you, the warrior salesperson? It may sound morbid, but if you imagine your deepest fears, death, humiliation, loss of pride, etc., and step into power, you will be in a better position to face whatever comes your way. It will start to develop the heart of a warrior, the type of person who does not let fear control them. You can be the type of sales professional who can face the toughest situations and call on their deepest resources to boost them into greater success. You may even use this to become the type of sales professional who looks forward to the cold call!

Now you are ready to become the ultimate sales warrior. The next few pages will teach you the secrets of advanced mind-control training.

Preparing Yourself to SELL

To become a master at the sales process, you need to be at the top of your game, and you need to stay there. The difference between the top performers and those who never quite make it is the ability to maintain high levels of performance on a consistent basis. To master these upcoming skills, I (WH) want you to think of yourself as a sales warrior, a martial artist for the business world. Now let us enter into the world of the elite martial arts training.

Entering the "Zone"

Have you ever watched a martial artist before a match? He is relaxed yet totally alert. His stance is straight; his hands loose but ready. His breathing is deep and rhythmic. His gaze is unfocused on any one object, but he can see the entire room. He offers no exotic defense postures. He is in what martial artists and athletes call "the zone."

When the attacker suddenly strikes out, he remains calm until the last instant —then becomes a blur of motion. If you were to change places with the martial artist, however, your perception would be different. To him, the attacker seems to be moving in slow motion, while he himself moves at normal speed. The two merge and, in a moment, the attacker is on the ground—leaving the defender to resume his relaxed but alert position.

Any martial artist who has trained long enough can relate to "the zone." Your vision is open and full. You feel centered and grounded—totally calm, yet very energetic. Your reflexes are awesome and there is no internal dialogue or indecision. This is what the Japanese call Zen—being in the moment.

Just think about it. How successful could you be if you started every encounter with a customer feeling calm, relaxed, and confident, yet with a keen awareness that allows a deep connection to others? You will discover that with a little practice you can achieve "the zone" state quickly and easily and use it to master the dynamics of great selling.

Zone State Exercises

1) Use this breathing technique to relax. Start with an exhalation through the mouth and slowly empty the lungs while counting to seven. Next, breathe slowly through the nose, taking in a nice, deep breath while counting to three. Repeat for a count of five. Once you feel truly relaxed, turn your attention inward and focus on your breathing. While doing this, make an O.K. hand sign and repeat "zone" to yourself several times.

2) Remember an occasion where time moved very fast. This can be a party, a celebration with friends, a sporting event, almost anything at all. Step into that experience and relive it.

3) Notice your vision. Is it wide and open? Are colors sharp and clear? Do you notice small movements?

4) Focus on your hearing. Are sounds clear? Are they loud or soft? Are they near or far? What about any internal sounds? What do you notice inside?

5) What do you physically feel? Centered and grounded? Calm yet energized? How do your stomach and chest feel? Do you feel light or heavy?

6) Do you notice anything different in your smell or taste senses?

7) Make a righthanded fist and think about your remembered fast time. Let a color come to mind that represents this state of mind-body.

8) Now think of a situation where time seemed to pass very slowly. This could be waiting in line at the bank, listening to a dull lecture, sitting in your car while you are stuck in traffic, etc. Step into the experience and relive it.

9) Notice your vision. Is it wide and open? Are colors sharp and clear? Do you notice small movements?

10) Focus on your hearing. Are sounds clear? Are they loud or soft? Are they near or far? What about any internal sounds? What do you notice inside?

11)What do you physically feel? Centered and grounded? Calm yet energized? How do your stomach and chest feel? Do you feel light or heavy?

12) Make a lefthanded fist and think about your slow time. Squeeze your fist and let a color come to mind that represents this state of mind-body.

13) Squeeze both fists together at the same time, telling yourself to be fast on the inside and slow on the outside. Let the colors mix as you now keep your right fist squeezed. Let this new state settle. Lock it in. Visualize it's becoming a permanent part of you.

14) Now keep squeezing the right fist and make an O.K. sign with your left hand and repeat "zone" several times. Now visualize locking in this new "zone state." Let it settle into every fiber and cell of your mental, physical, and spiritual being.

States of Excellence

Think of a time in your life when everything just seemed to come together. You were confident, you were happy, you looked forward to the day and what life had in store for you. Wouldn't it be great if someone could wave a magic wand and make every day like that?

Well, you don't need a magic wand. You can create your own state of excellence anytime you want by doing the following exercise.

Circle of Excellence

1) The first step is to identify your state of excellence. In what state would you have all of your resources available to you? Think of a time when you were at your very best and were mentally and physically very sharp. It could be when you scored the winning goal in the soccer game, an incredible sales presentation that knocked them off their feet, the time you got the only A in class on the science test.

2) Now imagine a circle on the floor in front of you. This is your circle of excellence and power. What color is the circle? Does it have a sound, a taste, or a smell? Do this until you've established a recognizable and identifiable presence for it.

3) Now think of your positive event and step into your circle. Pull your circle into you. Throw your shoulders back. Feel the focus and the power. Clasp your hands together so that you anchor this state.

4) Step out of the circle and relax. Then step back in the circle and recall your state of excellence. Again, throw your shoulders back and feel the focus and the power as you clasp your hands together.

5) Once again, step out of the circle and relax. Then step back in the circle and recall your state of excellence. Remember to throw your

shoulders back as you feel the focus and the power, while clasping your hands together.

6) Again step out of the circle and relax. From this point on, whenever you clasp your hands together you will step into the circle. Now think of a time in a future situation or context where you would like to have more of this special state of excellence.

7) Whenever you clasp your hands together you will step into the circle and recover your excellent state. Think of how this future situation will be different because you now have your circle of excellence when dealing with it.

What I'm about to share with you is one of the most amazing and empowering techniques ever devised. It's called the New Behavior Generator, and it allows you to model someone and blend his or her talents with your own at an unconscious level. Think of the greatest salesperson you have ever met. It could be the salesperson who sold you a beautiful new car, or the man on late-night television who convinced you to spend $49.95 to get his complete Maximum Wealth program.

This technique has been used by some of the greatest athletes of our time. But experience has shown that this technique can empower virtually any person in any area, including sales performance, acting, therapy, public speaking, sexual performance, and singing. The way you use it is limited only by your imagination.

As usual, the quickest, most effective way to do this is to walk through it. So let's up our skill level now.

First, think of a sales skill you would like to possess, or a sales skill that you would like to be better at, such as building rapport, demonstrating an expert knowledge of your product or service, or closing a sale.

Next, think of someone who has the talents, abilities, and skills you would like to have. This could be anyone—a public figure, a celebrity, or a leader in your field. In fact, this will be more effective if you do not personally know the person you are modeling. (We'll explain why in more detail later.)

Now imagine you are in a movie theater and you begin to watch a movie with your model on the screen. This person is doing the things you want to do, behaving the way you want to behave. Make this movie as vivid as possible. See how comfortable he is, how natural these skills are for him.

Watch the movie again; notice all the nuances. See the head movements, see the breathing patterns, and notice the eye movements. It's as if you can hear his thoughts, his internal subconscious strategies.

Now notice your model's energy field, his life force. It's as if you can see this force in, around, and through him. This aura is part of what makes him who he is. The more we give this away the more we have. Are there any special colors, vibrations, sounds, or feelings with this aura?

Now it's time to watch the movie again, except now you have replaced the model's physical form with your own, although still surrounded by the original model's life energy/aura.

Now, once again, "see" the movie in your mind. Rerun it from beginning to end. Notice all the intricate nuances, head movements, eye movements, breathing patterns, and subconscious strategies. Notice how you have absorbed his aura. Feel how comfortable and relaxed you are in this new aura. Be aware of how natural these new drills are for you—how right it all feels.

Now take a deep breath and as you exhale, step into the movie. See, hear, and feel everything, as you become this person. Feel the absorption of these talents, abilities, and skills. Let this aura mingle with yours. Experience everything.

Finally, replay the movie again as if you are acting in the movie, giving yourself a cue that you can use as an anchor. It could be an O.K. sign, a fist, pulling on your ear, etc. Lock this anchor in so you are able to call on these new skills at will. Use the same anchor that you used earlier.

The reason we stress that it is better if you are not well acquainted with the person whom you are modeling is because experience has demonstrated the power of your subconscious to take care of you. Here is an example to illustrate what we mean.

I was working with a salesman who wanted to increase his sales. We did some basic hypnosis and it improved his cold calls. The second session we did the New Behavior Generator, and this client decided to model a co-worker who could sell anything.

Unexpectedly, my client seemed to be having some problems with stepping into the movie, so I asked him about his co-worker. My client explained that this guy could sell anything. He always led the company in sales, made lots of money, and was treated like gold. Good, right? Not quite.

"Anything else about your co-worker, maybe something you don't like?" I asked.

"Well," my client went on, "he's a real jerk. He treats the office staff— you know, the secretaries and administrative assistants—like dirt just because he can. He also drinks too much and has been married four times."

Thank God his subconscious knew to block out this behavior. I decided the most effective method was to isolate the sales talent and explained to his subconscious, through a metaphor, using a sports analogy: "For every Dennis Rodman there is a Michael Jordan."

It worked. His sales went up to the top 10 percent of the company and he stayed a nice man.

Here are the steps again for the New Behavior Generator:

1) Pick a person you want to model, a person who has the skills and abilities you want.

2) Watch a movie of your model doing the things you would like to do.

3) Watch the movie again. Be sure to notice all the nuances. (See and feel how comfortable they are.)

4) See your model's aura, his life force. Notice the color, vibration, and sound. Notice how it gives them that special something, and know that the more we give this away the more we have.

5) Now watch the movie while replacing your model with yourself. Do everything your model did while keeping his aura around you.

6) Watch yourself again, noticing the nuances, and see how comfortable you are. Absorb the model's life force.

7) Step into the movie. See, hear, and feel everything as you replay the scene. Make it uniquely yours.

8) Give yourself a cue to have these talents and abilities emerge.

Now you are ready to unlock the true you, the master salesperson you have been working to be. Enjoy the journey.

CHAPTER 13

Changing How Customers See You . . . and How You See Yourself

How do customers perceive you as a salesperson? Have you considered what you can do ultimately to change that negative perception? When the term "salesperson" pops into your mind, what do you picture? What are some of the stereotypes that **you** have?

Is a salesperson someone who is pushing some service or product on you that you really don't want? Do you think of someone who is trying to coerce you into doing something you had never intended to do? Perhaps you think of someone who uses a certain degree of ruthlessness to get the sale.

We are all customers. All of us buy things and often our purchases bring us in contact with salespeople. Many of the complaints that people have about salespeople are the same from industry to industry. Salespeople are often viewed as pushy or aggressive. They argue with the customer and seem to care only about their commission.

Some salespeople turn their customers off because they call without an appointment or with no specific purpose in mind. Other salespeople do not take the time to know their product or service as well as they should, and find themselves saying things like, "Gee, I don't know," or "I'll have to get back to you on that."

Internal Misconceptions of Salespeople

What are your own personal feelings about salespeople? Do you have any negative feelings about sales as a profession? Most of your deep, sub-conscious feelings you developed in childhood. These feelings can become MAPS or patterns that you live out, and perhaps it's a good idea to become aware of them.

A student of mine (WH), Tim McBain, who was accustomed to telling people that he was a marketer, shared with me the experience he had the first time his parents told him he was a "natural salesman." Although they said it with pride, the term still made Tim feel bad. Then, when he overheard his mother telling friends he was a salesman, again he experienced negative feelings.

Remember, Tim was successful in the selling process, but he realized that he never acknowledged to people that he was a salesperson. He preferred to think of himself as a "marketer."

As Tim explored those feelings, he recalled a time when he was a small child and the family needed a new appliance of some sort, They went to the department store and began looking at several models. A well-dressed man approached them and asked if they required any help. Tim's mother replied, "No, we're fine. We're just looking." Tim asked his mother why she didn't let the man help her and she replied, "He's a salesman, Honey. You can't trust them." Strike one for the salesperson image.

Later, Tim recalled, how proud he felt when his father took him with him to buy a new car. They got to the showroom and were looking at the shiny, beautiful new cars. Tim was fascinated by the sports model. He saw his father looking at a beige sedan and overheard his dad say to himself, "I wonder if this comes in blue?"

When one of the car salesmen approached and asked if he could help, Tim's dad replied, "No, we are just looking around."

When he asked his dad why he didn't ask the salesman about the car he liked, his dad replied, "You don't talk to the salesman until the last minute. They only pressure you." Strike two for the sales image.

Tim also remembered a time when they were at home and the phone rang. He answered and it was someone who wanted to talk to his mom or dad. When he gave his parents the message, they told him to ask who it was and why they were calling. The caller told him that he was their insurance agent and he wanted to talk to his parents about insurance coverage.

That's when his mom got on the phone and told the agent they were just leaving the house and she would call him back. The young boy, overhearing her say this, was confused, because he knew they were staying home that evening. When he asked his mom why she told the agent they were leaving, she said, "I don't want to talk to a salesman. They only waste your time." Strike three for that good old sales image.

Now here it was some twenty years later and Tim was battling the negative feelings he felt when his mother proudly said he was a salesman. Tim understood he needed to change these internal perceptions if he ever wanted to be truly happy in his career.

Do You Have a Ph.D. in Sales?

I (WH) find it amazing that there is not a college that gives a degree in sales. Selling is the largest profession on the face of the earth. It is the one profession that every industry needs, and you cannot get a degree in it. You can get a degree in poetry, or literature, where you come up with ideas about what dead writers meant, but you cannot get one in sales.

Now, there is a degree in marketing, but they rarely teach basic selling skills. In the consulting world for small businesses, it is said, if you want to go broke, hire a person with a marketing degree. What businesses truly need is top-notch sales training.

I was watching an interview with a well-known actor, who talked about his training in that profession. He mentioned that he wished he had taken some sales courses, because he was struggling for acting work and he had noticed that the actors who could "sell themselves" got more work. He went out and got some sales jobs, he said, not just for the money but to improve his selling skills. Then these skills could be redirected so he could sell himself to directors and producers. The added benefit was that it had made him a better actor, since he has to sell himself to the public every time he portrays a character.

Another student, who had a marketing degree, mentioned that while he was in school it was stated that you might have to start in the sales department until you could get a real job in the corporation. After he got into the real world, of course, he saw that the true salespeople made more money and that it was their efforts that really drove the company. He thought back to the almost subliminal message from his college about salespeople.

Corporate Image of Sales

Many companies are also guilty of feeding the negative sales image. New hires are often told, "You have to start as a salesperson, but then you can move up." It gives you the impression that it is temporary menial position.

I have a friend who expressed his frustration at the fact that he is one of his company's top-producing salespeople, and he loves it, for all the reasons we talked about before. Yet he is looked down on for not moving into a management position. But that move, as he pointed out, would bring a huge cut in pay, more work, more pressure, and longer hours. That doesn't exactly sound like a win/win situation, does it? The upshot of it is that he is afraid he may have to switch companies to stay in his chosen career field.

Reprogram Your Self-image

Do you have any negative thoughts of being a professional salesperson? Do you hesitate to tell people you're a salesperson? Do you like the process of selling, but do not like the perception of sales?

If you can relate to any of the above items, the first thing you have to do is change your internal representation of a salesperson. Customers pick up on any negative feelings on your part and it will amplify the problem of gaining trust in a sales situation. As Dr. Hogan points out, we are attracted to people who have a strong self-image. It is important to remove any negatives from your past and then enhance your current beliefs of salespeople.

Most of your beliefs were formed when you were quite young. Before the age of twelve you really did not have the critical thinking developed to analyze the information presented to you. This is why you have many of the same beliefs as your parents and the people who reared you. You learned to believe most of the things they told you.

These are the same people who told you not to touch the stove, because it's hot. You will get burned if you touch a hot stove. So it's logical that if your parents/caregivers didn't like or trust salespeople, you may have these same beliefs tucked away in your subconscious.

These negative perceptions of sales will often come up when you are in a state where your resources are low, such as when you're tired or you've had a few rough sales calls. They will often impact hardest when you've hit a slump and have had several rejections. At this point, your subconscious will take over and you will find those old feelings coming to the surface. The more discouraged you are, the stronger those feelings become. (This may be the reason slumps are harder to pull out of than logically they should be.) Through my experience I have found this also to be true for athletes.

When I first started to work with salespeople and realized the need to reprogram their negative perceptions, I immediately thought of a friend of mine who is a professional salesperson. Bob is very successful, loves it, and does not seem to hit slumps. "Here is a great guy to model," I thought to myself.

When I talked to him and gathered information, I found out his father was a successful lifelong salesman, as were a few of his uncles. In fact, his grandfather had been in sales his entire life. The entire family enjoyed being in sales. Their upper-middle-class lifestyles were funded by the sales process. As Bob was growing up, he constantly received positive images of sales. The talk was always upbeat regarding sales and sales-people. He also remembered how his father, grandfather, and uncles would support each other through "slumps." They would stress that slumps happen, but "You snap out of them fast."

One of Bob's strongest memories of his childhood was a family vaca-tion they had taken, because his dad had had a great year. His father stressed, "This is what sales is all about; making the money to enjoy life, and enjoying the process."

What a powerful resource to draw from. Is it any wonder he is also a successful salesperson? Although he went to college and earned a degree, inside he always knew he would be a salesperson.

If you have these deep, subconscious negative beliefs about sales, you need to clean the slate before you can build a positive sales image. But you cannot rely on the use of simple affirmations, because they cannot overcome those beliefs. You can repeat to yourself constantly, "I love sales, I am a successful salesperson," but still those old feelings will sur-face. What you really need to do is to erase those old tapes.

When you need to reprogram your internal state, the fastest way is to "re-parent" yourself.

Doing It Right the Second Time

1. First, choose a comfortable, quiet location where you may either sit or lie down in privacy. Now, while you are in a relaxed state, think back to your childhood. Think of any negative beliefs, especially those pertaining to sales, that you have now and would like to see changed. An example would be the good fortune of having several influential people in your life who have been successful in the sales

profession. You may want to get out a picture of yourself when you were small to give yourself a reference point.

2. Now feel yourself becoming calm and centered. As you begin to feel centered, that sort of neutral, detached state, begin to focus on that younger you.

3. Begin to give yourself some self-love, that respect you deserve for all you've accomplished in your life up to this point, and the forgiveness of yourself for things that may have gone wrong up till now. Then tell that younger you all those things that you know now, that you wish you could have known then . . . the truth about sales . . . that it is a great career . . . it allows you freedom . . . the opportunity to earn large sums of money.

4. Stress to your "younger you" that sales is a normal, real career. It is a fun career and an honorable profession.

5. Don't forget to mention to your "younger self" that slumps are a natural occurrence with sales, something to be endured briefly, and to rebound from quickly.

6. Let that younger version of yourself see that your parents did not mean to pass their negative beliefs on to you. They were merely misinformed.

7. Now see yourself at that awkward age we all go through, the teenage years, and give yourself some self-love and appreciation.

8. Tell that younger you what you now know to be true about sales.

9. You may want to address another time in your past when you needed some extra self-love, appreciation, and self-forgiveness. We are often our own harshest critics.

10. Now come back to the present and let the past rewrite itself for your own good. Allow yourself to let go of those old beliefs that now no longer apply. You can review the negative beliefs and thoughts that you have now naturally changed into positive images.

You may want to do this exercise several times. Focus on any memories you may have of when you were given negative perceptions about sales. This will clean the slate. You can then replace these perceptions with positive beliefs.

These are some of basic steps you can take to help you change how your customers perceive you. The basics are here. Now it's up to you.

Let your customers know you care about them and their business. Don't leave them with the feeling that they are just another appointment on your calendar. Take the time to let your customers know that you understand and appreciate their unique problems and challenges.

Work on your listening skills and ask questions to uncover your customer's needs. Make sure that you are on time for any meeting with your customer and that you are prepared with all the proper information and materials. Organize your papers so that when the customer asks you for some price information, you can put your hands on it right away. Nothing looks worse than a salesperson who has to fumble through a stack of papers to find what he needs.

How can you avoid the fundamental pitfalls of those unsuccessful salespeople? First of all, make sure you do your homework. Know your product or service thoroughly, inside and out. Let your customers know where they can go for technical support. If possible, find out about your customers' business before you call on them. Make sure you understand their industry, their target market, and the positioning of their company. Think of it this way: the more you know, the easier it will be to demonstrate how your product or service is the solution to their problems.

We believe that for your customers to see you in a positive light, you first have to see yourself in a positive way. Here are some more examples to help you on the road to success, the types of models you want to consider.

Modeling Greatness

Selling plays a much greater role in life than simply moving goods and services from the person or company who produces them to the consumer who will benefit most from their use. The fact of the matter is that every product you use or see has a sales force behind it. The toothpaste you brush with in the morning, the cereal you eat for breakfast, the clothes you select to look your best for the big meeting—all of these products are part of your life because someone sold you on their value.

The process of selling has a big impact on many facets of your life in ways you may not have even considered. If you are with a group of friends about to go out to lunch, you may find yourself trying to talk the group into going to the new Mexican restaurant that just opened.

If you're a parent, you probably had to "sell" your child on the idea that green beans actually taste good. A friend of mine who works in television news goes into the morning story meeting every day knowing she'll have to "sell" the producers on the news stories she wants to cover.

From the moment in your childhood when you realized you needed other people (your parents) to fulfill your needs, you started learning the basic skills of a salesperson. You learned from your brothers and sisters (or from watching other children) and you discovered how to use these skills to get what you wanted.

Remember that giant coloring book with the jungle animals and the puzzles and the connect-the-dots? You already had a dozen or more coloring books at home, but you somehow managed to "sell" it to your mom by telling her it was the best coloring book in the whole world.

The simple truth is, we are all salespeople. Most of the time, however, we use the tactics of salespeople without even realizing it. I remember listening to my friend Mary describe her Toyota Camry at a party. The car had not been on the market for more than a few years, so people often asked her how she liked it. Her enthusiasm for the car came through loud and clear.

"I love it," she'd say with a big smile. "It has a four-cylinder engine, so the gas mileage is great, and yet it still has plenty of pick up. I've driven it 40,000 miles and all I've had to do is basic maintenance. It's the most reliable car I've ever owned."

Some of the most influential people of the past century, people who changed the way we live and how we do business, were first and foremost great salespeople, although they may not have considered themselves in that light at the time. An excellent example was Henry Ford, who improved the assembly line to such an extent that it made the automobile affordable for the average American.

In the early 1900s, cars were relatively expensive, a fact that pleased the stockholders of the emerging automobile companies. But Henry Ford believed that high prices ultimately slowed market expansion. In 1906 he decided that his company would introduce a new, cheaper model with a lower profit margin.

It was his dream to build a car for the "great multitude," the American people. The result was the Model T, and it appealed to the public like no other car ever had. On October 1, 1908, the first cars were offered at $825, which was well within the price range of many Americans. The Model T had a four-cylinder, twenty-horsepower engine, was relatively light—about 1,200 pounds—and was fairly easy to drive, with a two-speed, foot-controlled transmission. Henry Ford sold a record 10,000 cars the first year.

One of the most important characteristics of any great salesperson is sincerity. When you are talking about an issue you wholeheartedly believe in, when you share a dream or an idea you support passionately, often it is your sincerity that "sells" it to the other person. Probably one of the most famous "dreamers" who sold the world on his vision was Walt Disney.

Walt conceived the idea of a theme park one day while watching his daughters laugh and play on a merry-go-round. He decided to build a family park where parents and kids could go and have fun together. He arranged for the Stanford Research Institute to do a study to determine the ideal location. Shortly thereafter, he purchased sixty acres of orange groves in Anaheim, California, twenty-five miles south of Los Angeles near the Santa Ana Freeway.

In hindsight, it is difficult to imagine anyone turning away from Disney's creative genius. But at that time his animation studio was controlled partly by his brother, Roy, and several other important stockholders, all of whom were reluctant to invest in such a radical new idea as a "Disney theme park."

They were not alone in their doubt about making money with an amusement park that would appeal to both children and their parents. When Walt approached his business colleagues and sought their financial support, he found it difficult to find any backers. Undaunted and sure of his vision and determined to "sell" it to the American public, Walt started a separate company, Walt Disney, Inc., and used his life savings to make it a reality.

When Disneyland opened on July 17, 1955, there was live television coverage to record the historic occasion. And historic it was, as 170,000 people paid the admission price of one dollar per adult and 50 cents per child to enjoy the nation's largest entertainment complex.

Another way in which we use our "selling" skills is through personal interaction. When we enter into a new relationship of any kind, we want to be perceived as intelligent, caring, trustworthy, etc. So we put our best foot forward and try to "sell" the other person on our strong points.

For instance, a good friend of mine (I'll call her Susan) found herself out of a job through no fault of her own. I called her to see if she might be interested in a little freelance work, proofreading a workbook on NLP. When she answered the phone I could tell she was excited.

"Hey, Susan, how is the job hunting coming along?" I asked.

"Well, it's funny you should ask, Wil, because last week I used some of the skills I learned in your NLP sales class to "sell" myself to the interviewers—and it worked! They called me today and offered me the job! Full benefits, 401K, and I'm starting at the same salary I was making after eight years at my former job!"

The delight in her voice came across loud and clear.

"How did you do that?" I asked.

She explained:

> I had a job interview with the regional director. He told me his company makes one of the tools used in manufacturing semiconductor chips. Anyway, he said he wanted an office administrator to help the site coordinator with some of the administrative duties. To tell you the truth, I didn't really think I had a chance, because I don't have any background in engineering or technology. But I went into the interview determined to give it my best shot. I remembered what you said about mirroring and matching the other person to establish rapport.

(Those are skills that you, the reader, now know are essential in enhancing your expertise as a salesperson.)

Susan continued,

> Throughout the interview I paid careful attention to the nonverbal gestures of the interviewer. He began by clasping his hands together on the table and leaning forward. After a moment, I matched him by clasping my hands together on the table. When he changed position, leaning back in his chair and crossing one leg over the other, I did the same. I listened to what he said, trying to guess his preferred representational system by the words he chose. It soon became clear that he was a visual person.

> So I used words that I knew he would relate to, like "see," "perceive," and "imagine." I matched his tone of voice and his breathing patterns as well. I felt I had established a good rapport with him and I decided to check it about halfway through the interview. So I changed the position I was sitting in, by leaning back and placing my elbows on the arms of the chair. He mirrored me by doing the same thing a few seconds later.

By the time the interview was over, I knew I had made a good impression. He told me they would be making a decision within a few weeks. So you can imagine my surprise when, three days later, he called and offered me the job!

What Susan actually did, very successfully as it turns out, was "sell" herself to the regional director using some of the techniques you have learned in this book. The basic skill of establishing rapport, which Susan did right away, is essential for the successful salesperson. Rapport is achieved when two people are on the same wavelength, on the same page, as it were. Studies have shown that people are more inclined to buy from, agree with, and support someone they can relate to than someone with whom they feel no connection.

Selling has been defined as the ability to inspire another person to enter a state of believing he or she needs your product or service. Since all persuasion begins on an emotional or subconscious level, what the salesperson tries to do is to communicate to the customer using words, tone of voice, and gestures so that they non-critically accept the communication as fact. The moment the customer believes or changes the way he thinks, he is inspired to take a new action or to purchase the product or service.

One person who changed the way the customer thought was Bill Gates. His idea was to sell computers with the operating software already installed, partly because he was concerned about the amount of software "stealing" that was going on, but also because he wanted his operating system to become the standard worldwide. It was a revolutionary approach that quickly caught on in the late seventies. Within ten years Microsoft was providing the operating systems for roughly 80 percent of the personal computers sold each year.

Use these models to inspire you to reach for the stars. You are now a true black belt in the selling process. Remember it is said in the martial arts community that achieving your black belt means you are ready for the true journey. This is the journey where you internalize all the skills you have mastered.

Bibliography

Allesandra, Tony and Michael J. O'Connor. *The Platinum Rule: Do Unto Others As They'd Like Done Unto Them.* New York, NY: Warner Books, Inc., 1996.

Anastasi, Tom. *Personality Selling, Selling the Way Customers Want to Buy.* New York, NY: Sterling Publications, 1992.

Andreas, Steve and Charles Faulkner. *NLP: The New Technology of Achievement.* New York, NY: William Morrow and Company, 1994.

Aronson, Elliott. *The Social Animal.* New York, NY: W. H. Freeman and Company, 1995.

Bagley, Dan and Edward J. Reese. *Beyond Selling: How to Maximize Your Personal Influence.* Cupertino, CA: Meta Publications, 1988.

Bandler, Richard & John LaValle. *Persuasion Engineering.* Capitola, CA: Meta Publications, 1996.

Bethel, William. *10 Steps to Connecting With Your Customer: Communication Skills for Selling Your Products, Services, and Ideas.* Chicago, IL: The Dartnell Corporation, 1995.

Bloom, Howard. *The Lucifer Principle: A Scientific Expedition Into the Forces of History.* NY: Atlantic Monthly Press, 1995.

Brodie, Richard. *Virus of the Mind: The New Science of the Meme.* Integral Press. 1996.

Brooks, Michael. *Instant Rapport: The NLP Program That Creates Intimacy, Persuasiveness, Power!* New York, NY: Warner Books, Inc., 1989.

Brooks, Michael. *The Power of Business Rapport: Use NLP Technology to Make More Money, Sell Yourself and Your Product, and Move Ahead in Business.* New York, NY: Harper-Collins Publishers, 1991.

Buzan, Tony and Richard Israel. *Brain Sell.* Brookfield, VT: Gower, 1995.

Cialdini, Robert B. *Influence: The New Psychology of Persuasion.* New York, NY: Morrow, 1993.

Cohen, Allan R. and David L. Bradford. *Influence Without Authority.* New York, NY: John Wiley & Sons, 1991.

Dalet, Kevin with Emmett Wolfe. *Socratic Selling: How to Ask the Questions that Get the Sale.* Chicago, IL: Irwin Professional Publishing, 1996.

Dayton, Doug. *Selling Microsoft, Sales Secrets from Inside the World's Most Successful Company.* Holbrook, Mass.: Dayton, 1997.

Dawson, Roger. *Secrets of Power Persuasion: Everything You'll Ever Need to Get Anything You'll Ever Want.* Englewood Cliffs, NJ: Prentice-Hall, Inc., 1992.

Decker, Bert. *You've Got To Be Believed To Be Heard: Reach the First Brain to Communicate in Business and in Life.* New York, NY: St. Martin's Press, 1992.

Elgin, Suzette Haden. *Success with the Gentle Art of Verbal Self-Defense.* Englewood Cliffs, NJ: Prentice-Hall, Inc., 1989.

Farber, Barry J. and Joyce Wycoff. *Breakthrough Selling: Customer-Building Strategies from the Best in the Business.* Englewood Cliffs, NJ: Prentice-Hall, Inc., 1992.

Gitomer, Jeffrey. *The Sales Bible: The Ultimate Sales Resource.* New York, NY: William Morrow, 1994.

Grinder, John. *The Structure of Magic, Vol 1.* Palo Alto, CA: Science and Behavior Books, 1976.

Hamer, Dean. *Living With Our Genes: Why They Matter More Than You Think.* NY. Doubleday, 1998.

Hogan, Kevin. (Audio Program). "Mind Access: Beyond the Psychology of Persuasion." Eagan, MN: Network 3000 Publishing, 1997.

Hogan, Kevin. (Video Program). "Persuasion Mastery Course." Eagan, MN: Network 3000 Publishing, 1997.

Hogan, Kevin. *Life By Design: Your Handbook for Transformational Living.* Eagan, MN: Network 3000 Publishing, 1995.

Hogan, Kevin. *The Psychology of Persuasion: How to Persuade Others to Your Way of Thinking.* Gretna, LA: Pelican Publishing Company, 1996.

Hogan, Kevin. *Through the Open Door: Secrets of Self-hypnosis.* Gretna, LA: Pelican Publishing Company, 2000.

Johnson, Kerry L. *Sales Magic: Revolutionary New Techniques That Will Double Your Sales Volume in 21 Days.* New York, NY: William Morrow and Company, Inc., 1994.

Johnson, Kerry L. *Subliminal Selling Skills.* New York, NY: AMA-COM, 1988.

Keirsey. David and Marilyn Bates. *Please Understand Me: Character & Temperament Types.* Del Mar, CA: Prometheus Nemesis Book Company, 1984.

Kennedy, Daniel S. *The Ultimate Sales Letter.* Holbrook, MA: Bob Adams, Inc., 1990.

Kent, Robert Warren. *The Art of Persuasion.* Surfside, FL: Lee Institute, 1963.

Knapp, Mark and Judy Hall. *Nonverbal Communication in Human Interaction.* 3rd ed. Fort Worth, TX: Harcourt Brace College Publications, 1992.

Knight, Sue. *NLP at Work: The Difference That Makes a Difference in Business.* Sonoma, CA: Nicholas Brealey Publishing, 1995.

Kostere, Kim. *Get the Results You Want: A Systematic Approach to NLP.* Portland, OR: Metamorphous Press, 1989.

Lavington, Camille with Stephanie Losee. *You've Only Got Three Seconds: How to Make the Right Impression in Your Business and Social Life.* New York, NY: Doubleday, 1997.

Lewis, David. *The Secret Language of Success: Using Body Language to Get What You Want.* New York, NY: Carroll & Graf, 1990.

Linden, Anne with Kathrin Perutz. *Mindworks: Unlock the Promise Within—NLP Tools for Building a Better Life.* Kansas City, MO: Andrews McMeel Publishing, 1997.

Mehrabian, Albert. *Silent Messages: Implicit Communication of Emotions and Attitudes.* Belmost, CA: Wadsworth, 1981.

Moine, Donald J. and John H. Herd. *Modern Persuasion Strategies: The Hidden Advantage in Selling.* Englewood Cliffs, NJ: Prentice-Hall, Inc., 1984.

Moine, Donald J. and Kenneth Lloyd. *Unlimited Selling Power: How to Master Hypnotic Selling Skills.* Englewood Cliffs, NJ: Prentice-Hall, Inc., 1990.

Nicholas, Ted. *Magic Words That Bring You Riches.* Indian Rocks Beach, FL: Nicholas Direct, 1996.

Overstreet, H. A. *Influencing Human Behavior.* New York, NY: Norton, 1925.

Patton, Forrest H. *Force of Persuasion: Dynamic Techniques for Influencing People.* Englewood Cliffs, NJ: Prentice-Hall, Inc., 1986.

Piirto, Rebecca. *Beyond Mind Games: The Marketing Power of Psychographics.* Ithaca, NY: American Demographic Books, 1991.

Peoples, David. *Selling To The Top.* New York, NY: John Wiley & Sons, Inc., 1993.

Qubein, Nido. *Professional Selling Techniques: Strategies and Tactics to Boost Your Selling Skills and Build Your Career.* Rockville Centre, NY: Farnsworth Publishing Co., Inc., 1983.

Richardson, Jerry. *The Magic of Rapport.* Capitola, CA: Meta Publications, 1988.

Robbins, Anthony. *Unlimited Power.* New York, NY: Fawcett, 1987.

Robertson, James E. *Selling the Mind's Eye: What They Didn't Teach You In Sales Training.* Portland, OR: Metamorphous Press, 1990.

Sadovsky, Marvin C. and Jon Caswell. *Selling the Way Your Customer Buys: Understand Your Prospects' Unspoken Needs & Close Every Sale.* New York, NY: AMACOM, 1996.

Solderholm, Craig E. *How 10% of the People Get 90% of the Pie: Get Your Share Using Subliminal Persuasion Techniques.* New York, NY: St. Martin's Press, 1997.

Stiles, William H. *Hypno-Salesmanship: The Suggestive Art That Helps People Buy.* New Castle, PA: Bill Stiles Associates, 1996.

Thompson, George J. and Jerry B. Jenkins. *Verbal Judo: The Gentle Art of Persuasion.* New York, NY: William Morrow and Company, Inc., 1993.

Tracy, Brian. *Advanced Selling Strategies: The Proven System of Sales Ideas, Methods, and Techniques Used By Top Salespeople Everywhere.* New York, NY: Fireside, 1995.

Vitale, Joe. *Cyber Writing: How to Promote Your Product or Service Online.* New York, NY: AMACOM, 1997.

Vitale, Joe. *The Seven Lost Secrets of Success.* Houston: VistaTron, 1994.

Willingham, Ron. *The Best Seller: The New Psychology of Selling and Persuading People.* Englewood Cliffs, NJ: Prentice-Hall, Inc., 1984.

Contact the Authors

If you and your company are interested in having Dr. Hogan or Dr. Horton speak for your company or give seminars or sales training, simply call our corporate offices at 612-616-0732 or visit us on the net at http://www.kevinhogan.net/